An Economic History of Modern China

An Economic History of Modern China

Joseph C.H. Chai

Research Consultant, Research Grants Council, Hong Kong, China

Edward Elgar

Cheltenham, UK • Northampton, MA, USA

Published by
Edward Elgar Publishing Limited
The Lypiatts
15 Lansdown Road
Cheltenham
Glos GL50 2JA
UK

Edward Elgar Publishing, Inc.
William Pratt House
9 Dewey Court
Northampton
Massachusetts 01060
USA

A catalogue record for this book
is available from the British Library

Library of Congress Control Number: 2011922862

ISBN 978 1 84720 937 5

Typeset by Servis Filmsetting Ltd, Stockport, Cheshire
Printed and bound by MPG Books Group, UK

Contents

Acknowledgements   vii

Introduction   1

PART I   THE TRADITIONAL ECONOMY

1   Population   7

2   Agriculture   13

3   Urbanization and traditional industry   26

4   Trade   34

5   Social structure   45

6   Why China failed to industrialize   50

PART II   TRANSITION TO MODERN ECONOMIC
            GROWTH

7   Growth of foreign trade and investment   63

8   The rise of modern sectors and their impact   79

9   Why Japan succeeded and China failed   93

PART III   MODERN ECONOMIC GROWTH UNDER
             SOCIALISM

10   The Soviet model   109

11   The Great Leap Forward   120

12   The Great Famine   129

13   The Cultural Revolution   142

14   Socialist modern economic growth: the outcome   149

PART IV   REFORM AND GROWTH ACCELERATION

15   The reforms   163

16   Towards a new growth strategy   190

17   The rise of China   209

18   China's modern economic growth: retrospect and prospect   230

Appendix   242
References   243
Index   259

Acknowledgements

In writing this book, I was able to draw on all the advice, ideas and inspiration of my former teachers, colleagues and friends, especially Pikai Tchang who stimulated my interest in Chinese economy and Alpha Chiang who familiarized me with quantitative methods of economic analysis. Others owed gratitude are Carl Foehl for his inspiring insight into macroeconomic processes and Bruce Glassburner who stimulated my interest in development economics. I also acknowledge Dwight Perkins, Kenneth Walker and Christopher Howe, whose writings I have relied on heavily in this book. Needless to say, they should not be held responsible for my views. My thanks, too, go to Ronald Hsia and Clem Tisdell for their support and encouragement of my research. Special thanks go to Robert Ash for his inspiration and to Y.Y. Kueh for his healthy competition throughout my career.

Finally, I would like to dedicate this book to my wife, Karin, who gave me the strength to persevere under sometimes difficult circumstances. She is my best critic and creatively edited and typed the manuscript with patience and efficacy.

Introduction

The fall and rise of the Chinese economy over the last 200 years is nothing short of spectacular. In the time from the tenth to the fourteenth century the traditional Chinese economy outperformed its counterparts in the world, including European economies, for in that period it had the world's highest gross domestic product (GDP) per capita (Maddison 2001, 2007). But its lead began to decrease at the onset of the fourteenth century when Europe's GDP rose due to the medieval industrial revolution. From that time onward, up to the eighteenth century, its per capita income remained stagnant even though its population and GDP continued to grow and remained the largest in the world. By 1950 the relative decline was so great that China's income per capita amounted to only 10 per cent of that of its European counterparts. Thus China was among the poorest countries in the world with its economy ranking even behind that of India.

However, its powerful performance with consistently high economic growth over the last 30 years (1979–2009) has allowed China to work its way back into the international community and to become a dominant economy if not as yet a corresponding political power. In 2008 it replaced Germany as the world's largest exporter. In terms of GDP at conventional exchange rate, in 2010 it overtook Japan as the world's second-largest economy, and is set to overtake the US as the world's largest economy in the near future. It has already overtaken the US as the engine of world economic growth. China also has the world's largest foreign exchange reserves and is the second-largest recipient of FDI (foreign direct investment) after the USA.

The rise of China has attracted worldwide attention as evidenced by a wide range of voluminous books published on all aspects of modern China in recent years. Yet so far none has comprehensively dealt with China's economic history. The last English language text of this kind was published by Frank King some 40 years ago (King 1969), before China's modern economic growth gained momentum. The present volume is filling this gap and also provides the context of China's modern economic development. For, as the renowned economic historian Douglass North noted (North 2003), a country's development path is dependent on its past since it is shaped by its existing value system and institutions, without which the

1

country's current and future economic performance cannot be properly understood.

This book focuses on China's modern economic growth and comprehensively surveys the patterns of China's growth experience in the last 200 years. Its more important elements are traced back to their foundations in history in order to explain their impact on China's modern economic growth. The book is divided into four parts. Part I looks at China's premodern growth economy.

One of the great mysteries of China's pre-modern experience is that fourteenth-century China was well ahead of Europe in terms of scientific and technological development as well as in other areas, and that it apparently had all necessary conditions for an industrial revolution. Yet the industrial revolution started in eighteenth-century England instead of fourteenth-century China. The objective of Part I is to solve this mystery. Chapter 1 begins with an examination of the population dynamic of traditional China. The core sector of its economy, agriculture, is examined in Chapter 2, and the development of the non-agricultural sectors is discussed subsequently. Thus Chapter 3 discusses China's traditional handicraft industry and urbanization, and Chapter 4 deals with trade. China's unique traditional social structure which shapes all economic actions is discussed in Chapter 5, and Chapter 6 finally brings it all together in an analysis of why China failed to industrialize earlier despite its relatively advanced economic and technological development and its sophisticated social and political institutions.

Part II examines China's transition to modern economic growth after its forced opening for trade by the West in the middle of the nineteenth century. Another mystery in economic history is why it was Japan rather than China which became the first non-European country to industrialize successfully, for traditional China and Japan were very similar in many respects. Both had experienced the shock of being forced to open for trade with Western nations, and had been subjected to unequal treaties which restricted their tariff autonomy. In addition, both had to cede treaty ports where Westerners were given special rights to conduct their own business.

China and Japan both had a very low initial per capita income which was well below that of their European counterparts at their start of industrialization. Both were basically agrarian economies characterized by a high man–land ratio and intensive farming methods. Both used the same irrigation technology which had spread from China to Japan. And culturally the latter considered the former as a role model. Thus Japan had adopted many Chinese patterns and methods, including writing, paper making and many parts of Chinese tradition, including the Confucian value system.

However, Chinese society was relatively more advanced in that it was essentially a capitalist society with a free peasantry and private property rights and also a relatively high inter- and intraclass mobility with an incentive system based on achievement and individual merit. In contrast, traditional Japan was basically a feudal society with a rigid class system where farmers were essentially slaves of their feudal lords and were not allowed to leave the land or abandon agriculture. Neither were they allowed to sell or grow crops of their choice.

Given that China already had many of the building blocks of capitalism, one would expect that China would embrace industrialization more readily than Japan. However, it was Japan which experienced a swift and smooth transition to modern economic growth, which lasted for only about 20 years from 1868 to 1885. In contrast, China's transition to modern economic growth (MEG) was slow and painful. It started after the Opium War in 1842 but it was not until 1949 when the Communists took over control of China that the Chinese economy started to take off. Hence China's transition lasted for more than 100 years.

The aim of Part II is to unravel the mystery of why China's transition was so slow. It first examines changes in China's traditional economy after the European intrusion and discusses the growth in foreign trade and investment and their effects in Chapter 7. Chapter 8 considers the ensuing changes in agriculture and industry and the reasons why these significant changes in China's economic structure did not bring about MEG. Finally, Chapter 9 tries to identify the crucial factors responsible for the relatively slower progress of China to MEG than Japan.

The third part of the book scrutinizes the economic growth pattern in the Maoist period from 1949 to 1978. In this period China under the leadership of Mao Zedong pursued the twin goals of rapid industrialization and socialization. Initially it followed closely the Soviet model but the Great Leap Forward (GLF) from 1958 to 1960 and the Cultural Revolution (CR), 1966–76, were significant departures from that strategy.

In spite of these two significant departures, many China experts hold the view that China's development strategy was essentially a radical variant of the Soviet model in that it aimed at maximal speed of industrialization and the creation of a socialist state and society. However, Maoist economists and others in the West argue that Mao established a unique and different model of socialist development. They regard the GLF and the CR as genuine Maoist strategies aimed at rooting out a new bourgeois class which had consolidated its power in the bureaucracy and the economy. And they argue that this was an attempt to establish a more egalitarian, non-elitist and participatory type of socialism.

However, in the light of empirical data published in recent years, and flooding out of China in the form of memoirs of China's party elite members and monographs based on meticulously researched county records and party documents as well as interviews, this view has largely been discredited. These new data show convincingly that the Maoist model is just a figment of their imagination which was never realized. The objective of Part III is to identify the salient features of Mao's strategy and analyse their impact on China's MEG in this period. Chapter 10 highlights the Soviet approach to MEG that China initially adopted and Chapter 11 discusses its Maoist variant. Chapter 12 examines the causes of the failure of the Maoist strategy in the light of the Great Famine. Chapter 13 considers its culmination in the CR and Chapter 14 provides an assessment of China's achievements under Mao.

Part IV of the book focuses on the remarkable high speed of economic growth in China under the open door policy and the reforms since 1979. China was the first communist country initiating a transition from a planned to a market economy. It took the step in 1979, almost ten years earlier than the communist East European countries. And compared to the performance of these, China is the star insofar as it managed the transitions relatively smoothly. And in the early phase of transition it did not incur many of the high short-term transition costs that its European counterparts experienced in the form of dips in output, real wages and employment accompanied by increased political, social and economic instability. Some countries like the former Soviet Union, Yugoslavia and Czechoslovakia even disintegrated politically under reform pressure.

In contrast, China did relatively well: the level of real wages not only did not dip in the transition period, but actually rose, and the rate of inflation and unemployment were relatively modest. With the exception of the Tiananmen Square tragedy in 1989 and pockets of sporadic ethnic unrest in Tibet and Xinjiang in 2008–09, China has not experienced large-scale political and/or social upheaval in its transition. Not only did China manage to avoid the more drastic short-term costs of transition, but it actually managed to achieve and sustain a relatively high economic growth rate in that period.

Why was China able to avoid the short-run costs and what enabled it to achieve and sustain such a spectacular economic growth rate? The purpose of Part IV is to attempt to answer that question. Chapter 15 traces the evolution of China's reform strategy and evaluates its results. Chapter 16 examines the new growth strategy introduced since the reforms, and Chapter 17 provides a comprehensive assessment of its outcomes. The final chapter presents a summary of the conclusions derived from the analyses of the preceding chapters, and discusses the future growth prospect of the Chinese economy.

PART I

The Traditional Economy

1. Population

While traditional China and Europe were of similar size in terms of land area, the former was much more densely settled. Thus China's population between the tenth and nineteenth century was almost double that of Europe (Maddison 2001). This huge difference in population size needs to be explained.

The Chinese were originally a people of the steppes but had ceased being pastoralists before modern history began (Tawney 1964). Early Chinese agricultural settlements were widespread but concentrated mainly in the North China plain and in the central and lower valleys of the Yellow River. Their territorial expansion was, however, exceptionally fast. For example, from the Zhou to the Qing dynasty the size of the empire increased 27.3-fold and farming zones increased 12.7 times (Deng 1999). In fact it has been shown that the speed of the expansion averaged 1.26 kilometres per year during the Tang-Qing period – a development which has no match in Europe.

According to Ho (1959), the colonization of the land by the Chinese took three forms. Firstly, the military colonialization in frontier areas. This involved soldiers stationed in garrisons in the frontier areas having to cultivate the land in times of peace in order to become self-sufficient and keep their maintenance costs to a minimum. The second form was the civil colonialization with the assistance of the government. That is, the latter provided wide-ranging incentives to civilians to start cultivating land and to establish agricultural colonies in remote parts of the empire. The incentives could range from land tax exemptions to the provision of free draft animals or seeds. The third form was voluntary private migration, which is that people moved simply because of economic necessity or for fear of political persecution. The five successive migration waves of the Hakka people from North to South China are cases in point for this category.

While in early China the Yangzi River valley was the major destination for migration, the situation changed after the collapse of the Han dynasty (AD 220) with movement towards the south. The invasion of northern China by Central Asian nomads provided the impetus for many Chinese to escape even further south, and in the fourth and fifth centuries the Chinese actually started settling as far south as the tropical areas of Southeast Asia

(Perkins 1969). During the Song period the pressure to move continued and the whole of Guangdong province was settled (Fairbanks 1992). In the Ming period the expansion continued and the island of Taiwan was colonized.

By the time of the Qing, all good land had more or less been settled and so the direction of migration changed towards the previously only sparsely populated, less fertile regions of China, such as the Yangzi and Sichuan highlands in the West, the Han River drainage area in Gansu, Shaanxi, Hubei and Henan in the North as well as Manchuria in the Northeast (Ho 1959).

In 1819, on the eve of the Opium War, the Chinese population was concentrated in five major macro-regions, which were the Lower, Middle and Upper Yangzi, the Southeast coast and North China (Skinner 1977). Though the area of these regions together constitutes only a small fraction of land in China, they accounted for almost 90 per cent of the total Chinese population (Perkins 1969).

Many scholars have debated whether the Chinese population was, in fact, as large and so highly concentrated. However, in the absence of a regular population census data, only more or less reliable and varied estimates can be used. There are, for example, the records which the Imperial government kept to account for money payments in return for compulsory labour services. Since it is known that all adult males between 16 and 64 years were liable to render such services, this database could be used to extrapolate regional population figures. However, it is known that these registration figures are not very reliable since under-registration was a common phenomenon in order to escape the draft for compulsory labour and/or military services or to avoid payment of tax.

Nevertheless, on the basis of these figures, with chronic under-registration factored in, the best estimates, given in Table 1.1, show that the Chinese population fluctuated between 50 and 60 million in the early traditional period prior to the Song. In the Song period the population experienced a surge and by the late Qing period it had increased almost eight-fold to 423 million in 1910. In spite of the huge numerical increase the average annual rate of growth over this approximately 1000-year period was only about 0.3 to 0.4 per cent. Yet compared to Europe the growth rate of China's population was much higher, for in roughly the same period (AD 1000–1820) the former increased only 5.3-fold in contrast to China's 6.5-fold rise (Maddison 2001).

The rate of growth of the population of a country is simply the difference between the average birth and death rates. The former is, of course, strongly influenced by the fertility rate (the average number of children per female over a lifetime) and the net reproduction rate (the number of girls

Table 1.1 Population estimates, traditional and modern China

Dynasty	Population (in millions)
Traditional China:	
Early Han	60
Early Tang/mid Tang (618–762)	50–60
Early Song (960)	55
Late Song (1280)	100
Early Ming (1380)	68
Late Ming (1640)	130
Early Qing (1650)	123
Late Qing (1910)	423
Modern China:	
Republic (1915)	447
Republic (1945)	533
People's Republic (1950)	547
People's Republic (2008)	1327

Source: Fairbanks (1992) and Maddison (2007).

born per woman). The average death rate in the long run depends on the standard quality of nourishment of the people and of a country's health care facilities and their accessibility to the general populace. In the short run it is also influenced by the comparative regularity of disasters, both natural and man made.

The relatively high rate of growth of the population in traditional China can largely be explained by its relatively high birth rate. Obviously reliable data are not available for the whole period. But based on whatever data are available, Liu and Hwang (1979) infer that China's birth rate from 1380 to the 1950s ranged between 37 to 42 babies born per 1000 population.

The high birth rate is largely due to the high fertility rate, which in modern theory is largely explained in terms of a high incentive for households to have children, based largely on the cost and benefit calculation in regard to having children by households (Perkins et al. 2001). The cost of having a child can be seen in economic and psychological terms. The latter would include the risk-taking and burden of parenthood, while the former would include the outlay of child support and such opportunity costs as loss of earnings due to parental time spent on child care. The economic benefit–cost ratio of having a child was very favourable in traditional China, with older children expected to contribute to household income with their work in the labour-intensive agricultural sector. Moreover, in the absence of social welfare children were relied upon to support their parents in old age. And with high infant mortality a greater number of children was a better insurance against old age (Landes 1969). However, there was a real social pressure to have children, especially sons, not only as a guarantee against poverty in old age but also and especially to maintain the family lineage system with its associated ancestor worship.

The lineage consisted of a group of males with the same surname who descended from the same ancestor and lived together in the same settlement (clan village) under the leadership of the eldest of them. If they lived together as one unit, they formed an extended family, which was the major feature of traditional Chinese society. The lineage or clan together owned land in a trust, the income of which covered the costs of ancestor worship (Baker 1979). This was practised in China since ancient times and was based on the belief that there was a parallel spiritual world. Since this was ordered and functioned similarly to the earthly world, the departed needed heirs to look after their welfare and needs in terms of food, shelter and money in the other world to allow them to lead a comfortable and happy afterlife. In turn, children also needed the supernatural support of their parents (Baker 1979). Ancestors whose line became extinct or whose descendents failed to do the prescribed sacrifices would wander through the supernatural world as hungry ghosts, the beggars of afterlife (Baker 1979).

In view of this perspective on life and the perceived need to ensure their own long-term economic and spiritual welfare, the traditional Chinese family tended to have more than one son. Reliable estimates of China's fertility rate are not available, but the range of estimates is between six (Lee and Wang 1999; Pomeranz 2000) and eight to ten (Telford 1995). However, Tang (1979) argues that since the probability of having a male child is one-half and that of bringing them to maturity was one-third, traditional families would have to plan for six births to support the expectation of having at least one surviving male heir. Moreover, the actual cost of children in traditional Chinese society was comparatively lower to parents than in Europe as the burden was shared between members of the extended family.

Traditional Chinese families also practised birth control; for example poor people tended to marry relatively late and space their children carefully. Moreover, their malnourishment also led to a relatively lower fertility rate. In addition, infanticide of girls was not uncommon since female children would belong to another lineage after marriage and thus could not be relied upon for ancestor worship or old-age support. In addition, the poor who already worried about the costs of daily sustenance also felt heavily the burden of the dowry that girls were expected to bring into the marriage. Without the fairly widespread practice of female infanticide, the birth rate in traditional China would have been still higher. Again, no reliable figures for female infanticide are available, but it ranged from one-fifth to one-quarter according to Lee and Wang (1999) and Lee and Campbell (1997).

High birth rate was accompanied by high death rate. The average death rate per 1000 population in late traditional China ranged from 26 to 41 (Liu and Hwang 1979). Infant mortality was high, for fewer than 60 per cent of all babies born survived the first ten years. The general mortality rate was also high, as evidenced from the low life expectancy at birth. According to Buck (1937), 50 per cent of all people died before they reached age 28 in the early 1930s. A study by Barclay et al. (1976) of China's rural population in 1929–30 gives the male life expectancy at birth as 25 years. In contrast, that of England at the same time was 45 years (Wrigley et al. 1997). Other estimates of Chinese life expectancy at birth in the nineteenth century are higher, with an average of the high twenties for females and the mid-thirties for males (Lee and Wang 1999).

But man-made and natural disasters occurred regularly in traditional China, which also took their toll on its population. According to Tawney (1964), drought occurred every 8–12 years between 620 and 1619, and flood occurred even more frequently at once every 3–5 years in some provinces during 1644 to 1900. The great drought in 1877–78 in four northern provinces and the subsequent famine claimed 9 to 13 million lives. The great flood of the Yangzi River between 1931 and 35 and that of the Yellow River between 1938 and 1946 wiped out 4.5 per cent of the population of Henan, Anwei and Jiangsu (Ho 1959). Man-made disasters were usually wars. One outstanding event was the Mongol invasion in the thirteenth century which wiped out 75 per cent of the population in five major provinces in the North and Northwest (Perkins 1969). This caused the number of the total population to drop by one-third, partly due to the invasion and partly due to the spread of the bubonic plague in China by the invaders, parallel to the Black Death in Europe. In addition, the Mongols turned farms and highly productive agricultural fields back into pastures to feed horses and other animals, which caused a significant drop in food grain production.

The fighting between the Ming royalists and the Manchu during the Ming-Qing transition in the first half of the seventeenth century, which coincided with the arrival of the Little Ice Age in the Northern Hemisphere (Eastman 1988), also caused a significant drop in the size of China's population. In the Taiping Rebellion in the late Qing period (1851–64), some counties in Anwei, Zhejiang and Jiangsu lost between 50 and 90 per cent of their population (Ho 1959) to the uprising. The overall number of deaths from the rebellion is estimated at around 20 million (Maddison 2007). Another 14 million people lost their lives in the three Northern provinces of Gansu, Shaanxi and Shanxi as a result of the brutal suppression of the Muslim rebellion there.

From the collapse of the Qing dynasty up to the establishment of the People's Republic in 1949, China was rocked by a series of wars. For example, between 1917 and 1927 the Republican armies launched the Northern Expedition to eradicate warlordism in Northern China, and a short time later the Nationalist government was engaged in a civil war against Communist insurgents. This was interrupted by a short period of a United Front to unify forces in the fight against the Japanese invasion of China. But the civil war was promptly resumed thereafter and lasted until 1949 when the Nationalists were driven off Mainland China and fled to Taiwan. The population losses due to these wars are hardly ever exact, but Rawski (1989) estimates that the casualties from the warlord years amounted to roughly 400 000, and Ho (1959) estimates that the Sino-Japanese War alone wiped out 15–20 million people.

In summary, the traditional Chinese economy was characterized by its huge population, the size of which was almost double that of Europe. The higher population of China can be explained by the faster speed of the expansion of the Chinese empire and its relatively higher rate of population growth. The latter, in turn, is due to its relatively higher birth rate. Incentive to have more children was high in traditional China because of lack of social old-age security, and China's peculiar family lineage system with its associated ancestor worship. The high birth rate was accompanied by a high death rate, due to high infant mortality, female infanticide and the regularity of both natural and man-made disaster. As a result, the population growth rate was moderated to less than 0.5 per cent per year on average. Nevertheless, population density was high, as the population was mainly concentrated in five regions which constituted a small fraction of land in China, but accounted for almost 90 per cent of total population. This exceptionally high-population density resulted in low labour productivity in agriculture, and at the same time generated a large pool of surplus labour in the traditional economy.

2. Agriculture

The importance of agriculture for traditional China can never be over emphasized because it has always been an agrarian economy. Between the ninth and eighteenth centuries agriculture accounted for 80 per cent of all employment and 70 per cent of national gross domestic product (GDP) (Feuerwerker 1984). Thus Chinese economic history in the pre-modern period is simply the history of Chinese agriculture (Perkins 1969).

One of the main reasons why traditional China outperformed Europe in terms of population and per capita income was the unique perform-ance of China's agriculture. It brought much higher yields than that of Europe. This was partly due to comparatively better conditions, for in many parts of China there were regularly two harvests per year, and in the warmer southern rice-growing regions even three. However, the com-paratively better performance of China's traditional agriculture was also due to better technology, institutional arrangements and more favourable government policies. In the early period agriculture was confined to the North China dry lands which has similar farming conditions to those of Northern Europe. But due to population pressure and the general scarcity of farmland the Chinese farmers were inspired to improve and perfect their cultivation techniques early on.

The first step was to shorten the period during which land was left fallow after harvesting to allow the soil to reaccumulate nutrients before the next sowing. In the early times, from Shang to Zhou times, slash-and-burn cultivation was practised, with long periods for land recovery in between. However, in Zhou times the fallowing of land was shortened to three years (Deng 1999). During this period China adopted the famous well-field system in which each community divided its fields into nine plots, eight of which were allocated to private households for cultivation. The ninth plot was held by the community and was cultivated by all households together to pay their taxes (Bray 1984; Deng 1999) and to fund general welfare.

From the end of the Zhou dynasty on, according to Bray (1984), the length of time that a field lay fallow declined steadily as is evidenced by the slow but steady increase of the multiple cropping index from 0.6 in the Han period to 0.8 through the Tang dynasty, and to 1 in the Song period in AD 1040 (Chao 1986). Thus, by about 1100 the land was cultivated each year and no land was left fallow. In contrast, fields in Europe were left fallow every other or every third year before the eighteenth century (Bray 1984).

The second step in improving the yield in China's agriculture consisted in economizing on the amount of seed used in the sowing process. This was made possible when seed drills were invented which allowed the careful selection and placement of seeds in rows. In addition, seeds were treated with insecticide or fertilizers. In contrast, seeds in Europe were sown by the broadcasting method which resulted in wastage of seed and a comparatively lower yield–seed ratio. In Medieval Europe it was about 4 to 1 for wheat whereas in China it was about 10 to 1 in the twelfth century (Maddison 2007). In South China's wet rice cultivation the transplanting technique was used where seedlings were grown in seedbeds and then individually planted in fields. This method resulted in an unprecedented high yield–seed ratio of 500 to 1 (Bray 1984).

The third method to improve the yield in traditional agriculture was the development and use of efficient tools in the processes of soil preparation, sowing, fertilizing, watering and weeding. In this respect the Chinese farmers had the best tools from early on, for wooden ploughs were already used in the Lungshanoid period in 3000 BC (Bray 1984). These were replaced by iron ploughs during the period of the Warring States (475–221 BC), and their use was widespread in Han times (206 BC to AD 220). In sowing, seed drills used in North China since Han times were unknown in Europe until the sixteenth century (Bray 1984).

According to Perkins (1969) the development and use of fertilizer went through three stages in China. In the first, the type of fertilizer used was mainly greenstuff, for instance grass. In the beginning of the second stage, in the early Yuan dynasty (1271–1368), night soil was used, and later other commercial fertilizers such as manure, dried fish and oilcakes were used. With an increasing ratio of men, pigs and draft animals per unit of land it became possible to intensify the use of fertilizer, and its application per unit of land doubled between 1400 and 1957 (Perkins 1969).

In contrast, the application of fertilizer in pre-industrial Europe was limited. The main source was animal manure and in some regions night soil. Bray argues that the former tended to be in short supply in the winter months when the harsh weather conditions took their toll on livestock (Bray 1984). However, fertilizer in traditional agriculture in Europe was generally applied only once to every crop, before sowing in spring. After the harvest, greenstuffs or husks or similar tended to be used to help the soil to recover over the winter.

Another vital factor in improving the yields of agriculture was the timely supply of water. Its regulation started from early on in China with the use of the water wheel. Large-scale irrigation and flood control projects were begun as early as the period of the Warring States (Bray 1984). However, the rate of construction of irrigation works was moderate until the beginning of Tang times when it accelerated. From then on it remained high through both the Tang and Yuan–Ming periods, for the percentage of irrigated acreage tripled between 1400 and 1820 and reached 30 per cent (Maddison 2007). In contrast, only about 3 per cent of all cultivated land in Europe was irrigated.

For their weeding, from at least the sixth century Chinese farmers had a variety of horse-hoes and ridges at their disposal which allowed them to weed their rows of plants in a careful and effective manner. In contrast, horse-hoes were developed in Europe only in the eighteenth century, with the agricultural revolution (Bray 1984).

Apart from improving cultivation techniques by way of invention of newer and more efficient new tools, farming in China kept improving its performance and yield due to its adoption of ever new varieties of seeds. Over the past three millennia thousands of new varieties of grains and seeds have been discovered and adopted in China. Perkins (1969) makes the point that for rice alone an average of 19 varieties were discovered every year. In contrast, European farmers tended to be more conservative and to persist with the seeds that they knew, and, unfortunately, only a few good strains of seeds were available to pre-modern European agriculture (Bray 1984).

The above points and data provide evidence that China had improved and perfected traditional agricultural techniques for farming as early as the Han period (206 BC to 220 AD), whereas similar techniques and tools were unknown in Europe through most of the traditional period and were introduced there only in the course of the eighteenth century, lagging China's development in agriculture by roughly a millennium. This is also attested to by the fact that a handbook called 'The Essential Technique for the Common People' (*Qimin Yaoshu*), a treatise on agricultural technology, closely described agricultural techniques in eighteenth-century Europe – except that it was written in China in AD 534.

The institutional framework of agriculture plays a very important role as well: for example the organization of property rights and room for individual freedom and initiative are crucial in the promotion of productive entrepreneurship (Powell 2008) and in providing farmers with incentives to work hard. Furthermore, the development of a land market is important as it ensures that the most precious agricultural resource is allocated to those who can manage it most efficiently. And as in the case of agricultural technology, the institutional framework in China was far more efficient than that of feudal Europe.

Private property rights on land were introduced in China as early as the Zhou dynasty, as there was provision for both private and communal landholding in the well-field system in non-feudal areas as well as in the feudal landownership system. Yields in communally held plots tended to be low as peasants had little incentive to put much work into them. Private ownership of land was institutionalized in the Qin period (221–207 BC) with the introduction of the Shan Yang reforms. These abolished the communal land of the well-field system and replaced it with taxable family farms (Deng 1999). By the time of the Qing dynasty 92 per cent of land was privately owned (Feuerwerker 1984). Private ownership was initially in the form of freeholds, with the sole owner having the exclusive right to the land. Later on, ownership developed into a leasehold type with multiple ownership, with rights over the land divided into topsoil and subsoil rights. This meant that if there was a tenant the latter held the right to the topsoil and the landowner held that to the subsoil (Deng 1999).

The reason for this evolution, according to Palmer (1987) and Deng (1999), was that freeholding of land was comparatively less profitable as the landlord had to pay a land tax and the rent collected was fixed. In contrast, leaseholding tended to be more profitable since the landowner had no tax obligation and the rent collected tended to be sharecropping. Consequently the market price for freehold property was usually lower than that of leasehold. Hence landlords were very tempted to sell their freehold rights and to retain their leasehold rights in order to capture the benefits of the tenants' labour.

The rate of tenancy in traditional China was not particularly high. According to the statistics of the Department of Agriculture and Commerce, in 1918, 50 per cent of China's peasants were owner-occupiers, 30 per cent were tenants and 20 per cent were part owner and part tenant (Tawney 1964). According to Bray (1984) and Perkins (1969) the rate of tenancy in China remained relatively stable and changed little in the millennium between the Song and Qing periods. However, there were some regional variations in the rate of tenancy which tended to be lower in the North than in the South because of the former's relatively lower population density.

The tenant's rights were well protected in traditional China which provided a good incentive for them to work hard and invest in the property. The duration of the rental contract tended to be relatively long, with most of them being either semi-permanent or completely permanent since the Song period (Golas 1980). The tenancy rights were hereditary in the sense that they were usually passed from father to son, but they could also be freely sold or mortgaged without the permission of the subsoil owner (Watson 1977). Thus the relationship between the landlord and his tenants was based on contract rather than on a feudal relationship between lord and serf.

In the Song, Ming and Qing periods rent was usually paid in three forms, namely fixed rent in kind, fixed rent in cash or sharecropping. The latter was relatively common earlier but declined since the Song period. This was partly due to the high transaction cost for the landlord which required close supervision of the tenant's efforts, and the difficulty in determining the share of rent after the harvest (Golas 1980). By the late nineteenth and early twentieth centuries 75 per cent of rent on agricultural land was fixed, and 25 per cent remained in sharecropping which was more common in the North, whereas the fixed rent tended to be more prevalent in the Yangzi area.

Chinese farmers tended to pay on average about 50 per cent of their crop as rent, a figure which appears to have been relatively stable over the Song, Ming and Qing periods (Golas 1980; Tawney 1964). A fixed rental contract appears to have provided a better incentive for hard work for tenants, but it also carried a relatively higher risk than sharecropping where the risk of a bad harvest was shared by both parties. From the theoretical point of view, however, the incentive effects of both methods for peasant tenants are more or less the same (Cheung 1969).

Contrary to the assertion by Chinese Marxists, the tenant–landlord relation was not based on exploitation but on contract. A review of 175 volumes of Ming and Qing dynasty archives of rent-collecting records by landlord families in various prefectures of the lower Yangzi Delta (Chao 1981) shows that landlords had no effective control over their tenants. And the records show that it was not uncommon for tenants to fail to pay their rents in full, and yet delinquent tenants were not dismissed from the contract.

While in traditional Europe the peasants were bound by many restrictions, their Chinese counterparts enjoyed a relatively high degree of economic freedom in terms of their movement, activities and crop decisions. European peasants were tied to the land; they could not forsake agriculture or move to another area. They also were restricted in their decisions about which crops to plant in their fields. For instance, in Medieval England under the three-field system and prior to the enclosure movement each farmer had to follow a communally agreed plan. According to this, one field would typically be planted with rye or wheat; a second with barley, oats, beans or peas; while the third was kept fallow. Each year the field was shifted to the next phase in sequence. It was only after the enclosure movement that peasants assumed exclusive control rights to their property and could then plant whichever crop they pleased without reference to the rest of the community (Allen 2004).

In contrast, the system of a free peasantry existed in China as early as the Qin dynasty, after the abolishment of the well-field system and its replacement with taxable family holdings in the Shang Yang reforms discussed earlier. The relatively early institutionalization of private property rights for land allowed its free selling and buying and the relatively early development of a land market, perhaps as early as Tang times (Schurmann 1956). However, the transfer of a land title was subject to restrictions. To begin with, it was subject to pre-emptive rights. These were exercised either by: (1) a direct relative, such as the brother or a descendant of a brother; (2) a neighbour; or (3) mortgage holders or people who occupied the property by virtue of limited tenure but did not yet own it. Another restrictive practice in the sale of land was that it was subject to redemption, a rather common occurrence in traditional China. This meant that land could be purchased by a tenant, but they would receive only limited ownership since the seller would retain the right to repurchase the land at the original price after the expiration of a specified period. If the seller was unable to do so, the full rights would revert to the tenant. During the redemption period the occupant was not allowed to sell or otherwise dispose of the property.

Another difference is that land in China was vested in the family on a joint basis, where each family member was deemed to be a participant in the possession of the property. Thus, upon the death of a father the land was equally divided among his sons. Land was crucial to the Chinese family: it determined their status in society, their wealth and their social security. Moreover, land was symbolically important since deceased family members would be buried in family-owned fields. Descendents honoured their ancestors and would on no account relinquish their landholding unless they had no other option for survival (Schurmann 1956). For these reasons the transferability of ownership of land, in particular that of subsoil rights, while theoretically free was in practice severely restricted. In the above-mentioned survey of 57 volumes of local government records of land and household registers and 84 volumes of land purchase records of private households in the Lower Yangzi area in the Ming and Qing periods by Chao (1981), it was found that the turnover rate of ownership of land was relatively low, for it covered only 1.3 per cent of available land per year.

Though the transaction of subsoil rights was restricted, the exchange of topsoil rights was not. In fact, according to Palmer (1987) the very factors which restricted the trading of subsoil rights worked to facilitate the trading in topsoil rights. For one, the topsoil owner had no tax obligations and his name did not even appear in state registers. Exchanges of topsoil deeds were carried out by unofficial 'white deeds' (*baiqi*) and did not attract the 3 per cent government fee for official 'red deed' (*hongqi*) transfers for subsoil rights. Secondly, by only selling the topsoil rights, disguised as a permanent lease, and keeping rights to the subsoil families were able to comply with the lineage rules forbidding the sale of land to people who were not related to the lineage.

To sum up, the Chinese system of split land ownership and permanent tenancy, which had evolved over centuries, was optimal in that it provided not only enough security of tenure but also flexibility and incentives for all stakeholders.

Another important factor besides the institutional framework was government policies which were rather favourable to agriculture in China and supported its good performance. Traditionally, China was a physiocratic state which saw the promotion of agricultural development and, consequently, the better welfare of farmers as a guarantor of political stability. Hence governments tended to adopt low tax regimes with a comparatively low rate of land tax, which was the main tax on agriculture in general. The tax was very narrowly based on land area and, therefore, remained inelastic in respect to income and price. To avoid tax, farmers tended to under-register their land and thus the real burden of land tax (tax as a percentage of land produce) was low. In the Han and Tang times the burden was only between 1.6 and 2.5 per cent of total grain output for peasant households (Deng 1999). In the late Qing period land tax as a percentage of land produce was only 2–4 per cent. In contrast, the Japanese land tax in the Meiji period amounted to 10 per cent of land produce (Wang 1973).

Besides a low rate of taxation, the government supported agriculture by providing assistance to farmers in various ways over the centuries. For example, there was a public granary system to store grain. These granaries were of three types according to Bray (1984). Firstly, granaries for produce collected as tax or as tribute. Secondly, there were normal granaries to control fluctuations in grain prices and ease shortages. The earliest of these granaries was established in 54 BC and they were widely adopted in the Tang dynasty. The third type of granary was charitable: community granaries for the support of widows and their children, especially in times of famine. These were quite important and in the late Qing period they held between 3 and 4 per cent of the total national grain output and were capable of feeding 5 per cent of the provincial population for 15 per cent of the year (Will and Wong 1991).

From time to time the government would also step in to rescue poor and landless peasants. For instance, in the Song period poor peasants could make use of specially provided low-interest loans made available by the government. Under the Wang An Shi reform (1021–86) special cheap bridging loans were also given to needy peasants to tide them over the period when the grain from the old harvest was consumed but the new crop was still in the blade (Deng 1999). The government also issued state-controlled land to landless citizens, a practice which had begun as early as the Han period. The final and not the least important measure was that the government periodically controlled or banned the trading of land in order to counter a tendency towards concentration of land in the hands of a few rich peasants (Deng 1999).

Thus China's institutional framework and supportive government policies provided favourable conditions for China's agriculture, and land productivity reached its pinnacle during the Song dynasty. Between 960 and 1279 during the Song dynasty, or within a period of about three and a half centuries, China's population growth started to accelerate and it actually increased by 82 per cent from 55 million people in 960, to 100 million in 1280. In the same period, China's per capita income surged by 33 per cent (Maddison 2007). Thus the Song period seems to have been critical for China's economic development in the past, and the question is how this staggering performance in the Song period can be explained.

During the Song period agriculture was still contributing about 70 per cent of China's GDP and thus the surge in per capita income must have been due to improvements in agricultural performance. Since per capita agricultural output is simply a product of yield (Q/Ld) and the land–man ratio (Ld/P) the source of its increase must have come from these two factors. Reliable estimates of the land–man ratio are not available but there are strong indications that this was drastically reduced due to the population explosion. This implies that the surge in income per capita during the Song period must have come entirely from a tremendous spike in agricultural yields in that period. How can this be explained?

The productivity of land can be increased in different ways, for example: (1) one can plant higher yield varieties of crops; (2) one can work the land more intensively by double cropping; and (3) one can grow other crops which are more suitable to the given climate and conditions and bear a higher yield. It seems that the rise in productivity was due to all three factors of which the first, namely the planting of higher-yield varieties, played a dominant role. For although no reliable cropping data for this period are available, the shift of the population to the South must have been accompanied by an increase in the acreage planted with rice instead of the traditional northern crops of wheat, millet and barley. Data from the 1929–37 period suggest that the national average of rice yield was 342 catties per *mu* (1 catty is equal to 0.5 kg, and 1 *mu* to 0.067 hectares), which was about 2.4 times that of wheat, for example 141 catties per *mu* (Perkins 1969). And since this ratio would be fairly constant it seems logical that the increase in the acreage of rice crops during the Southern

Song period was a significant factor in explaining this rise in agricultural productivity.

A second factor contributing to the higher yield of agriculture in the Song period was the introduction of cotton, for before it was introduced to China the Chinese used to wear clothing made of hemp. According to Bray (1984), cotton spread via two routes: a southern route from Indo-China to Guangdong and Fujian and a western route from Turkestan to Gansu and Shaanxi. By the thirteenth century it had reached the Yangzi delta. The yield of cotton fibre per unit of land is about 10 times higher than that of hemp (Elvin 1973).

A third factor which contributed to the revolution of agriculture in the Southern Song period was the introduction of Champa rice from Indo-China which came to Fujian in 1012, and later into the Yangzi and Huai River deltas (Bray 1984). It was so successful that by the end of the twelfth century 80 to 90 per cent of the rice crop in the lower Yangzi area was of this variety.

The difference between other varieties of rice and Champa is that the latter halves the growth period from six months to three months only (Ho 1959), which enabled peasants to achieve much more intensive use of land through double cropping. Champa rice is also much more drought-resistant than other varieties, and enabled the peasants living in drier and hillier regions with an unreliable water supply to grow rice as well.

Increased marketization and specialization also contributed significantly to the increased yield of Song agriculture. While agriculture in Han and Tang times was largely on a subsistence scale, with little trade other than luxuries and salt, Song agriculture was different. The shift of the population and the move of the capital to the South required an efficient transportation network. Thus the Song government set out to construct a national water-way network (Hartwell 1971), with rivers and canals as the main routes. And by the end of the tenth century all economically important regions of China were linked into a single 48 000 km network of canals and navigable rivers (Chi 1936). The availability of cheap water transport in turn supported the development of markets and reinforced specialization in agriculture.

How high the degree of market specialization actually was in the Song period is not exactly known, but according to Golas (1980) large quantities of rice were shipped from South China to the north along the Grand Canal and also over land. And a flourishing sea trade brought rice from the surplus regions of the lower Yangzi and Pearl rivers to the rice-deficit areas of the Southeast coast. This trade made it possible for farmers to specialize in cash crops and handicrafts.

The Song government played an important role in promoting agricul-tural development by building a transport network, but it is also credited as the first government in the world to adopt an integrated approach to rural development. In contrast to industry, many inputs in agriculture are complementary and cannot be substituted. Hence individual policies are not likely to be effective unless reinforced by a set of complementary policies. For instance, if the government provides peasants with new seeds it also has to support the adoption of new seeds by way of an agricultural extension service. Since new seeds may also need more water, the construction of irrigation projects becomes necessary. And more intensive cropping requires more fertilizer which needs to be commercially available in sufficient quantities. These tasks all need to be done or promoted by the government, which also has to ensure credit facilities for peasants to enable them to buy agricultural inputs. In addition, the government also needs to reform the institutional framework to suit changed circumstances, to ensure that farmers have enough incentives to work hard and invest.

The various forms of assistance described below, provided by the Song government to agriculture a few centuries ago, bear an uncanny resemblance to the integrated rural development strategy recommended by the International Organization for Asian Developing Nations in the 1960s and 1970s:

1. Introduction of new seeds. In 1012 some 1 092 000 litres of the early-ripening Champa rice were delivered to key agricultural areas together with precise instructions by the government on how to cultivate it (Bray 1984).
2. The establishment of a rural extension service. The extension officers, known as master farmers, were appointed to instruct their peers in new techniques and they were also authorized to report farmers to local authorities if they failed to adopt new techniques.
3. Dissemination of agricultural technology. The invention of block printing in the ninth century was utilized by the government to print handbooks on agriculture. Some 78 of them had been published previously, but in the Song dynasty another 105 volumes on agriculture were added.
4. Extension of credits. As mentioned before, credit was extended to peasants in the form of 'green sprout agricultural loans' at or below the market price.
5. Tax incentives. Agricultural products and implements were exempted from commercial tax. In addition, the rate of land tax was reduced to below the value of one-tenth of the harvest. Thus, the Song period was the only time in traditional China when the share of land tax in revenues of the central government fell below 50 per cent (Golas 1980).

Table 2.1   Grain output performance in the Ming and Qing periods

	Population (million)	Cultivated land (in mill. *mu*)	Land–man ratio	Grain yield (catties per *mu*)	Output per capita (catties)
1400	72	296	4.11	139	570
1770	270	760	2.82	203	570
1850	410	960	2.34	243	570

Source: Perkins (1969).

6. Protection of tenants from exploitation by landlords. There were decrees which limited the power of landlords over tenants and, in some cases, made them pay compensation if tenants were displaced. There was also a decree forbidding landlords to charge rent on the second crop.
7. Measures against concentration of land in the hands of a few. The Song government introduced the public field law as part of a land reform policy. This countered concentration of land in the hands of a few and distributed it to landless peasants (Bray 1984; Golas 1980).

After the successes of the Song period in promoting agricultural development, Chinese traditional agricultural performance stagnated. Since Chinese traditional agriculture is mainly grain-based (Perkins 1969) its performance can be measured in terms of grain output, as shown in Table 2.1. It presents the major findings of Perkins's study of this period. It shows that while grain output itself kept increasing, the output per capita stagnated.

Perkins sees the reason for this in two factors, namely the worsening land–man ratio and the very slow increase in land productivity after the spurt in the Song period. In the almost 500 years of the Ming and Qing periods, China extended its territory due to the colonization of Taiwan and Manchuria and a westward migration of the population towards Sichuan, Yunan and the Yangzi highlands. Thus the area of cultivated land increased 3.24-fold. However, while the size of farmland more than tripled the population increase was 5.7-fold, that is, nearly twice the rate of the former. Hence the land–man ratio shrunk nearly by half, dropping from 4.11 *mu* per capita to only 2.34.

At the same time, land productivity increased steadily but slowly, just enough to offset the fall in land–man ratio and keeping per capita output constant. Over the 500 years land productivity increased by only 75 per cent in total. The main reason for this seems to have a considerable slowing of innovation in agricultural techniques. There was the development of new seeds, with an average of nearly 500 new varieties of rice seeds discovered during the Ming and Qing periods. There was also the introduction of new crops from America, such as potatoes, tobacco, corn and peanuts. These contributed significantly to growth in agricultural output because of their high yield and their suitability to grow in poor land and mountainous areas. In addition, best practices of farming methods developed during the Song period spread to the more backward areas.

However, on the whole there was relatively little innovation of cultivating techniques in the Ming and Qing dynasties. That these remained essentially the same is shown by the three major agricultural handbooks published in 1313, 1628 and 1742 respectively, containing almost identical numbers and kinds of farm tools (Perkins 1969). The same occurs with respect to water wheels and irrigation techniques.

As mentioned before, agriculture in the Song period was already relatively highly marketized and commercialized. Thus there was little room to push this further in the following periods of Ming and Qing. Hence, there was no significant rise in per capita trade between 1400 and 1800. Thus trade remained unimportant in respect to the rise in yield.

A greater application of labour and capital per unit of land associated with a greater cropping index explains most of the yield increase. In the Ming and Qing periods the cropping index increased from 1.0 to 1.4 (Chao 1986) as double and triple cropping became increasingly widespread in the South. This in turn led to a much greater application of labour in sowing, transplanting and harvesting, to an extent that labour even became scarce in certain seasons. Multiple cropping also led to a more intensive use of capital because of the greater use of water controls, seeds and fertilizer. Using the growth accounting framework, Perkins shows that the greatest part of the increase in grain output in the Ming and Qing periods can be explained by greater inputs, with only a minute percentage due to a change in agricultural techniques (Perkins 1969).

In conclusion, agriculture was the mainstay of China's traditional economy and the Chinese pre-modern economic history is simply the history of Chinese agriculture. One of the main reasons why traditional China outperformed its European counterparts in terms of output and output per capita was the superior performance of its agriculture. This was in turn due to its better technology, institutional arrangements and favourable government policies. Chinese traditional agricultural performance reached its pinnacle during the Song period and stagnated thereafter. The land–man ratio worsened due to rapid increase in population, whereas land productivity increased only slowly due to a lack of significant technical change. The productivity increase was just sufficient to offset the decline of the land–man ratio, and as a result the output per capita remained constant over the 500 years during the Ming and Qing periods.

3. Urbanization and traditional industry

URBANIZATION

Urbanization in feudal Europe was due to two major factors, namely agricultural surplus and, equally important, trade by craftsmen and merchants. Cities often developed along trade routes and functioned as shelter for escapees from nearby manors. In contrast, urbanization in traditional China was directly correlated to the growth of agricultural productivity and it can be shown that there were two distinct phases of urbanization, an earlier one and a later one. Thus cities in China had a pattern different from that of Europe in two ways. Firstly, they were multifunctional, for in addition to being marketing centres for handicraft industries they served as the nation's administrative centres and garrison posts. And secondly, while cities in Europe were fairly evenly distributed, the majority of China's cities were concentrated around the Yangzi River and in the Southeast coast with Beijing being the only important city of more than 100000 people in the North.

The unique features and trends in urbanization in China are best explained by a model developed by Chao in 1986. According to this, the growth of cities is constrained by three factors on the supply side, namely: (1) peasants' productivity; (2) peasants' consumption standards; and (3) the cost of transport of agricultural goods to the city. The growth of cities is limited by the share of the urban population in agricultural output, Q. Assume that farming population is Pa, urban population is Pu, the share of urban population is defined by the following relation:[1]

$$Pu/P = (1 - ca/Q/Pa)(1 - t) \qquad (3.1)$$

where ca is the average farmers' consumption; Q/Pa, farmers' productivity; and t, transport efficiency indicator, which measures the percentage of food grain eaten by transport workers. Thus the growth of cities can be accelerated: (1) by a lowering in farmers' consumption standard; (2) by increasing farmers' productivity, Q/Pa; and (3) by lowering the cost of transport, t.

This model is useful in explaining the unique features and trends in urbanization in China. Its merits are that it, firstly, emphasizes the cost of transport of farming products to the cities as a decisive factor in the location of cities in traditional China. Perkins (1969) shows that before 1900 most of the larger cities were located in the South. Out of the total of 46 large cities with a population of more than 100 000 that existed in China, 24 relied on the Yangzi River and another eight were located on the Southeast coast. In contrast, the only city in the North was Beijing, a mainly administrative city, which had to be supplied with grain shipments via the Grand Canal. The reason for this was that the cost of grain transport was cheaper in the South than in the North, because in the former goods were moved mainly in bulk by junk on the Yangzi, whereas in the latter on comparatively more expensive overland transport. This could be 20 to 30 times more expensive (Perkins 1969). Thus North China experienced a growth in large cities only in modern times with the construction of railway lines and advanced industrialization.

Secondly, the two-stage model of urban development can be explained by the rise in agricultural productivity. There are no official figures for the urban population, for the Chinese government did not distinguish between urban and rural population in its population statistics. Thus we must rely on two well-known guesstimates, namely those by Chao (1986) and Rozman (1973). According to Maddison (2007) Chao's relatively high estimate of urbanization for the Southern Song time is not credible as it relies on dubious accounts of Marco Polo and Hollingsworth (1969). That of Rozman (1973) is more reliable. Table 3.1 compares the degree of urbanization in traditional China according to Rozman's data with comparative estimates for three European countries by de Vries (1984).

Table 3.1 shows the two stages of urbanization in China clearly. In the earlier phase, due to increased agricultural productivity and surplus the rate of urbanization rose steadily from 4.7 per cent in mid-Tang times to 6.5 per cent in the middle of the Ming period. Compared to Europe, the degree of urbanization and its rate of growth were much higher and the average size of Chinese cities was much larger than in Europe.

In the second phase of China's urbanization from mid-Ming times to the late Qing period, agricultural productivity in China stagnated and, as a direct consequence, so did the rate of urbanization. In the last stage of the Qing dynasty it even started to decline and fell by 1 per cent to 5.9 per cent. In contrast, in this time the rate of urbanization in Europe soared due to higher agricultural productivity as a result of the agricultural revolution, combined with the revolution in transport technology with the arrival of railways and steam ships, and the industrial revolution in the seventeenth

Table 3.1   Comparative urbanization in traditional China and Europe

Period	Degree of urbanization (%)	Number of cities (10 000 or more)	Average size of cities (000s)
I. 762 to 1506			
China			
762	4.7	50	60
1120	5.2	91	41
1506	6.5	112	44
Europe			
1000	0.0	4	n.a.
1500	5.6	154	22
II. 1650 to 1820			
China			
1650	6.8	112	44
1820	5.9	136	48
Europe			
1650	8.3	197	31
1820	10.0	364	34

Source: Rozman (1973) and de Vries (1984).

and eighteenth centuries. Thus in 1820 the number of large cities in Europe was almost triple that of China.

TRADITIONAL INDUSTRY

Traditional cottage industry was the second most important economic sector after agriculture. Table 3.2 shows that in 1890, relatively late, it still accounted for 8 per cent of gross domestic product (GDP), thus its share in GDP in earlier periods must have been significantly higher. A comprehensive survey of the industry in the Qing and Ming periods by Xu and Wu (2000) shows that it covered diverse product lines, such as tea, sugar, tobacco, oil, silk, cotton textiles, paper, porcelain, iron, copper, coal and salt. It was well developed and its products had a superb quality of craftsmanship so that they were internationally renowned and sought after.

The relatively early and rapid development of the handicraft industry is strongly related to the existence of labour surplus in China's agriculture. The modern concept of surplus labour is based on the definition that labour is employed to the point that its marginal product is less than the subsistence wage. Traditionally Chinese farms are family based and

Table 3.2   Share of economic sectors in China's GDP, 1890

Sector	Share in GDP (%)
Agriculture	69
Handicraft industries	8
Modern manufacturing	negligible
Mining, electricity and construction	2
Transport	6
Trade	8
Government	3
Finance	negligible
Personal services	1
Residential services	4

Note: GDP in 1933 prices.

Source: Maddison (2007).

differ significantly in their operation from the capitalist farm postulated by neo-classical economics. Chinese peasants did not hire labour at subsistence wages and did not operate for the sake of making a profit. Since everyone in the Chinese peasant family was a co-owner, they were all given subsistence wages, independently of whether they actually contributed to the economic operation of the farm. Similarly, any surplus was divided equally among family members. Thus, Chinese peasants actually treated family wages as a fixed cost. In order to maximize the surplus income above the fixed cost, traditional Chinese farmers tended to maximize their output subject to the constraints of their supply of labour. In Figure 3.1 if L_2 is the total labour supply of the family farm it will employ L_2 units of family labour where output, employment and the income from the land is maximized. Thus there was a tendency to overemploy labour with the result that its marginal product was less than its average subsistence wage rate. This led to an L_1L_2 amount of surplus labour. Traditional industries, such as handicrafts, provided an opportunity for peasants to reduce surplus labour and to increase family income. In order to maximize the surplus income, the family farm will allocate labour in such a way that the marginal revenue productivity of labour in agriculture, MRP_a, is equal to that in the cottage industry. In other words, the marginal productivity of labour in agriculture, MP_a, is equal to the marginal productivity of labour in handicraft production, MP_h, expressed in terms of agricultural product according to the relevant relative price ratio of handicraft versus agricultural products, that is, $P_h/P_a\ MP_h$.

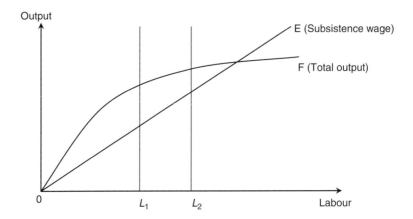

Figure 3.1   Employment of labour in the traditional Chinese family farm

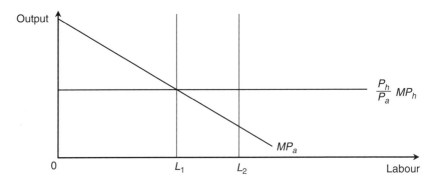

Figure 3.2   Labour allocation in the traditional family farm

In Figure 3.2 if L_2 is the total supply of family labour, to maximize both output and income a family farm would allocate OL_1 amount of labour to agricultural production and the rest, namely $L_1 L_2$ would be used for handicrafts. The relative amount of labour allocated to the latter would under these circumstances depend on: (1) the productivity of the cottage industry; and (2) the relative price levels of agricultural and handicraft products. An increase of either would shift the $P_h/P_a \, MP_h$ relation up and lead to the family farm's reduction in agricultural production in favour of that of the cottage industry and vice versa.

As mentioned before, China's traditional cottage industries covered a broad range of products. From early on the textile industry was important, with the spinning and weaving of hemp mainly in North China (Elvin 1972). Since the thirteenth century the processing of cotton became dominant and the centre of the traditional Chinese textile industry consequently shifted to the Yangzi River delta. The bulk of handicraft production was done in individual rural or urban households which brought their surplus to the periodic markets and exchanged it for other commodities and, occasionally, for goods of a more distant origin (Feuerwerker 1976). Much of the exchange took place without involvement of merchants.

There also existed a rudimentary putting-out system in which merchants supplied raw input materials, such as cotton, to individual households and later collected the finished products for sale on the market. However, this never gained significance. According to Elvin (1972) the reason for this was the growing number of markets in China which made supplies of the daily necessities and of raw materials for input readily available. They also provided price information for decision-making by producers of handicrafts (Golas 1980).

Skinner, in his study of marketization and social structure (1964), found that the average Chinese peasant was served by a hexagonal market area. This typically had a market town at the centre surrounded by an inner ring of six and an outer ring of 12 villages, with major routes radiating out from the town to the villages. The market areas were dispersed in such a way that even the most distant villages were within 3–6 km of the town. Thus the putting-out system was adopted only in special circumstances, for example in the tea industry which existed only in hilly areas, with often poor communication routes and few markets. It also was used in the silk industry when increasing foreign demand for silk inflated the price of silk cocoons so much that it required substantial working capital to purchase the raw material (Elvin 1972).

There were also handicraft workshops of the type which Chinese Marxists consider as the sprout of capitalist organization. These workshops were either controlled by cloth merchants in the case of textiles, or by individual craftsmen in the other industries, who employed hired labour to carry out their operation. Some well-known examples include the pottery kilns of the Jingdezhen in Jiangsu, the copper mines in Yunan and the salt wells and refineries in Sichuan (Feuerwerker 1976). However, they were hardly significant in term of output and employment compared to the household production of manufactured goods.

There are several reasons for this. Firstly, assuming that both individual and workshop production adopt the same techniques and face the same resource constraint, the output and employment of individual households would be higher. This is simply because households would maximize output while workshops would maximize profits. Secondly, apart from wage costs, workshop production would incur additional costs of the supervision, coordination and monitoring of hired labour. Hence work-shop production is worthwhile only if labour productivity is significantly raised due to the installation of labour-saving devices. However, Huang (2002) forcefully demonstrates that household production could hold its own even with a much lower labour productivity of one to four compared to machine production, for example, in weaving because of low-cost family labour. In contrast, the labour productivity gap in spinning by hand versus by machine was 1 to 40 and the introduction of workshops actually wiped out home spinning. Thirdly, since workshops would substi-tute machinery for labour until the ratio of rental cost of capital to wage of labour (i/w) is equal to that of their marginal productivities (MP_k/MP_l), the installation of labour-saving devices is worthwhile only if i/w is very low. However, this is unlikely in traditional Chinese society due to the scarcity of capital and the surplus of labour, especially in the key industrial area of the Lower Yangzi delta where the population density was much higher than in Northern China.

In Jiangsu, for example, the population density per hectare is alleged to have been 3.1 in the eighteenth century and over 3.9 in the middle of the nineteenth century (Elvin 1972: 154). This also explains why inventions such as the multi-spindle wheel, which was a powerful time-saver in the spinning of cloth, were not generally adopted in China, and why people stuck to the single spinning wheel although the multi-spindle wheel had been introduced in China in the thirteenth century (Elvin 1972).

SUMMARY

Growth of cities in traditional China was constrained by the size of agri-cultural surplus available to feed the urban population, which in turn depended on agricultural productivity, peasants' consumption standard and the cost of transport of agricultural goods to the city. Due to the prim-itive transport technology, traditional Chinese cities were concentrated along the Yangzi River and the Southeast coast to take advantage of the cheap water transport. There were two phases of urban development in traditional China. During the first phase, due to increased agricultural productivity and surplus, the rate of urbanization was higher than that of Europe; whereas in the second phase, due to stagnant Chinese agricul-tural productivity and the revolution of transport technology in Europe, Chinese rate of urbanization lagged behind that of Europe.

Traditional industry was the second-largest sector in China's traditional economy. It included traditional manufacturing, such as handicrafts and mining. The handicraft industry was highly developed and internationally renowned owing to the existence of the large pool of surplus labour and a high degree of marketization in traditional society. Handicrafts were carried out as a by-employment in agricultural areas, mainly in individual households. The putting-out system involving merchants, and the establishment of workshops with hired labour, was rare due to the limited scale of production and degree of mechanization due to the availability of cheap surplus labour.

NOTE

1. Let Ca represent the consumption of peasants, Cu consumption of city folks, then total food consumption is given by $Q = Ca + Cu$ (1) and the share of urban population in agricultural output is given by $Cu/Q = 1 - Ca/Q$ (2). Since $Ca = caPa$, where ca is average farmers' consumption and Pa, farm population, hence $Cu/Q = 1 - caQ/Pa$ (2a). Given that total population, P, is equal to farm population, Pa and urban population, Pu, hence, $Pu/P = Cu/cu/(Ca + Cu)/ca$ (3), where cu is the average consumption of the urban population. Assume further that $cu = ca$ and because of (1), then, $Pu/P = Cu/Q$ (4). With positive transport cost, $Pu/P = Cu/Q = (1 - ca/Q/Pa)(1 - t)$ (4a), where t is percentage of surplus food grain eaten up by transport workers.

4. Trade

Compared to agriculture, trade played a minimal role in China's traditional economy. It consisted of local market trade, regional long-distance and foreign trade. The first was small in volume and usually involved an exchange between peasants of their respective surplus products, such as grain for cloth and vice versa (Huang 1990). Nevertheless it was by far the most important type of trade in China and accounted for 77 per cent of all trade before 1910 according to Perkins (1969).

The distinction between local market and long-distance trade is important from the point of view of economic development, as the latter involves a certain degree of division of labour, specialization and economies of scale and enables producers to capture the resulting productivity gains and, hence, leads to Smithian growth (Wrigley 2002). However, this type of trade was rather limited prior to 1910 and accounted for less than 20 per cent of gross domestic product (GDP) (Perkins 1969). The long-distance trade that was generated was largely regional trade based on the comparative advantage of each region in terms of resources and climate conditions. Thus tea was exported from Fujian, Zhejiang and Anwei, raw cotton and cotton textiles from the Yangzi delta, opium from Yunan, sugar from Guangdong and Fujian, and silk from Jiejiang, Jiangsu, Guangdong and Sichuan. Salt was exported from Sichuan; wheat, soybeans and cotton from North China; and rice from the Yangzi delta (Chen and Meyers 1989). Table 4.1 presents the main commodities entering regional long-distance trade in China in the mid-nineteenth century.

Table 4.1 shows that long-distance trade in China consisted mainly of a small number of commodities, such as grain, cloth and salt, which together accounted for 80 per cent of trade volume. Grain constituted the basis of exchange, and salt and cotton cloth were its main object (Xu and Wu 2000).

Foreign trade involved even fewer commodities, such as tea, silk and cotton textiles, and it was insignificant in total trade. In the mid-nineteenth century, according to one estimate (Xing 2000), exports accounted for only 3 per cent *ad valorem* of marketed goods. This is partly due to the relatively high costs of the primitive transport technology, since goods for overseas trade had to be shipped by junk. Since most of this trade

Table 4.1   Volume of long-distance trade in China, c. 1840
          (in million taels)

Commodity	Value	%	Net import (−) and net export (+)
Grain	138.8	39.7	
Cotton	10.9	3.1	−3.0
Cotton cloth	94.6	27.0	−0.8
Silk	10.2	2.9	+2.3
Silk fabric	14.6	4.2	
Tea	27.1	7.8	+11.3
Salt	53.5	15.3	
Total	349.6	100.0	

Note: The figures exclude goods traded on local markets and the share of grain, cotton etc. sold to meet tax payments.

Source: Xu and Wu (2000).

involved fairly long distances, the value per tonne of traded goods had to be very high to make it worthwhile. Therefore, foreign trade mainly involved luxury goods, such as exports of Chinese manufactured silks against imports of spices from Southeast Asia. These luxury goods were beyond the means of the average Chinese and therefore foreign trade was not generally appreciated as a means of economic development in traditional China. For example, the famous Ming dynasty Admiral Cheng He failed to bring back from his seven voyages any valuable goods to China other than luxury items or biological specimens from other countries and continents. Because of such low regard, foreign trade was more or less forbidden in the Ming and Qing periods.

The relative significance of trade for the Chinese traditional economy can be assessed in terms of its share in GDP. It is obvious that the share of trade in China's GDP was relatively small. In the 1890s trade still accounted for only 8 per cent of GDP (Chapter 3, Table 3.2) and it must have been even less in earlier times. This compares to nearly 20 per cent in 1920 in the USA. And even low-income countries in 1958 had a higher average share of trade in their GDP, at 13 per cent (Kuznets 1971).

Since the lion's share of GDP in traditional China was made up by agriculture, the importance of trade can also be measured in terms of the marketed agricultural output. According to Perkins's estimate (1969) this was quite high before 1910, with about one-third of farm output traded, including handicrafts. However, three-quarters of this trade was just local. Regional long-distance and foreign trade were limited with the former covering only 6 per cent and the latter 0.5 per cent of agricultural output. Similarly, trade per capita in 1910 was still rather small and had not grown significantly between the fifteenth and the nineteenth centuries. This is quite different from the development in Europe where trade had flourished, and the question needs to be asked why China failed to develop a significant long-distance and foreign trade.

One of the reasons for this is that in an agriculture-based economy there is a limit to specialization and, hence, to trade simply because the scope for vertical disintegration of production in agriculture is limited. Specialization requires division of labour and the breaking-up of the production process into stages, each of which produces a different intermediate good, as input for the next one. Thus at every stage a producer on one site can specialize in the production of one good, buying his inputs from producers on other sites and selling his output as input to another producer in a different location. However, agricultural production, such as the growing of rice, is tied to a certain location and plot in which all the preparation of soil for planting, weeding, fertilizing, watering and so on needs to be done.

Moreover, Chinese peasants were aware that excessive dependence on the market for their grain supply carried with it the risk of starvation, and hence they tended to be risk-averse and unlikely to give up their self-sufficiency in food grain production for the sake of specialization (Perkins 1969). Last but not least, due to the existence of surplus labour in the family, farmers were able to satisfy a large amount of their own need of handicraft products rather than purchasing them from the market.

Another major reason why trade remained stagnant in traditional China was that the government had adopted a non-interventionist approach towards business. The size of the government is a major indicator of economic freedom for business (Lawson 2008), and it can be measured in terms of the rate of taxation of business activities. Using this indicator, the size of government in traditional China was very small because in 1908 the share of tax in net domestic product (NDP) was only 2.4 per cent (Wang 1973). In contrast, Japan's rate of taxation in the Meiji period in 1888 was 11 per cent (Minami 1994).

Moreover, the tax burden of business was very light, and a glance at the tax structure of the late Qing dynasty in 1753 in Table 4.2 shows that almost three-quarters of all tax revenues were collected from peasants as land tax, with only one-quarter of revenues from business. It was not until the early twentieth century that business taxes became an important

Table 4.2   Tax structure of the Qing government (%)

Item	1753	1908
Land tax	73.5	35.1
Other tax	26.5	60.9
Salt tax	11.9	15.4
Domestic customs	7.3	2.3
Maritime customs	–	11.3
Likin	–	13.6
Miscellaneous taxes[1]	7.3	22.3
Total	100.0	100.0

Note: 1. These included property deed tax, pawnshop tax, commercial tax, household tax, licence fees, tax on slaughtered animals, prostitute tax, gambling tax and other levies.

Source: Wang (1973).

source of revenue, and by 1908 they accounted for well over half of tax revenue.

The most important taxes for trade were the sales tax, known as miscellaneous surcharge, and domestic customs tax (see Table 4.2).The rate of the former in Qing times ranged from a low 0.5 to 2 per cent of value (Mann 1987). The latter was an internal tariff levied on goods in transit and was collected in the centres of commercial activities. This kind of tax was not conducive to trade development but hindered it, because rather then freeing the domestic market, it fragmented it (Wang 1973).

Similarly, the government's regulation of business was limited as well. The government only owned a few businesses in certain industries, such as in salt, ginseng, pearls and a few in porcelain manufacturing and silk (Feuerwerker 1984; Naquin and Rawski 1987). Most businesses were privately owned and subject to various government regulations. The Tang period was the only time in traditional China when foreign trade flourished and the government took a more active role to regulate it. For example, official market inspectors were sent to all the major trade centres to collect commercial taxes and supervize activities. They stopped monopolizing practices, controlled competition, enforced fair pricing and arbitrated trade disputes (Mann 1987). But from then on the degree of official involvement in local affairs, in marketing and trade declined steadily. Skinner (1977) argues that this was due to the growing size of the empire.

In Song times, in view of the high administrative costs, lack of information and poor staffing, the government contracted the collection of taxes and market regulation out to market brokers and this system was retained until the Qing dynasty. Brokers in rural markets were middlemen, *yahang*, who brokered grain, livestock and other transactions (Mann 1987). Those in urban centres were trade guilds or *hangtous*. Each broker was responsible for the collection and payment of sales taxes (Mann 1987). They also provided the central government with a crude formal bureaucratic control mechanism over the price, personnel and organization of the rural marketing system, though it is not clear to what extent these controls were enforced.

The contracting-out system works well if the contractors and contractees are not corrupt. In traditional China broker licences were issued by the county magistrate subject to a quota set by the provincial government. Since the magistrates were paid only one-third of their official wage and had to earn the rest through their activities, corruption seems to have been widespread, especially among officials in the Qing dynasty (Naquin and Rawski 1987). Therefore it seems very likely that the government's regulation of trade through the brokerage system in Qing times was ineffective. That the government's regulation of trade and enforcement of rules of commerce was lax is borne out, for example, by the fact that while the official monthly interest on a cash loan was limited to only 3 per cent, pawn shops in some instances charged interest as high as 36 per cent (Bernhardt and Huang 1994).

On first glance the non-intervention policy of traditional government should have favoured the development of business. However, unlike in Hong Kong and Singapore, such non-intervention in the context of traditional society is not positive but negative, for the Chinese government was more interested in system maintenance than in growth and expansion. Hence it tended to overemphasize the role of agriculture and neglected trade and business. It had failed to establish and maintain a proper infrastructure for trade development as there was: (1) no uniform system of weights and measures; (2) no sound monetary system; (3) no national banking system; (4) no uniform taxation; and (5) no adequate institutional framework to support private contracts (Eastman 1988). In addition, the transport and communication system was rather primitive.

There was no uniform system of weights and measures in late traditional China, as evidenced by Table 4.3. The units of weight and other measures differed between regions as often also between types of goods. For instance, while the official weight measurement of rice was 1 *picul* being equal to 100 catties, in Amoy it would be worth 140 and in Fuzhou 180 catties. Similarly, while 1 Chinese foot was officially equal to 10 Chinese inches, in Shanghai, 1 tailor's foot was equal to 13.85 Chinese inches and one carpenter's foot equal to 11.1 Chinese inches. The length of the foot used to measure land was 12.1 Chinese inches. The measures of volume

Table 4.3   Weights and measures in the Qing period and their variations

Official measure	Regional variations	Items of variations
1. Weight 1 picul (*dan*) = 100 catties	Amoy: 1 picul of rice = 140 catties Fuzhou: 1 picul of rice = 180 catties	Amoy: Indigo: 1 picul = 110 catties White sugar: 1 picul = 95 catties Brown sugar: 1 picul = 94 catties
2. Length 1 yard (*zhang*) = 10 feet (*chi*); 1 foot = 10 inches (*cun*)		Shanghai: Tailors: 1 foot = 13.85 Chinese inches Carpenters: 1 foot = 11.1 inches Land: 1 foot = 12.1 inches
3. Volume		Grain: 1 pint (*dou*) = 176 cubic Chinese inches Liquid: 1 pint (*dou*) = 1800 cubic inches
4. Area	1 *mu* = between 3840 to 9964 square feet	

Source: Eastman (1988).

also had great variations, with one litre being as low as 309.8 or as much as 3169 cubic Chinese inches. The purpose of the transaction also made an impact, for in buying merchants used a long pint, whereas in selling they used a short one (Eastman 1988).

In the absence of a sound monetary system, economic growth cannot be sustained. Moreover, its lack does not only hinder development of trade but also undermines it. An unsound monetary system also fails to protect private property rights as inflation erodes the value of a property held in terms of money because the government could simply expropriate private property by printing money and causing runaway inflation (Lawson 2008). Of course, the incentive to save and invest would have lessened with such measures.

Traditional China had a bimetallic system based on silver and copper, using three kinds of money, namely silver, copper cash and paper notes. Silver was used for large transactions and wholesale trade as well as for payment of land tax, whereas copper was usually the medium for retail and wage transactions. The official exchange rate between silver and copper was fixed at 1 *tael* of silver to one string of 1000 pieces of copper cash. However, in practice the exchange rate tended to fluctuate, at times violently, because the government was not able to control the supply of both metals (Wang 1979). The supply of silver was especially problematic because the output of domestic silver mines was limited and most had to be imported. The government did not cast silver coins itself and imports and exports of silver and its coinage were free.

However, it did try to control the supply of copper coins by controlling the output of the Yunan copper mines by tax and forced acquisition at fixed prices. Export of copper was banned and imports of copper were contracted out to a small number of merchants. But these controls were not effectively enforced and in the eighteenth century 80–90 per cent of copper production was sold against government regulation (Wang 1979). Similarly, the attempt to control copper coinage was not very successful. The government set up mints in the capital and various provinces and assigned each an annual quota of copper cash to be struck. However, counterfeiting and illegal melting of copper cash was rampant. Sometimes the government's own actions led to misuse. For example, in the early nineteenth century the government regularly debased the value of copper cash because of a shortage of revenues. It also reduced the copper content so that in the period 1821–50 a copper coin was 20–30 per cent less worth than it had been in 1736–95 (Wang 1979), with the result that its intrinsic value was smaller than its nominal one, which again was an incentive for forgers to counterfeit the coins.

In addition to the lack of a fixed exchange rate between silver and copper coins there was also lack of uniformity in both coins. Silver was circulated in bullion without standardization, so that each transaction required a professional money-changer to ascertain the weight and fineness of the metal. The matter was made even more complicated because the official weight unit of silver, the *liang*, was not standardized and experienced great regional variations.

The situation in respect to copper coins was no less confusing because there was nearly as much variety of coins, from government-issued to counterfeited ones, to foreign coins from Japan and Annan, as there were differences in weight and size between them. Thus it was hardly surprising when in the late Qing period due to the law of good money chasing out bad money, the Spanish or silver dollar struck in the West grew in popularity because of its standard weight and fineness.

The third kind of money used in traditional China took the form of paper notes and transfer of accounts. Although China had been the first nation to invent paper money and use it on a large scale, its volume and circulation declined rapidly after the thirteenth century, and it had virtu-ally disappeared after the sixteenth century. However, a paper currency revived in the nineteenth century in the form of paper notes of which three kinds were issued. These were, firstly, silver or cash notes issued by native banks, money and pawn shops initially as receipts for customers in return for deposits of silver or copper cash. Secondly, the native bank order was a kind of promissory note which was generally payable within 5–10 days; and thirdly, the Shanxi or remittance bank issued drafts. Transfers of current accounts were handled by domestic banks usually on the basis of oral instruction only, without the use of cheques.

The most commonly used of these four types was the silver and cash note equivalent of paper notes. These made up about one-third of all money circulated in the late Qing period (Wang 1979) because of their convenience and ease of transport. However, the issue and supply of paper money was not controlled by the government since there was no central bank and no reserve requirement. As a result, runs on banks, suspension and redemption of currency notes occurred all too frequently in tradi-tional China.

There were several kinds of credit institutions in traditional China. The most numerous were the pawn shops, which advanced cash against prop-erty pawned, usually at the high rate of 36 per cent interest per annum. There was also a type of self-help mutual finance association to which each member contributed a specified amount and could then borrow from the association either by lot or by bid (King 1965). However, since they provided only small loans their place in the finance business was limited.

In the eighteenth century the emerging local or native banks and the Shanxi or remittance bank played a much more important role. The local banks accepted deposits, maintained current accounts and paid inter-est. They also gave out small loans and issued paper money and, more importantly, issued native bank orders. A local bank order constituted an advance of credit for merchants which allowed them to finance their pur-chases on wholesale markets. Since the wholesaler could cash the note in only after 5–10 working days, this arrangement helped the merchant who, in turn, would repay the loan from the bank after having sold his goods (Eastman 1988). Thus while the local banks were important, their role in financing trade in traditional China should not be overestimated because their business was restricted to a local area and clientele. The appear-ance of their notes outside the local area was a rare occurance (Eastman 1988).

Since traditional China had no integrated national commercial banking system there was no facility for the mutual clearing of indebtedness. The

Shanxi bank was mainly engaged in the interregional remittance of money to facilitate long-distance trade. It only accepted a few current accounts and issued no bank notes, so its contribution to the creation of credit was rather limited (King 1965).

The most important institution to support private contracts in impersonal exchanges is the establishment and enforcement of contract law. This, however, was virtually non-existent in Qing times. The Qing Code of law – which had its origin in the Ming Code which in turn was derived from the Tang Code of law – was by and large a criminal law and failed to address areas usually covered by civil law. For example, only eight of its 436 statutes dealt with commerce (Brockman 1980). These Articles were:

- 149 Usury.
- 150 Bailing of pawned property.
- 151 Lost property.
- 152 Licensing of commercial agents.
- 153 Valuation of merchandise.
- 154 Monopoly practices and unfair trade.
- 155 False weights, measures and scales.
- 156 Substandard manufactured goods.

Contracts existed in traditional China within the framework of customary law which was not proscribed by the government but which was enforced through the legal institutions through the application of informal social sanctions.

A study of contract enforcement in Taiwan province in the late nineteenth century by Brockman (1980) shows that local courts were not effective as instruments of contract enforcement simply because the parties to the contract did not perceive that court-imposed sanctions would or could be enforced. Few contract disputes were even brought to the courts or the magistrate, either because people had no confidence in him, or because it caused too much hassle and distress, and was costly in terms of time and money. And as a rule magistrates had little time because of their multiple functions as policeman, detective, district attorney, judge and jury. If a trade dispute was brought to the court the magistrate would decide the case in accordance with local customs after consulting with local assistants, village headmen, guild leaders and local gentry members. Generally magistrates were rather flexible with the application of law and would often prefer a non-judicial settlement of disputes by passing the case to the authority of village headmen for private settlement (Brockman 1980).

In traditional China, informal settlement of conflicts and enforcement of rules was much preferred to formal enforcement mechanisms. These were in the form of pressure from the community on the defaulting individual or family through guilds, clans or other village organizations, or else through the self-enforcement of the contract system itself. The self-executing contract involved the simultaneous performance by both parties. Thus goods would be paid for when transferred, with no responsibility of the seller for defects after the buyer had accepted the delivery of goods. Each side could effectively withhold his performance to force the partner to perform.

Guilds were important for trade and commerce in traditional China because they reduced transaction costs considerably. They were trade and area based. Thus there were merchant, craft and professional guilds with members from the same county or district engaged in the same occupation. They provided members with information; quality control of goods or services; the standardization of market weights, measures and money exchange rates; and with mediation in the case of disputes between one of their members and other parties when contract enforcement was required (Chang Chan and Myers 1989). Often they also had their own quarters in other regions which served as hotels for members. Guilds lowered commercial transaction costs because they were cheap and convenient, but in the absence of formal contract enforcement mechanisms they were essential in the settlement of disputes. Because of their importance they were able to exert considerable pressure on their members and could impose fines or expel individuals, who would then be left in an organizational limbo.

However, contract enforcement by way of pressure from the community, too, had its limitations. Llewellyn (1931), for example, demonstrates that such informal pressures are effective only in a static society with long-term mutual dependence of members on each other. They are no longer effective in a dynamic society where people constantly change their occupation, residence and association. Furthermore, a guild could only control its own members in a contract dispute, but was powerless if a dispute involved another guild (Brockman 1980). Hence trade based on community relationships for contract enforcement tends to be restricted to personal trade relationships and thus remains small in scale.

Greif (2001) demonstrates that guilds in Europe, in contrast, developed contract enforcement mechanisms which were not only guild-specific and could, therefore, also enforce contracts with members of another guild. This enabled the development of impersonal trade by effectively attributing collective responsibility to all guilds or to the local community for any breach of contract by a trader. Guilds in China, however, showed little interest in the standardization of contract enforcement or in practising collective responsibility.

In general, in order to facilitate impersonal exchange, commercial customs and rules were arranged in traditional China in such a way that they could enforce themselves without the need to go to court. Besides the above-mentioned self-regulating exchange which required the simultaneous performance of both partners, there was one, often used in local trade, which required only a partial performance of one partner, for example the payment of a deposit in exchange for goods or services received. Failure to perform would then mean forfeiting the deposit. In regard to loan contracts the property or a third-party guarantor acted as security that the loan would be repaid with interest, or the property would be forfeited, or else the third party had to pay off the debt if the debtor failed to pay. The incentive of the self-enforcing contract lies in the fact that the gain from contract compliance is larger than the cost of cheating. This sort of contract, however, unfairly distributes the risk of loss to the buyers; however, the remedies available to the buyer in case of a breach of contract by the seller were strictly limited (Brockman 1980). Prepaying buyers possess no security or leverage at all to enforce the full delivery of goods if the price of the goods rises after the signing of the contract. A buyer in this position could only remedy the situation by cutting his losses and recouping the deposit without any compensation.

Thus self-enforcing contacts restrict trade as they cannot accommodate changing circumstances. They cannot prevent purely executory contracts with performance from both sides from occurring in the future as well as other non-self-enforcing contracts. This explains why interregional long distance trade and foreign trade in traditional China remained so underdeveloped.

In summary, trade in traditional China was highly developed. Yet in spite of this, it did not lead to Smithian growth. The main reason for this was the limited development of long-distance trade. Foreign trade was banned in late traditional China, and most trade was confined to local trade which was small in volume and involved an exchange among peasants of their respective surplus products. The limited development of long-distance trade was partly due to the nature of the agrarian economy under which the scope of vertical integration of the production process, and hence, specialization and trade, is limited. It was also due to the government's negative non-intervention policy toward business. The government failed to maintain a proper infrastructure for trade development. There was no uniform system of weights and measures, no sound monetary system, no national banking system and no uniform taxation system. Worst of all, the government in traditional China had failed to provide an adequate institutional framework to support private contracts.

5. Social structure

Chinese traditional society was strictly hierarchically ordered, with the population basically divided into two different classes, the rulers and the ruled. The rights, obligations and privileges of each class were clearly delineated and left little room for individual freedom or initiative. Box 5.1 depicts the social structure which developed in the Ming–Qing period and remained stable up to the modern period. At the apex of the Chinese social pyramid stood the Emperor, the Son of Heaven, whose function was to guarantee the harmony between heaven and earth. Closest to him was the hereditary imperial nobility, made up of the Emperor's clansmen. The next level, the non-Imperial nobility, was created as status reward for exceptional, mostly military, services and these positions were not hereditary. The next level was made up by the scholar-officials or the gentry.

The gentry, the scholar-elite, were given the power to govern the country because of their scholastic achievements which comprised both academic achievements and character-forming Confucian ethics. According to the monumental studies of Chang (1955) and Ho (1964) the Chinese gentry can be further subdivided into two main groups. The first of these consisted of degree holders with official appointments. Government officials were further divided into nine ranks. The first three ranks were made up of senior government bureaucrats at the central and provincial government levels, such as the Prime Minister, the Governor General and other provincial government officials. The second tier, which included the 4th to 7th rank, was constituted by mid-level bureaucrats, such as the junior officials at the central government level and senior officials at the local government level such as the county magistrates. The third tier of 8th and 9th-rank officials typically included junior officials of local governments.

The second group of the gentry class was made up of degree holders without official appointments. In traditional China, a degree was the passport to officialdom. A degree could be obtained either through the regular route, namely by passing a series of gruelling, competitive examinations at various levels, or sometimes through the purchase of a degree. It is unknown when this practice started but it obviously became more prominent in times of dynastic decline as a means of revenue-raising. At the height of the Qing dynasty, before the Opium Wars, only 3 per cent of the

---

BOX 5.1 CHINA'S TRADITIONAL SOCIAL STRUCTURE

Emperor and nobility
Emperor
Imperial nobility (Royal family, clansmen)
Non-Imperial nobility

The gentry

A. Degree holders with official appointments
1. Upper level: Officials of the 1st, 2nd and 3rd rank
2. Middle level: Officials of the 4th to 7th rank
3. Lower level: Officials of the 8th and 9th rank

B. Degree holders without official appointments
1. *Jinshi*
2. *Juren*
3. *Gongsheng*
4. *Shengyuan*

The common people
1. Scholars
2. Peasants
3. Artisans
4. Merchants
5. Soldiers

Source: Ho (1964).

---

holders of degrees obtained through exams were appointed government officials. The purchased degree holders appointed as officials numbered about 11 000. The total number of officials appointed was 35 000, of which 27 000 were active and the rest were retired officials (Feuerwerker 1976).

There were four distinctive types of degree holders, namely the *Jinshi*, the *Juren*, the *Gongsheng* and the *Shengyuan*. The latter, as the lowest level, were undergraduates at the district or prefectural colleges who had already passed a series of local government exams and, therefore, had gained the privilege of studying at these colleges. The examination that granted this access was held only twice in three years and was extremely difficult, with a quota of only 1–2 per cent of all candidates being allowed to pass. The *Shengyuan*, being undergraduates, were not entitled to official appointment without obtaining a higher degree. They were subject to periodic tests, which if not passed could lead to their demotion or even dismissal. If their results were good they could be promoted to *Gongsheng*.

Degree holders from the district and prefectural colleges were chosen to further their studies at the Imperial Academy for their eventual appointment as minor officials. Successful candidates of the provincial examinations were awarded the degree of *Juren*, the second-highest degree, which entitled them to the appointment as a minor official. Since the quota for passing this exam was as low as 1–2 per cent each year there would be many disappointed candidates. However, they could always resit the exams, which had no age limit.

The highest degree of *Jinshi* could only be gained by successfully passing the metropolitan examination, which was sat triennially. This degree entitled its holders to a middle-level official appointment. The highest exam for scholars was the Imperial Palace examination and those who passed were awarded the highly respected title of Champion of Examinations.

The numbers of the various degree holders on the eve of the Opium Wars were, according to Feuerwerker (1976) approximately as follows: 2500 *Jinshi*, 18 000 *Juren*, 27 000 *Gongsheng* and 460 000 *Shengyuan*. Altogether they made up only 0.1 per cent of the total Chinese population which stood at 400 million at that time. Since the numbers of active officials, which totalled 27 000, were not enough for the effective administration of the population, the scholars who held degrees but no official titles formed a unique informal layer of government. They were relied upon to liaise between the local government officials, such as the county magistrates, and the local communities. They performed various important government functions, such as the collection of taxes, the promotion of the general welfare of the population and protecting the interests of the residents of their area. Thus they were a part of the Chinese ruling class even though they did not hold what counted as official positions.

The mass were known as the common people and they occupied the lowest rank. This was further segregated into different groups according to their occupation. Those who laboured with their minds, for example scholars (as teachers) held the top position, followed by those who did physical labour. Here the peasants ranked ahead of artisans and merchants, and soldiers ranked last.

In the Ming and Qing periods there existed another layer below the ordinary, common people: a class of inferior commoners, a Chinese version of the Indian Untouchable caste. They included singers, dancers, entertainers and acrobats, and, of course, beggars and prostitutes, who were all denied the rights of commoners to sit for exams. They and their descendants were barred from marriage into the normal class of commoners. However, in the Qing dynasty in 1723–35 these distinctions were abolished (Ho 1964).

The status of the gentry was well guarded and associated with certain privileges which were denied to commoners (Chang 1955). The gentry's right to wear special, luxurious garments including decorative hat buttons was protected, with punishment of contraventions by commoners, even if the latter had become wealthy. The gentry were also a privileged group before the law – justified by their Confucian education and assumed adoption of high ethical standards – and could not be humiliated before a commoner in court, even if one had committed a crime. The gentry also had exclusive rights to participate in certain ceremonial rituals and enjoyed important economic privileges, such as exemption from labour service to the state, reduced rates of property tax, plus a monthly allowance from the government for *Shengyuan* degree holders. Last not least, an official who had served to satisfaction over a certain period of time was able to recommend that their status be granted to their son as well. However, this privilege was limited to one descendant only and was seldom extended to more than two or three generations (Ho 1964).

There has been considerable debate about whether China's traditional society was feudal or not, and there are good arguments on both sides. The key criteria of feudal societies are: firstly, a closed social system; secondly, a well-defined status and associated socio-economic hierarchy; and thirdly, the distribution of goods and services in accordance with the respective hierarchic ranking and their associated obligations.

On the basis of the first criteria, namely a closed society, China certainly was not a feudal society. China's society was a relatively open, not a closed traditional system, and there was a relatively high degree of both horizontal and vertical social mobility. Horizontal mobility was very wide spread and common, even though there were at times legal barriers to it. For example, in the early Ming period families were required to register their occupational status and not to change it under pain of punishment. However, because of lack of enforcement this restriction had lapsed by the second half of the Ming period (Ho 1964) and was completely abolished in the Qing period. Vertically, the ruled class or commoners were able to climb the social ladder potentially as far up as they merited on the basis of their results in the competitive civil service examination system.

These examinations were introduced during the Tang dynasty and lasted until 1904. They not only served as a selection mechanism for the most capable bureaucrats, but could be used for political control as well. In addition, they channelled the energies and ambitions of the most intelligent people in the country. Moreover, commoners paid for their own education and the privilege to sit these examinations. And since the curriculum was largely made up of Confucian classics, all candidates were homogenously moulded into malleable bureaucratic behaviour by its doctrine of loyalty and service (Elvin 1973).

While there were some restrictions of access to the civil service exams and upward mobility, these were mostly temporary. For example during the Song period merchants, artisans and their families were barred from sitting exams, However, this discriminatory restriction was abolished in the Ming and Qing periods (Ho 1964).

The examination system in China was a key selection method for its civil service for more than 13 centuries. In the Qing period the content of the exam consisted of three parts. According to Chang (1955), the first was writing an essay based on the classic four books *The Analects*, *The Doctrine of the Mean*, *Mencius* and the *Great Learning*, and writing a poem. In the writing of the essay a definite scheme of composition, the 'eight-legged style', had to be followed and the length was limited to 500 to 700 characters. The main criteria for the essay and the poem were calligraphy and poetic composition. The second part addressed any of the questions raised in the five classic works *The Book of Change*, *The Book of History*, *The Book of Odes*, *The Spring and Autumn Annals* and *The Book of Rites*, and the third part involved discussion questions.

This shows that the content of the exams was more concerned with writing style and moral content rather than with current political affairs and a problem-solving approach. Moreover, since the pass quota was so low and the stakes very high, candidates tended to concentrate their studies on model answers of recently successful scholars rather than focusing on the classics themselves.

The purchase of degrees by wealthy commoners was the second channel of upward mobility in times of dynastic decline. However, up to the Taiping Rebellion in 1851 the government ensured that the examination system remained a primary channel of selection of government officials and sale of degrees and offices a secondary channel. It was only in the late nineteenth century when the government faced dwindling revenues and soaring expenditures that it had to rely on the sale of government positions to a greater extent.

In conclusion, it must be argued that on the basis of the openness of China's social structure, as evidenced by the selection of officials through the competitive examination system, China was not a feudal society, even though it had a well-defined status and socio-economic hierarchy, and the distribution of goods and services was, by and large, in accordance with the respective hierarchic ranks.

6.   Why China failed to industrialize

There are several reasons why industrialization is an absolute necessity for modern economic growth. First, there is a specialization limit to growth in the traditional agricultural economy since, as mentioned earlier, Smithian growth is based on the division of labour. Unlike modern industry, there is a limit to vertical disintegration of the production process and hence division of labour in agriculture, as discussed before. Second, there is a biological limitation to growth in an agrarian economy which uses land as its main production factor. According to Wrigley (1988) and Landes (1969), agrarian economies are organic because they largely rely on plants for their raw materials and main sources of energy. And human and animal power, the traditional sources of their energy, rely on the supply of food which in the long run is constrained by the fixed production factor of land. Thus growth and productivity are limited, and once the land cannot be expanded diminishing returns set in and the traditional economy stagnates. In contrast, an industrial economy relies on stored energy in the form of fossil fuels. Through the development of the engine which converts heat into work, fossil fuels provide a not entirely unlimited but nevertheless huge supply of energy which largely replaces the need for human and animal sources of power. Furthermore, the fossil fuels also provide an unlimited supply of mineral raw materials. Thus land as a fixed factor of production no longer restricts growth.

In view of the importance of industry to sustained economic growth, the question thus arises as to why traditional China did not embark on industrialization after it had encountered limited growth. Was China not ready for it?

TECHNOLOGICAL CONSTRAINTS

One of the explanations why China failed to industrialize in the traditional period is its alleged lack of science and technology, both of which are prerequisites for industrialization. However, this has been clearly refuted by Needham who in his 13 volumes of *Science and Civilization in China* (1954–97) demonstrated that China not only had the required scientific knowledge, but before 1400 also led Europe by centuries in such areas as mathematics, astronomy, physics, engineering and material and civil technology, medicine and agricultural technology. Many Chinese inventions, such as gunpowder, paper, printing and the compass were well known in the world and, for example, were regarded by Francis Bacon as the most important inventions that facilitated the transformation of society from the Dark Ages to the modern world. Many of these subsequently found their way into Europe, either by direct importation or by independent reinvention (Mokyr 1990; Jones 1990).

In a recent paper Lin (1995) blames the lack of modern sciences for China's failure to have a scientific and, ultimately, an industrial revolution. He argues that scientific discovery in China remained pre-modern in that it relied on trial and error and remained experience based. He argues that with knowledge based on trial and error China should have experienced at least parallel development to Europe, which had a scientific revolution around the fifteenth and sixteenth century. However, this did not happen because China failed to make the transition to modern science.

Modern scientific discoveries are driven by abstract problem-solving through mathematization, and by posing and testing hypotheses about nature which are then tested in controlled experiments. Though China had many gifted and inventive people they did not embrace this path of inquiry, since the institutional framework in which they operated motivated them to compete successfully in the civil service exams and thus to emphasize the study of the Confucian classics. Science in traditional China was always a subsidiary subject and was not valued in its own right. Lin explains why China failed to develop modern sciences but he does not explain why it did not experience an industrial revolution.

In Europe there were actually two phases in the industrial revolution, the first of which was the result of innovation gained through experience-based knowledge. It depended on the experiences of skilled craftsmen like James Watt who invented the steam engine. It was only in the second phase of the industrial revolution that modern science, based on controlled experiments, played a vital role. Since China had a larger population and arguably more gifted peasants and craftsmen, the question is why it did not produce its own equivalent of James Watt to kick off the industrial revolution.

THE HIGH-LEVEL EQUILIBRIUM TRAP

The most sophisticated theory advanced so far to explain why traditional China failed to industrialize is the 'high-level equilibrium trap' theory. It

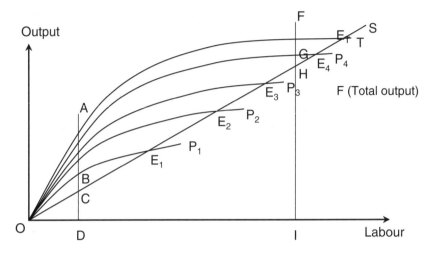

Figure 6.1   High-level equilibrium trap

is advanced by Elvin (1973) who argues that the agricultural output in traditional China was near its pre-modern limit as a result of diminishing returns induced by the rising man–land ratio within the stagnant confines of traditional technology.

In Figure 6.1, OT is the potential output curve which shows the maximum output obtained under full exploitation of traditional technology at a given size of agricultural labour and population. OS is the total 'subsistence' consumption requirements of the farm population. The intersection of OT and OS produces Elvin's equilibrium trap E_T. As long as the agricultural output per capita is greater than subsistence, the population grows and continues to do so until the excess is eliminated and E_T is reached. No further growth takes place beyond E_T because then subsistence exceeds availability and the mortality rises. OP_1 to OP_4 represent actual output curves which shift continuously upwards due to the combined influence of improved traditional technology, institutions, commercialization, discovery of new land and so on. In the short run population, OD, is determined by the short-term surplus, such as at BC. As long as this surplus is positive, the population and labour force expand and there is movement along P_1 towards the short-term equilibrium, E_1. However, the latter is shattered with a shift of the short-run output curve upwards due to improvements in traditional technology and other factors. This would cause the short-run surplus to reappear, which allows the population to expand until it hits E_T. The argument continues that with China's agriculture increasingly approaching E_T, the agricultural surplus per capita dwindled, which in turn implied an absence in effective demand for goods other than those needed for bare survival. Hence there was a reduced incentive for technological innovation to produce new types of goods, such as manufactured goods. Furthermore, with a rising man–land ratio labour became cheaper and capital relatively more expensive. This thwarted any move to invent labour-saving devices or machines.

The high-level equilibrium trap theory has proved popular with China scholars and has been expounded by Fei and Liu (1979), Tang (1979) and Chao (1986). But it has also attracted many criticisms. One of the most important ones argues that it is not at all clear when China's traditional agriculture had reached the point of severely diminishing returns. Elvin claims that this had happened in late traditional China, but Perkins (1969) shows that even in the early 1950s agriculture in China was still some distance below that point.

Another criticism is that Elvin's theory is hard to square with the facts, for the key claim that there was little surplus in late traditional China cannot be verified. Riskin (1975) set out to estimate the actual and potential surplus of China's economy in 1933, and found both to have been substantial, for in that year the actual surplus accounted for 27 per cent and the potential surplus 37 per cent of the net domestic product. Thus in spite of the relatively low per capita income there was a substantial surplus in traditional China. This is partly explained by the relatively high income inequality in traditional China where the gentry, who made up only 2 per cent of the population, received an annual income 16 times that of the rest of population in 1880 (Chang 1962).

Moreover, the claim that a high man–land ratio reduced the incentive to develop labour-saving devices is questionable. As discussed in Chapter 1, the Chinese population experienced great short-term fluctuations due to war, epidemics, bad harvests and so on. For instance there was a sharp drop in the population from 100 million people in 1280 (late Song) to only 68 million in 1380, early Ming (see Chapter 1, Table 1.1), as a result of which the man–land ratio was reduced by almost 40 per cent. Yet the rate of innovation in the Ming period was much slower than that of the Song. Thus, the rate of innovation is not dependent on, and cannot be explained by, a high man–land ratio. Finally, according to Mokyr (1990), Elvin's argument that the population growth reduced surplus and demand for manufactured goods, and therefore made profitable innovation more difficult, involves a circular argument, as innovation would have raised the surplus and real income and would have made itself profitable.

INSTITUTIONAL FAILURE?

Institutions play an important role in facilitating or preventing development in a country. The institutional structure is a combination of formal rules and informal constraints and their respective enforcement mechanisms. 'Institution' is a broad concept and there are many kinds. However, it is those institutions which define the incentive structure which have a special relevance for economic development.

In his book *Structure and Change in Economic History* (1981) North singles out two institutions vital to economic change, namely that of contracting and that of property rights. In a recent study Acemoglu and Johnson (2005) attempt to gauge the relative importance of these two types of institutions for the long-term economic development of a country. They studied 71 former European colonies in the 1990s and found that property rights are more important for development than contracting. Specifically, countries with greater constraints on politicians and elites and, therefore, with greater protection against expropriation by the powerful group, show relatively higher growth rates in the long term than those that do not have equally protective institutions. They found that the contracting institution affects the form of financial intermediation but has less impact on economic growth and investment. According to the authors the reason for this is that in contracting individuals often find ways of altering the terms of their formal and informal contracts in order to protect their own interests, such as the use of community-based enforcement mechanisms or self-enforcement mechanisms. However, property rights relate to the relationship between the state and citizens, and when checks on the state, the elite or politicians are absent private citizens find it harder to mitigate the risk of expropriation. In such a case they do not have the security of property rights necessary for investments.

In late traditional China, as discussed earlier, the contracting institution was weak and therefore self-enforcement and community-based enforcing mechanisms were the dominant form of contracting in economic and financial exchange. Though transaction costs were high, individuals could protect themselves against exploitation. Therefore, a weak contracting institution could not be the main reason why late traditional China failed to industrialize, as suggested by Feuerwerker (1984) and Jones (1990). Thus, a weak property rights institution must be one of the main culprits for lack of economic change in traditional China. Formally, China had a long tradition of property rights protection; however, the protection was ineffective for several reasons. Firstly, as mentioned earlier, there was no independent judiciary, and local courts and judges or magistrates usually lacked legal competence and often were corrupt when judged from a modern perspective. Moreover, disputes often faced long delays, both in being dealt with in the courts and in executing judgments; thus as a rule courts were unreliable instruments of law enforcement and property rights protection.

However, the state and the powerful elite, the gentry, posed a much more profound threat to the property of citizens. One reason is that in traditional China the Emperor, as the Son of Heaven, held absolute power, and constitutional restrictions on the monarchy like those in England would have been unthinkable. Moreover, since the Emperor was responsible for maintaining balance with the universe and harmony in society, there was no concept of a system of counterveiling powers or an independent judiciary. The Emperor was the sole source of law and its principal executor (Feuerwerker 1976) and could infringe upon or violate property rights at will. He could do so: (1) by direct expropriation of assets; (2) by debasing the currency; (3) by prohibiting any transactions other than those at officially established prices; and (4) by blocking entry of new groups and producers to the market.

China's history is full of examples of the government directly expropriating private assets. For instance, in early Qing times the law theoretically protected private real estate against encroachment; however, the large-scale seizure of land by bannermen (Manchurian elite soldiers) was initiated and directed by the royal family of the Emperor (Bernhardt and Huang 1994). Debasing the currency in order to boost government coffers was, unfortunately, a rather regular occurrence, especially in respect to coins. As mentioned earlier, in Qing times the government regularly debased copper cash by reducing its copper content. The blocking of entry of private enterprise in business was a favourite practice from early on since it allowed profiteering by the government. In Han times the government had established a monopoly in key commodities, such as wine, iron and salt (Deng 1999). And in the Tang dynasty the monopoly was expanded to foreign trade. In Qing times the government still maintained this monopoly but used a more elegant method of employing agents, the *hong* merchants, to avoid dirtying its hands.

However, the direct exploitation of individual business by the central government pales in comparison with that by local officials and the gentry. According to Balazs (1964) local officials and the scholar-elite were quintessential rent-seekers. However, to some extent they had to be, because their official income would not even have covered official expenses. Consequently, money bribes and rake-offs were commonplace (Naquin and Rawski 1987) at all levels of government, so that in Imperial China the holding of office was closely associated with wealth (Chang 1962). Chang in his study of the gentry gives a detailed account of their rent-seeking behaviour. For example, there was a provincial governor in Jiangsu whose annual regular income amounted to 12 857 *taels* per annum. However, he managed to rake in an extra annual income of 180 000 *taels*, which was 14 times more than his official income (Chang 1962). Similarly, a district magistrate whose annual regular income was between 1145 and 1945 *taels* made another 30 000 *taels* a year which was 2.6 times his official annual income, though it has to be kept in mind that official salaries would generally not have been enough to live on or to cover official expenses. Most of the extra income was made up by gifts and 'take'.

But the section of the Chinese gentry which was not officially employed by the government also profiteered handsomely as a result of rent-seeking activities. Their regular income was largely derived from performing their gentry function which included: (1) retainer fees for settling disputes and handling lawsuits in clan and local affairs; (2) managerial income from undertaking various local and clan projects such as local transportation networks, irrigation facilities, defence works, schools and temples; and (3) income from teaching (Chang 1962). Their extra income consisted of gifts and 'take' connected with the provision of these services, as well as rent-seeking because of their special privileges. For instance, as mentioned before, the gentry paid less property tax than commoners. Thus they often engaged in tax farming, where they paid land tax on behalf of common proprietors at the rate for the gentry, and pocketed the difference (Wang 1973). Their land tax privileges were substantial since commoners paid per *mu* double to five times the amount paid by the gentry (Chang 1962). Because of this some commoners registered their land under the name of a member of the gentry and were, of course, later unable to reclaim their property (Chang 1962).

It was also not uncommon for members of the gentry to appropriate the land assigned to temples as their own private property. Chang (1962) estimates that in Qing times one-quarter of cultivated land was controlled by the gentry, who could own as much as between 40.5 and 405 hectares. Because of their special relationship with the government the gentry incurred fewer constraints than commoners and had substantial advantages in respect to business. These included, firstly, that big business required a relatively large amount of capital which was only available to the upper gentry or officials with a high income. Moreover, big business was usually handled in the form of a monopoly which required approval and protection by the government. Only members of the gentry were in the same social rank as, and connected with, officials. Thus it is not surprising that in the late nineteenth century most of the 10 000 merchants controlling salt and foreign trade, pawn shops, native banks and the Shanxi banks were members of the gentry (Chang 1962).

The breakdown of total annual income by the Chinese gentry according to their sources (Chang 1962) shows that they received more than half of their annual income from business transactions. The adverse combined impact of government exaction and rent-seeking by the gentry on business, investment and economic growth was immense. Many government practices led to uncertainty, to which people reacted by concealing wealth and hoarding. Thus investment was discouraged and money was spent on activities which lent themselves to concealment (Landes 1969). Secondly, government exactions made entrepreneurial activity very risky since any profitable business would be subject to a bureaucratic squeeze (Maddison 2007).

The rent-seeking activities of the gentry in traditional China can be regarded as seeking monopoly profit, since unlike the English gentry they derived their position not from land but from their monopoly in education. Tullock (1987) shows that the social costs of such practices are far greater than the deadweight costs of a monopoly, because the total resources committed to rent-seeking are much greater than all the profits from the monopoly. To obtain gentry status or educational monopoly through the civil service examination system absorbed a large amount of resources in terms of time, talent and energy on the part of exceptionally talented individuals. It also incurred high opportunity costs, because these highly intelligent people could otherwise be more productive than studying Confucian classics and engaging in long periods of political maneuvering in the hope of being appointed as government officials. Moreover, in the course of time the Chinese gentry became a distributional coalition (Olson 1982), for their relatively small size in relation to the society gave them little incentive to make society more productive. On the contrary, they had a powerful incentive to seek a larger share in national income even with reduced social output. Thus they constituted the single most important stumbling block to innovation and economic change in traditional China.

LACK OF ENTREPRENEURSHIP?

Institutions are crucial for economic change and development because of their powerful incentive effect, but the initiation of change ultimately lies with the entrepreneur, without whom economic growth does not occur. The conventional theory of entrepreneurship developed by Schumpeter (1934) emphasizes entrepreneurs' role in the disequilibrium since they are creative destroyers of the existing equilibrium through innovation. Kirzner's (1973) newer theory introduces entrepreneurs as restorers of equilibrium, since a disequilibrium motivates them to act by

providing opportunities for profit-taking. Thus economic development
can be explained in terms of alternate disturbance and restoration of the
market equilibrium by the two types of entrepreneurs (Holcombe 2008).
Entrepreneurial activities are closely linked to Smithian growth which is
driven by a greater division of labour in a limited market. The market can
be extended by entrepreneurial activities which create new market niches
as a result of innovation. Furthermore, entrepreneurial activities generate
wealth and increase the market, and thereby create more opportunities for
greater specialization.

However, China had many inventors and inventions but this did not
generate an expansion of the market or more specialization. Thus the question is why there was such an obvious lack of entrepreneurs who applied
the inventions and thereby initiated economic change in traditional China.
Could it have been due to a lack of entrepreneurial spirit? McClelland
(1983) operationalizes this as achievement motivation, and the argument
is that entrepreneurial spirit, initiative and risk-taking activities would be
high if the level of the culturally imbued need for achievement is generally high in a society. Traditional China's dominant value system which
largely determined motivation was Confucian, which according to Kahn
(1979) has a very close association with achievement, on which it places
great emphasis, especially in terms of self-cultivation. A recent world value
survey by Granato et al. (1996) provides direct evidence for this hypothesis. The authors constructed an index of n-achievement based on their
results from 25 countries which shows that on a scale from 125 to minus
125 the index for China stands at 87.5 and is among the highest in the
world. In comparison, India's index is minus 44.

That there was no lack of supply of entrepreneurs in traditional China
is also corroborated by the rapid growth of the 'miracle' economies
in East Asia in the twentieth century. These consist of the four 'little
dragons' (Hong Kong, Singapore, Taiwan and Korea) and the three
'tigers' (Malaysia, Indonesia and Thailand), and in most of these growth
in post-war years was largely driven by traditionally educated resourceful
entrepreneurs of Chinese descent.

Thus the question remains why, with no shortage of achievement
motivation and inventions, this supply failed to provide productive entrepreneurs in traditional China. Baumol (2008) proposes an important
hypothesis which argues that what counts in modern economic growth
is not the total supply of entrepreneurs, but rather the allocation of
entrepreneurial activities between productive and unproductive activities;
that is, whether they are applied to innovative practices or rent-seeking.
He argues that whether allocation takes place in one or the other area is
largely determined by the rules of the game, that is, the reward structure of

society. And the previous chapter discussed that this in traditional China was clearly biased against productive activities and favoured unproductive activities.

As mentioned, traditional Chinese society was divided into the ruling and ruled classes, with the former made up by the Imperial family and the gentry elite. The gentry not only enjoyed prestige because of their education, and power through office-holding, but also possessed considerable wealth as a result of landholding and business activities. This wealth was well enhanced by their notorious rent-seeking activities, which could provide many times their official income.

The extent of these rent-seeking activities can be seen from the fact that, for example in the late Qing period, per capita income of the gentry with 90 *taels* per annum was 16 times that of a commoner with 5–6 *taels* (Chang 1962). The total number of gentry in the late nineteenth century was estimated at 1.5 million, and including immediate family members their number would have been around 7.5 million. This constituted only 2 per cent of the total population which, however, according to Chang's calculation, received about 24 per cent of gross national product (GNP) (Chang 1962). However, Chang seems to have underestimated the total GNP by about a quarter, judging from official data of the cultivated area of land and the income from agriculture (Feuwerker 1969; Perkins 1969). Thus using Feuerwerker's corrected figure of a GNP of 3339 million *taels* in the 1880s instead of Chang's 2781 million, the gentry's real share was probably in the region of 22 per cent (Lippit 1978).

Chinese traditional society was relatively open and there was no status or class barrier to vertical mobility. Since the reward structure heavily favoured the gentry in terms of status, power and wealth, everyone aspired to become a scholar and to sit the competitive entrance exams at as high a level as possible. Since the success quota was very low at only 1–2 per cent and exams were sat only every three years, people would make repeated attempts and not give up until completely frustrated. Then they would pick up a trade and accumulate savings in order to facilitate their sons' pursuit to become a degree holder (Ho 1964). As a result, all effort went into the acquisition of Confucian education, and a lot of talent, time and resources was wasted on unsuccessful attempts to pursue elite status with its licence for rent-seeking behaviour.

PART II

Transition to Modern Economic Growth

7. Growth of foreign trade and investment

Many hypotheses have been advanced to explain the relatively slow progress of China compared to Japan during its transition to modern economic growth (MEG). One of the more popular explanations is that while foreign trade played a crucial role in early Japanese development, their role in China at the onset was modest at best, if not negative (Hou 1965; Dernberger 1975; Mah 1979; Rawski 1978). The purpose of this chapter is twofold: (1) to re-examine this hypothesis in the light of available evidence; (2) to assess the contribution of foreign capital to early Chinese MEG.

FOREIGN TRADE

The Growth of Foreign Trade

Despite the Western countries' attempt to force China to open to free trade, the late Qing government resisted these attempts because the country was largely self-sufficient and had a highly developed system of internal trade which assured sufficient supply of goods for traditional demand to most of China's regions. Thus China's foreign trade during this period grew only slowly (see Table 7.1), but its pace picked up with the steady weakening of the government. This was true especially after the Treaty of Shimonoseki, with China's external trade volume doubling between 1891–95 and 1906–10.

During the Republican period (from 1912 to 1949) the trade volume continued to surge and reached its peak in 1926–30 at almost $1400 million. However, in the 1930s China's external trade was heavily impaired by external and internal political and economic factors, such as the Great Depression of 1929–39, the restoration of China's tariff autonomy and the subsequent revision of the tariff rate by the Republican government. This changed from 4.3 per cent in 1928 to about 35 per cent in 1936 (Fan 1987). The loss of Manchuria to Japan in 1932 and the outbreak of the Sino-Japanese War in 1937 had a severe impact as well. Thus the volume of foreign trade in the early 1930s dropped by almost one-quarter.

Table 7.1   *China's average annual trade volume, 1871–1940 (current price, in million USD)*

Year	Exports	Imports	Total trade	Balance
1871–75	126.7	91.8	218.5	34.9
1876–80	121.9	93.1	215.0	28.8
1881–85	109.2	95.2	204.4	14.0
1886–90	122.5	114.7	237.2	7.8
1891–95	123.6	123.1	246.7	0.5
1896–1900	134.3	142.3	276.6	−7.9
1901–05	153.8	222.6	376.4	−68.8
1906–10	211.7	296.6	508.2	−84.9
1911–15	266.6	347.3	613.9	−80.7
1916–20	611.3	703.9	1315.0	−92.6
1921–25	582.4	767.2	1349.5	−184.8
1926–30	622.3	763.4	1385.7	−141.1
1931–35	220.8	375.9	596.8	−155.1
1936–40	176.9	203.7	380.5	−26.8

Source: Chen (1979).

The above picture of growth of China's trade is not quite realistic because it is described in nominal terms. Deflated by the adjusted Nankai's price indices (Hou 1965) the trade volume in 1913 prices grew only marginally from $481.6 million in 1871–75 to $524.5 million in 1906–10; for example at an annual average rate of only 0.3 per cent. It was only during the Republican Beijing government period (1912–26) that the annual average growth rate of China's external trade volume, in 1913 prices, accelerated and reached 2.4 per cent.

Thus the growth rate of foreign trade in pre-war China was a far cry from that of Japan in the comparable period of late Tokugawa and early Meiji. In nominal terms Japan's external trade volume exploded after its opening for free trade: it more than tripled within two decades, or grew at an annual average rate of almost 6 per cent from 1860–67 to 1879–86 (Howe 1996). In real terms it grew at an average annual rate of 7 per cent between 1874 and 1887 (Ohkawa and Shinonhara 1979).

Trade Share

While growth rates are a good general indicator, the relative importance of foreign trade to a country's economy and its impact can be assessed more precisely by the share of trade (imports and exports) in national income. Initially trade soared in both China and Japan after their respective opening to the West. Measured in current prices China's trade share was about 5 per cent in 1871–84 (Dernberger 1975; Chen 1979) and rapidly rose to about 16 per cent in 1920–29. However, for the above-stated political and economic reasons it dipped to about 9 per cent in 1933 (Rawski 1989). No trade share figures are available for Japan's transition period. But it is safe to take 1887 as the initial condition prior to MEG (Ohkawa and Shinonhara 1979), when its trade share stood at 14.7 per cent, much higher than that of China in 1933. If the trade share is measured in constant prices, the same picture emerges, for the average trade share in real terms in 1931–36 was 3.3 per cent in China (Yeh 1979), whereas that of Japan in 1885–1900 was 18 per cent (Minami 1994). Hence, China's trade share was much lower than that of Japan during their respective transition periods.

Up to the 1930s the relatively low share of China's external trade can be explained by two factors, namely China's domestic economic environment and its trade policy. While both had some effect it is uncertain which was more detrimental to the development of external trade: whether it was mainly the huge size and traditional patterns of China's domestic economic environment, or the failure of its trade policy to utilize its trade potential fully.

According to Kuznets, the trade share is negatively correlated with the size of the country measured in terms of its gross national product (GNP) and population, but positively correlated with its stage of development measured in terms of its national income per capita. The size of China's economy is and was much larger than that of Japan, and its stage of development was much lower. Furthermore many provinces of China are landlocked and were insulated from foreign economic influence, whereas Japan is an island economy which facilitates transport. On the basis of these factors one would expect Japan's trade share to be much larger than that of China. On the other hand, policies played a decisive role as well, for whereas Japan actively implemented an export expansion policy, this policy was virtually non-existent in China. Hence, the difference in trade policies of the two countries also affected their trade shares. However, due to lack of good data it is not possible to determine whether China undertraded in this period of its economic history.

Growth Contribution

Foreign trade spurs a country's economic growth through either the demand side or the supply side. Export accelerates economic growth through its effective demand-creating effect. Its relative contribution to

*Table 7.2   Relative growth contribution of investment, consumption
            and exports to China's GDP, 1914–18 and 1931–36
            (in billion 1933 yuan)*

	1914–18	1931–36	Relative growth contribution in %
GDP	22.84	29.13	100.0
Investments	1.60	3.20	25.4
Consumption	20.26	24.26	63.6
Exports	0.76	1.25	7.8

Note: Relative growth contribution are the ratios of the relative increases of the three sectors to the increase in real GDP.

Sources: GDP, investment and consumption: Rawski (1989); current prices export data from Yeh (1979) which are converted to 1933 prices using the adjusted Nankai export price index (Hsiao 1974).

output growth over a period can be measured by: (1) its increment as a percentage of the increase of gross domestic product (GDP); or (2) as the ratio of its growth rate compared to that of GDP weighted by its share of GDP in the base period (Yeh 1979). Using the latter approach it can be shown that the relative growth contribution of exports in the late Qing period was virtually nil. Real trade volume grew by 0.1 per cent between 1871–74 and 1906–10, and its share in GDP in 1871–74 amounted to a mere 5 per cent. Hence its relative contribution to growth can be considered negligible.

In the early Republican period, the increase in exports caused their relative growth contribution to soar to nearly 8 per cent (Table 7.2). However, because of the small share of exports in GDP, their relative growth contribution was dwarfed by those of consumption and investment. These growth rates confirm Rawski's observation that Chinese economic growth in the Republican period was mainly driven by domestic rather than external economic forces (Rawski 1978).

As can be expected, the relative growth contribution of exports in Japan was much higher than that of China due to its relative higher export share in GDP and export growth. It stood at 10 per cent in 1888–1900 (Minami 1994). Analysed from the supply side, the sources of output growth are: increase of capital through investment, increase in employment and technological progress. Foreign trade spurs economic growth through its impact on all three factors. However, in a labour-surplus economy like China's, the major effect of trade on growth is through its positive impact on capital growth and technological progress. Export expansion increases a country's ability to import foreign capital and, hence, contributes directly to the growth of capital stock.

A less obvious but equally important effect is the greater exposure to the outside world that trade brings, for example the contact with new ideas, technology, organization, standards, values and attitudes. These all together enable a country to accumulate knowledge and allow a gradual learning process known as technological transfer. Finally, foreign trade also allows a country to specialize in certain products and services and thereby to realize economies of scale. However, to what extent this is possible depends on a country's ability to adjust to the world market demand, and to reorganize its production which had previously been geared to supply domestic segmented markets.

Unfortunately, there is a lack of accurate data to determine the contribution of exports to these growth factors from the supply side. There is only fragmentary evidence that imports of machinery and large equipment increased fairly rapidly between 1893 and 1930, though from a low base. By 1933, 37 per cent of total equipment installed in China was imported (Yeh 1979). This must have enhanced the quality of China's capital stock significantly.

Industrialization Effect

Though the volume of trade of a country may be small and its growth effect may be limited, its impact on the country's structural change may nevertheless be highly significant. In Japan, modern industry was initiated by trade with Western countries. After its opening to foreign trade with the West, its industrialization began first with the importation of new foreign products (I). When this process had taken root, a phase of import substitution occurred (IS) which in turn led to a phase of export expansion (ES). This pattern of trade-initiated industrial growth is known as the 'flying geese pattern' of economic development (Akamatsu 1962) or 'catch-up' industrialization (Yamazawa et al. 1991).

Evidence of this pattern can also be found in China after its opening. Catch-up industrialization can be illustrated by either an increased production–consumption ratio (P/C) or a declining import–consumption ratio (M/C). As P/C exceeds unity the export expansion phase begins. Consumption is estimated as production plus net imports. For China, the aggregate M/C ratio for all industries (agriculture, modern and traditional manufacturing, and mining) is estimated as follows (Wu 1994):

1840	0.01
1869	0.08
1908	0.20
1920	0.13
1936	0.09

This shows that the M/C ratio increased steadily during the late Qing period but declined in the early Republican period, indicating that import substitution had begun. Evidence of catch-up industrialization for individual industries, where relevant data is available, is presented in Table 7.3. This shows that for cotton yarn the P/C ratio declined during the late Qing period, suggesting that imports were replacing traditional production. The P/C ratio began to rise and hence the IS stage began during the Republican period. It exceeded unity in the late 1920s, suggesting that the export expansion phase had begun.

For cotton cloth, however, the picture is different. Although the P/C ratio increased, it was still below unity at the outbreak of the Sino-Japanese

Table 7.3   Production (P) and consumption (C) in selected industries, China, 1871–80 to 1934–36

	1871–80	1901–10	1923–24	1925–27	1928–30	1931–33	1934–36
Cotton yarn (mill. picus)							
P	4.9	3.4	11.0	11.5	11.0	11.4	12.1
C	5.0	5.8	11.6	11.8	10.9	11.0	12.3
P/C	0.98	0.59	0.95	0.98	1.01	1.04	1.0
Cotton cloth (mill. sq. metres)							
P	1348	1567	2704	3403	3143	3219	3461
C	1662	2113	3205	3929	3670	3520	3712
P/C	0.81	0.74	0.84	0.87	0.86	0.90	0.93

Matches (mill. cases)		1913	1930	1931	1932	1933
P		0.18–0.29	1.17	1.32	1.20	1.39
C		0.75–0.86	1.34	1.37	1.21	1.41
P/C		0.23–0.34	0.87	0.96	0.99	0.98

Iron and steel (000 tonnes)		1912–14	1915–19	1920–24	1925–29	1930–34
P		296	419	427	438	582
C		451	437	577	734	880
P/C		0.66	0.96	0.74	0.60	0.66

Sources: Rawski (1985a, 1975).

War in 1937. Thus in regard to this industry, China was still very much in the IS stage at that time. In the match industry, import substitution accelerated from 1929, when the match import duty was raised to 40 per cent, after China recovered its tariff autonomy (Rawski 1989). The P/C ratio approached unity in the early 1930s.

However, the above three cases are exclusively from light industry. In heavy industry, import substitution proceeded much more slowly as is typical for catch-up industrialization, which is characterized by varying speeds of development for different industries and imbalanced growth. This is due to the fact that heavy industry requires more capital, has more difficulties in technological absorption and experiences a slower growth of the domestic market than light industry (Yamazawa et al. 1991). Thus, for instance, for iron and steel products the P/C ratio in China initially rose but declined later in the Republican period. The failure of import substitution in this sector was due to the existence of indivisibilities, for example high fixed costs, scarce capital and the prolonged depression of iron prices after the First World War (Rawski 1975). Similarly, import substitution in the engineering industry had barely started. Most needs for basic, intermediate and capital goods still had to be satisfied by imports. However, an embryonic engineering industry appeared in the first three decades of the twentieth century in Shanghai (Rawski 1989).

There can be little doubt that the speed of China's catch-up industrialization was much slower than that of Japan. The differences are clearly shown by the example of cotton yarn. Japan quickly developed its own cotton yarn industry after a massive increase of cotton yarn imports in the 1870s and reached the EE stage by 1900, within a span of 30 years (Minami 1994). China, on the other hand, lagged far behind: at the turn of the century its P/C ratio was only 0.59 and it had to rely on imports from Japan. In fact, the Chinese market, including Hong Kong, absorbed 94 per cent of Japanese yarn exports at that time (Howe, 1996). It entered the EE stage only in the late 1920s. Thus the shift from I to EE in China in the case of the cotton yarn industry was not completed until half a century later. By that time, Japan was already headed toward the mature or reverse-import stage in that industry.

Trade Structure

A change in the structure of outputs leads to a change in trade structure. Thus industrialization reduces the share of primary exports and increases that of manufactured goods. In imports, share of manufactures declines, whereas that of primary product imports increases. Thus China's exports were initially dominated by primary and handicraft products, with tea

Table 7.4   China's and Japan's trade structure in their transition phase to MEG (%)

	Export composition	
Japan	1874–80	1881–90
Primary products	47	34
Handicraft and manufactures	53	66
China	1912	1933
Primary products	39	36
Handicraft and manufactures	61	64
	Import composition	
Japan	1874–80	1881–90
Primary products	8	16
Manufactures	92	84
China	1912	1933
Primary products	28	46
Manufactures	72	54

Sources: Japan: Minami (1994); China: Yuan (1996).

and silk together accounting for 94 per cent of total exports in 1868 (Cheng 1956). The predominance of these two commodities persisted until the turn of the century. Japan's initial export structure was similar to China's. Silk and tea accounted for 94 per cent of its exports in 1865 (Howe 1996). In the Meiji period (1874–80), primary products such as tea, marine products, copper and coal made up 47 per cent of Japanese exports, while silk and other handicrafts accounted for 53 per cent of its exports (see Table 7.4).

China's import structure was initially dominated by opium, which accounted for 55 and 46 per cent of its total imports in 1842 and 1867, respectively (Huang 1992). Towards the end of the nineteenth century, manufactured goods, especially light industry products, had replaced opium as China's major imports. By 1912, light industrial goods, especially textiles, and heavy industrial products together made up 72 per cent of China's imports, with primary products taking up another 28 per cent (Table 7.4).

Japan's major imports were initially similar to China's, for manufactured goods accounted for 92 per cent of Japanese imports in the period 1874–80 and the remaining share was accounted for by primary products. Most of the manufactured imports were light industrial products, and especially textiles. However, in its transition to MEG Japan's share of primary exports dropped from 47 per cent during 1874–80, to 34 per cent in the late Meiji period 1881–90, while the share of manufactured goods in exports soared from 53 to 66 per cent in the same period. Textiles was the lead industry in this period and its share in Japan's total exports rose from 39 per cent in the period from 1874–80 to 45 per cent in 1881–90 (Minami 1994).

In contrast, the pace of change in China's trade structure was relatively slow in the transition period. From 1912 to 1933 there was initially a slight decline in the share of primary exports, parallel to a rise of the share of handicrafts and manufactured exports. The declining share of primary exports was in part due to the fact that China had lost its market share of tea and silk to Japan, India and Ceylon. The share of tea in Chinese exports fell from a high of 54 per cent in 1868 to a mere 4 per cent in 1936, whereas that of silk fell from 39.7 per cent in 1868 to a mere 8 per cent in 1936 (Howe 1996). On the import side, the change was faster: the share of manufactured goods declined steadily between 1912 and 1933. For example, the share of textiles in total imports declined sharply from 35 per cent in 1912 to 5 per cent in 1936 (Yuan 1996). At the same time, the share of raw materials such as fuel and other primary products increased steadily, indicating that import substitution industrialization was well on its way in China.

FOREIGN LOANS

Foreign investment is a key factor in industrialization and played a critical role in the early industrialization of both the old and new industrialized countries. Foreign investment consists of both foreign loans and foreign direct investment (FDI). In pre-war China the bulk of foreign investment was in the form of FDI (Table 7.5). Altogether foreign loans accounted for only 30 per cent of China's foreign investment in the period 1902–36 (Hou 1965). Most of pre-war China's foreign loans were public foreign loans which the Chinese government largely used not to finance development of infrastructure but to cover budget deficits and foreign obligations. The pattern started in 1861 when the Qing government tried to crush the Taiping Rebellion and needed money which it borrowed from overseas. Later on, three foreign loans (one Russo-French and two Anglo-German loans) were sought to finance the indemnity payment resulting from the Sino-Japanese War and the Boxer Rebellion, as well as

Table 7.5   Foreign loans and FDI in China, 1894–1936 (in million current yuan)

	1894–1901	1902–13	1914–30	1931–36
Foreign loans:				
In-payment	21.3	61.0	23.8	
Out-payments	20.9	89.2	70.9	
Balance	0.4	−28.2	−47.1	
FDI:				
In-payment	60.0	52.8	73.6	
Out-payments		69.3	138.8	
Balance		−16.5	−65.2	
Foreign loans and FDI:				
In-payment				68.9
Out-payments				162.2
Balance				−93.3

Note: Manchuria is excluded after 1931.

Source: Hou (1965).

to finance railway construction (Huang 1992). All together, in the period 1861–1911 the Chinese government borrowed £156 million in 1913 constant prices with a weighted average interest rate of 4.5 to 9 per cent per annum (Hou 1965).

Following the collapse of the Qing dynasty the Nanjing government in the Republican era stepped up its foreign borrowing in order to meet the foreign debt servicing and indemnity payment obligations that it had inherited from the Manchu government. As a result, public foreign borrowing surged to a new high of £96.7 million in 1913 constant prices during the period 1912–27 (Liu and Fang 1991). The weighted average interest rate of these loans increased to between 7 and 9.5 per cent per annum (Hou 1965).

China's foreign debt in this period would have been much higher without the First World War and the October Revolution in Russia. Due to China's early participation in the war, it was granted a five-year moratorium on Boxer Uprising indemnity payments. In addition, due to the defeat of Austria and Germany in the First World War, as well as the collapse of the Czarist regime in Russia, indemnity payments to these three countries, which alone accounted for 49 per cent of total Boxer Uprising indemnity payments, were cancelled (Ma 1987).

The default of several foreign debt payments by the Beijing government forced the Nanjing government to exercise restraint in foreign borrowing. It also tried to accelerate the repayment of old debts in order to boost its international credit rating (Liu and Fang 1991). As a result, foreign borrowing declined during this period. Nevertheless several small loans were sought in this period, mainly to finance railway construction (Feuerwerker 1977).The average interest rate of these borrowings declined to between 5 and 6 per cent (Hou 1965).

Debt Ratio

As a result of successive public foreign borrowing, China's debt ratio (debt–GNP or D/Y) rose between 1894 and 1930 from 0.3 to 7.0 per cent (Chen 1995). Analytically, the debt ratio is positively correlated with the investment–saving gap $(I - S)$ to be financed, and is negatively correlated with the gap between the growth rate of GNP (Gy) and interest rate (i) (Perkins et al. 2001).

$$D/Y = ((I - S)/(Gy - i)) \qquad (7.1)$$

Thus, given the investment–saving gap the debt ratio will remain unchanged as long as Gy is greater than i and the positive gap between the two is maintained. The debt ratio will fall if Gy is increasing faster than i. Thus to utilize foreign loans optimally, they should be invested in productive investments which spur the growth rate of the GNP. In pre-war China, however, foreign loans were not invested in productive investments. This is evidenced from the fact that during the late Qing period, 73 per cent of foreign loan proceeds were used to finance indemnity payments as well as military and administrative expenditure; 26 per cent for railway construction; and only 1.2 per cent for industrial purposes (Hou 1965). In the Republican period, the utilization of foreign loans improved slightly with 52.3 per cent of loans used for indemnity payments as well as military and administrative expenditures. The share of loans used for railway construction and industrial purposes rose to 37 and 11 per cent, respectively (Hou 1965).

In addition to the unwise use of foreign loans, their burden was increased with the rise of their average interest rates from between 5.3 to 7 per cent in the period 1886–94 to between 7.5 and 9.5 per cent in the period 1916–29. Both sets of interest rates were significantly higher than China's nominal average annual GNP growth rate of 4 per cent during this period (Chen 1995).

The rising interest rate of foreign loans was largely due to a shift in the source of borrowing (Chen 1995). While in the first period foreign loans were raised on the European money markets where interest rates were relatively low, in the second period foreign loans were made by foreign banks operating in China, which charged interest rates according to the much higher ones prevailing on the Chinese money market. Thus, the rise of China's debt ratio between 1894 and 1930 was, among other factors, largely the result of inefficient use of foreign loans coupled with rising interest rates.

However, even the rising debt ratio was relatively low compared with the 30 per cent ratio of contemporary low-income countries (World Bank *World Development Report* 1994). China's debt service ratio in the late Qing dynasty was only 7.7 per cent and rose to 10 per cent during the Beijing government period (1912–27). It was brought back to 9 per cent during the Nanjing government period (1926–36). In contrast, the average debt service ratio of contemporary low-income countries ranged from 21 to 29 per cent in the 1980s.

Net Resource Transfer

Foreign loans normally entail a positive net resource transfer for the debtor countries. In pre-war China, however, the reverse was the case, for foreign loans did not result in net resource transfer to China but vice versa. A total of approximately 477 million *taels* in principal and interest was paid between 1895 and 1911 to foreigners as indemnity payments for the Boxer Uprising. This amount alone was more than twice the size of the total initial capital of all foreign, Sino-Japanese and local enterprises established in China between 1895 and 1913 (Feuerwerker 1969). The indemnity payments to Japan amounted to a quarter of the Japanese national income at the time and contributed to almost 10 per cent of Japanese gross capital formation during the period 1895–1900 (Minami 1994).

During the periods 1920–23 and 1928–30 the annual outflow of capital in connection with foreign loans is estimated by Hou (1965) to have averaged $30 million, which was equivalent to 0.2 and 0.4 per cent of China's GNP, respectively. Thus the political penetration of China by the West brought the irony that China's pre-war foreign borrowings, instead of being used to augment domestic savings in China to finance capital formation, were effectively used as a vehicle to channel domestic savings out of the country to finance the capital formation of other countries, especially that of Japan.

FOREIGN DIRECT INVESTMENT

The significant influx of FDI into China can be traced back to the Treaty of Nanjing in 1842 under which foreigners were given extra-territoriality rights in the treaty ports and were allowed to set up their own enterprises in China. Initially, they were restricted to the non-manufacturing sector. Nevertheless foreigners found ways to circumvent the rules and in the period from 1842 to 1894 set up 142 manufacturing enterprises (Zhang 1992). Most of these were located in Shanghai and were largely confined to ship repairing and building and the processing of primary products for export (mainly tea and silk). But there were also a few FDIs geared towards the domestic market in such diverse products as matches, paper and soap production (Zhang 1992).

The manufacturing sector was opened for FDI under the Treaty of Shimonoseiki in 1895, first to Japan and later to all other countries by virtue of the most-favoured nation (MFN) clause (Huang 1992) causing the number of manufacturing FDIs to increase by 337 during 1895–1916 (Zhang 1992). Those in the non-manufacturing sector also soared, with the number of foreign trading firms jumping from 579 in 1892 to 3805 in 1913 (Liu and Fang 1991). In roughly the same period seven new foreign banks were established (Huang 1992). However, it was the sectors of railways and mining which attracted the largest amount of foreign direct investment in term of value (Hou 1965).

During the Beijing period of the Republican government (1912–26) the number of domestic market-oriented manufacturing FDIs soared, partly as a result of the disruption of foreign supply caused by the First World War and partly in anticipation of a pending upwards revision of China's tariffs after the restoration of tariff autonomy. In contrast, there were few new FDIs in China proper during the Nanjing government period (1928–37), though of course Japanese FDI in Manchuria kept growing fast (Hou 1965).

The Pattern of FDI

The average annual FDI inflow, which had remained relatively stagnant during the late Qing period (Table 7.5), jumped sharply in the early Republican period and declined thereafter. By 1936 the accumulated stock of China's FDI had risen from $503 in 1902 to $2681.7 million (Hou 1965). Prior to the First World War the main investors were Britain, Russia, Japan and Germany. By 1930–33 the order had changed, with Japan having second rank, followed by Russia, the US and then Germany. Geographically, the FDI was heavily concentrated in the Treaty or Open Ports along the Eastern seaboard, dominated by Shanghai with 34.3 per cent and Manchuria with 27.1 per cent of all FDI (Feuerwerker 1977).

Most of China's pre-war FDI was in the service sector, especially in import–export trade, banking, finance and transport (chiefly railways). In 1914 these three sectors alone accounted for 46 per cent of China's total stock of FDI and by 1936 their share had shot up to 62 per cent (Hou 1965). The share of foreign capital in China's manufacturing sector rose from 10 per cent in 1913 to 20 per cent in 1936. Foreign investments in mining, on the other hand, were negligible, and practically non-existent in agriculture.

Benefits of FDI

The benefits of FDI for the host country can be real and financial (Lim and Fong 1991). They arise from the extra financial resources which fill in the foreign exchange and investment savings gap, and FDI also impacts on economic growth and structural change. However, in pre-war China the direct financial benefit of FDI was largely negative since annual out-payments connected with FDI constantly outstripped in payments. China's FDI account showed a persistent deficit (Table 7.5). Whether China reaped any indirect financial benefits from FDI is questionable since this depends on the trade balance and since most FDI was concentrated in the service sector in connection with China's foreign trade. However, FDI doubtlessly promoted China's exports significantly, with the number of exported goods increasing by 152 from 1912 to 1931 (Hou 1965). Obviously, in the later Nanjing period of the Republican government the increase in the number of manufacturing FDIs oriented to the domestic market contributed significantly to import substitution and foreign exchange savings.

But unlike FDIs in contemporary China the pre-war FDIs in China were as much export-oriented as they were import-oriented, for investors were working hard to promote the sale of Western-made goods to China. As a matter of fact, purely export-oriented FDIs in China were an exception. The fact that very few FDIs went into agricultural products, such as tea, silk and beans, which accounted for the bulk of China's traditional exports (Hou 1965), is strong evidence for this. In terms of gross products, only 5 per cent of total manufacturing FDIs were in the export industries.

Furthermore, there are indications that foreign firms, together with their Chinese purchasing agents, the *hongs* or compradores, acted as a monopsony in the purchase of traditional Chinese exports from peasants and manipulated prices at the expense of the sellers. The result was that the low prices discouraged production and retarded the growth of exports (Chen 1979; Hou 1965). In conclusion, evidence of FDI's negative impact on China's trade balance far outweighs the positive. From 1871 to 1930 the growth of imports outstripped that of exports by 7 to 4, with the consequence that China's trade balance slid into an ever bigger deficit. It grew from $8 million in the second half of the 1890s to $155 million in the second half of the 1930s (Chen 1979) .

Theoretically FDI has the potential to accelerate economic growth: (1) by boosting capital and export growth; (2) by absorbing underemployed labour; (3) as a source of new technology; and (4) as contributor to export growth. It also promotes economic growth through backward–forward linkages with domestic enterprises. In pre-war China the capital contribution of FDI to growth was negative since, as mentioned, there was a net outflow of capital. Its contribution to employment was not significant either for it did not even make a dent into China's huge supply of labour. Undoubtedly FDI played a critical role as a source of new technology which helped China to launch its modern sector, as discussed later. But it seems that the impact of FDI on productivity was largely confined to the tiny modern sector (Hou 1965; Rawski 1989) which in 1933–36 contributed only 8 per cent to the Chinese economy (Yeh 1979). Hence, growth in pre-war China was mainly driven by internal forces, especially growth in the agricultural sector (Rawski 1989). Since most FDIs were not export-oriented their contribution to China's exports was rather limited. Because of the locational and structural constraints of the FDIs their linkages were weak (Dernberger 1975). The confinement of FDIs to the Treaty Ports and the structural linkage to the domestic producers through the comprador system had the effect of insulating FDIs, and severely limited what positive linkage they might have had.

By far the most significant real benefits of FDI on pre-war China was its structural effect, for it helped to create and shape the modern sector comprising factory industry, mining, modern transport, utility, construction and communication. In the late nineteenth century foreign capital held a dominant share in this sector and still accounted for 70 per cent of total capital in 1931–36 in this sector (Hou 1965). The setting up of the modern sector by the foreigners provided a strong stimulus for the development of a domestically owned modern sector of the Chinese economy. Government officials and the business community, including compradores, soon began to set up their own modern enterprises in the Treaty Ports (Hou 1965). As a result, the modern sector grew rapidly from a share of 3 per cent in GDP in 1890 to 8.5 per cent in 1933 (see Table 8.3 in the following chapter).

SUMMARY AND CONCLUSION

In spite of the fact that Japan and China were opened up to free trade at about the same time, China's foreign trade grew much slower than Japan's and remained relatively unimportant to the Chinese economy in the pre-war period. Its structure also remained relatively unchanged with traditional exports of primary and handicraft products still dominant in 1935. However, imports to China experienced significant changes with a declining share in manufactured goods, especially in light industry, due to growing import substitution. At the same time there was a greater share of primary products in imports.

The contribution of trade to the growth of the economy in the Qing period remained negligible and even in the Republican period trade accounted for only 8 per cent of Chinese GDP growth. However, it did contribute to the structural change of the Chinese economy in the form of catch-up industrialization based on the 'flying geese pattern'. The impact of foreign loans on the Chinese economy was largely negative because they were in most cases used to finance indemnity payments or to cover military and administrative expenditures. Between 1894 and 1930 China's debt ratio rose due to the increased cost of borrowing and the ineffective use of foreign loans which resulted in the growth rate of GNP being lower than the interest rate on foreign loans. Worst of all, foreign borrowing did not augment domestic savings to finance domestic capital formation. Foreign borrowings were used as a channel to transfer domestic savings out of the country to finance the capital formation of other countries, especially in the case of Japan. The role of FDI was crucial and positive only in respect to technology transfer for it initiated and helped to shape the very small modern sector of the Chinese economy.

8. The rise of modern sectors and their impact

MODERN INDUSTRY

Chinese modern industry is defined here as factories using mechanical power and employing more than 30 workers. This industrial sector was driven by three groups of entrepreneurs, namely foreigners, government officials and private Chinese entrepreneurs. As discussed, foreigners began to set up their own manufacturing enterprises immediately after the Treaty of Nanking in 1842 and their number soared after the Treaty of Shimonoseiki in 1895 which officially opened China's manufacturing sector to foreign direct investment (FDI). Initially it was foreign enterprises which dominated China's modern industries; however, they were soon taken over by Chinese nationals (see Table 8.1). By 1933 the Chinese accounted for three-quarters, or the lion's share, of modern manufacturing output, with foreign firms only one-quarter (Rawski 1989).

China's early industrial entrepreneurs largely were either gentry officials, merchants or compradores. The earliest Chinese-owned modern factories were established during the Self-Strengthening Period (1842–1904/05) by gentry officials led by Governor Zeng Guofan and Zou Zongtang and Li Hongzhang.

Though adopting Western practices, Chinese officials still upheld the ideology of the gentry class under the policy of 'Chinese learning as essence, Western learning for practical use'. They were convinced of the superiority of China's traditional value, culture and institutions and were only prepared to borrow elements of Western military and industrial technology in order to gain sufficient strength to resist foreign incursion. Thus modern factories were established in the mining, ship building, armaments and machinery industries which included, for example, the Kaiping coal mines in Tianjin, dockyards in Fozhou and arsenals in Shanghai and Nanjing. The government later also invested in iron and steel and in light industries, such as cotton textiles and matches (Eastman 1988).

Industrial plants were usually sponsored by the provincial rather than the central government. They were financed mainly with capital from Treaty Port merchants but were controlled by gentry officials under the

Table 8.1   Ownership structure of modern manufacturing in China (number of enterprises)

	1895	1913	1933
Foreign	142	479	822
Chinese	94	594	2978
Total	236	1143	3800

Sources: Hou (1965), Richardson (1999) and Eastman (1988).

so-called 'official supervision and merchant management' system. As a rule they were given monopoly rights over a certain market and were subject to constant official exaction because of the ambiguous management system. Thus foreign competition, official indifference and a shortage of capital and personnel hampered the growth of these pilot industrial plants (Feuerwerker 1958).

Merchants played a very limited role in China's early industrialization (Hao 1970), where compradores were the major driving force because of their expertise and connections. In 1842, after the abolition of the foreign trade monopoly by *hong* merchants, foreign firms had appointed Chinese managers for their firms to serve as the commercial intermediaries. These were known as *mai-pan* and were up-country buyers who purchased goods such as tea and silk in China's interior on behalf of Western firms in the Treaty Ports. Though the official salary of the compradore was fixed at an average of about 1000 *taels* per year, as a rule they were able to amass a fortune. They had many opportunities to do so because: (1) they received commissions from Chinese and foreign merchants for each business transaction; (2) they could squeeze foreign employers by accounting for higher prices of goods purchased and pocketing the difference; and (3) they derived income from their own business (Hao 1970). As a result they became the richest merchants in China and their number soared from only 250 in 1854 to around 20 000 by the end of the nineteenth century.

They used their newly amassed fortune, their knowledge of how to operate modern factories and their business connections to invest in industrial enterprises in the Treaty Ports which provided stable conditions for business. Under foreign protection their property rights were secure and the accumulation of wealth was possible in the absence of official exaction (Hao 1970). They invested in a wide range of industries, such as coal mining, cotton textiles, machinery, matches, rice mills and so on. But beyond manufacturing they also invested in shipping, railways, banking, insurance and public utilities (Hao 1970).

In the early twentieth century the role of the compradore in China's industrialization declined and they were replaced by the newly emerged merchant class. The ending of the civil service examination system in 1905 had led to the weakening of the gentry, whose activities were now redirected from achievement in terms of examinations and bureaucratic positions towards success in industry and commerce (Sheridan 1975; Eastman 1988). Thus merchants competed for status as the leading social class. Their growth is evidenced from the rise in membership of the Chamber of Commerce, which in 1919 stood at 162 500 (Sheridan 1975).

Modern industry in China experienced a golden age from 1914–18 to 1931–36 when it had a rapid annual growth of between 7.7 per cent (Liu and Yeh 1965) and 8.1 per cent (Rawski 1989). The factors responsible for this high growth rate were, firstly, the improved competitiveness of modern Chinese industrial enterprises in this period vis-à-vis foreign imports as a result of the combined influence of the First World War, the currency depreciation and tariff protection.

The First World War had disrupted the supply of foreign imports from the West and Japan. This was followed by the fall in the international market price of silver in 1922, which constituted a de facto depreciation of China's silver-based currency and increased the competitiveness of Chinese products against foreign imports. Following the restoration of China's tariff autonomy in 1929, China raised its import tariffs from an average of 4.3 per cent in 1928 to 35 per cent in 1936, which gave Chinese entrepreneurs another price edge against foreign imports.

Another factor contributing to rapid industrial growth in this period was the expansion of the money supply. The establishment of modern banking and the increasing substitution of cash payment with the use of bank notes, bank drafts, bills of exchange and cheques caused the supply of M2 (currency in circulation plus bank deposits) to soar by 76 per cent between the First World War and 1933 (Rawski 1989).

The rapid industrial growth was also due to greater foreign investments, especially those by Japan in Manchuria which it had occupied since 1931. Japan wanted to use Manchuria as a base for heavy industry to support its military conquest in Asia and, therefore, invested heavily in the mining of iron and coal, the generation of electricity and the production of iron, steel, machinery and chemicals (Eastman 1988).

Despite its high rate of growth the contribution of China's industry to the overall growth of gross domestic product (GDP) was insignificant in this period because of its small share in Chinese GDP, which stood at less than 1 per cent in 1916 and only reached 2 per cent by 1933. In terms of employment its share was even smaller and did not even reach 1 per cent in 1933 (Rawski 1989). Most modern industries were located in the provinces of Liaoning in Manchuria and Jiangsu in the Yangzi delta, which together accounted for two-thirds of China's total modern industrial output, while Shanghai alone accounted for 40 per cent of Chinese manufacturing output and Manchuria for another 14 per cent (Rawski 1989). It was only in the mid-1930s that modern industries spread to other urban centres as a result of both the demonstration effect of Shanghai and the extension of transport and communication along the coast and to the inner cities. Another push factor was the rise of wages and land prices in Shanghai.

In this period Chinese modern industries largely confined themselves to the production of consumer goods, with textiles, clothing, footwear, food, beverages and tobacco accounting for two-thirds of total value-added of the manufacturing sector in 1933 (Rawski 1989). The share of producer-good industries, such as iron, steel and cement production, remained insignificant in this period.

MODERN INFRASTRUCTURE INDUSTRIES

Modern infrastructure industries, such as transport, communications and public utilities were rapidly developed in the phase of China's early industrialization. Railways were first introduced in 1876 and the length of tracks had grown from 410 km in 1895 to 20 746 km in 1936, including Manchuria. Steamships were introduced in the 1850s and in 1936 the number of motorized ships had grown from 30 in 1882 to 3895 (Rawski 1989). The first motorway was built in 1913 and road length grew from 29 000 km in 1927 to 111 000 km in 1936. Airlines were introduced in the Republican era and by the mid-1930s 40 major cities were linked by passenger flights.

In communications the first post office was established in China in 1896 (Rawski 1989). Telegraphs and telephones were first introduced in the Treaty Ports. By 1935 the length of telegraph lines was 99 000 km, up from 62 000 km in 1912. And by the mid-1930s, telephones existed in 25 Chinese cities. The improved transport facilities considerably reduced the time and cost for freight and passenger transport. For example, steamships and railways cut the time needed for travel between Chengdu and Beijing from 80 days in late Qing times to 10.3 days in the mid-1930s (Rawski 1989). And a shipment from Guangdong to Beijing was cut from 90 days to only 3.3 days with the opening of the Beijing–Guangdong railway line. Railway and steamship transport drastically cut the freight cost per tonne and kilometre to only 0.02 yuan in the 1930s, which was one-tenth of that relying on human porterage.

Similarly, modern communications like postal services, telegraphs and telephones facilitated trade and massively improved factor mobility because of the reduced cost and time needed for the transmission of information. Together with improved transport they laid the basis for the formation of a nationwide commodity market which, however, was not complete until after the economic reforms in the late twentieth century.

IMPACT ON TRADITIONAL SECTORS

Agriculture

The actual rate of growth in agricultural output in China's transition period to modern economic growth (MEG) has caused considerable controversy. Early estimates by Perkins (1969) and Liu and Yeh (1965) suggest that it grew at the same rate as the population, with per capita agricultural output remaining steady between 1814 and 1936. The implied average rate of growth per annum is 0.6 per cent. However, in a more recent study Brandt (1989) suggests that agricultural output in the later part of that period from the 1890s to 1930s grew at least twice as fast as the population, with a rate ranging between 1.2 and 1.5 per cent a year.

Much of the controversy is due to the lack of hard data, and there may be wide margins of error in these estimates (Brandt 2000). For the first part of the period up to 1920, where no field research exists, students rely on a range of sources such as county gazettes, official reports, travellers' tales and newspapers (Faure 1984). Such information is usually inconsistent and often unreliable. For the second part of the period, field research data are available; however, their method of data collection leaves much to be desired since they are often inferred, sometimes simply from impressions on the basis of travels or the opinion of local informants.

Thus economists need to employ economic models and their predictive power to reconstruct the missing pieces of information. However, the models often make assumptions which are unrealistic in the Chinese context. For example, Brandt's high estimate of agricultural growth results from the assumption of the neo-classical model about farm households which do not apply in China. In this model the product and factor markets are assumed to be perfectly competitive, with peasant households striving to maximize profits. The theory holds that in order to maximize profits a household will equate the marginal product of farm labour with its minimum wage. And there is no surplus labour as unemployed family members can be hired out or be employed on additionally rented land. Consequently the marginal product of farm labour is equal to that of its alternative employment, factors are remunerated at their marginal products and the real wage of labour is highly correlated with its productivity

(Brandt 1989). Since real wages of rural labour increased between the 1890s and 1930s by 60 to 70 per cent or at an annual rate of 1.3 per cent, it can be concluded that the productivity of family farm labour must have risen at the same rate as hired rural labour. Hence, the per capita output in agriculture should have increased by the same percentage and not remain unchanged as implied by the Perkins (1969) and Liu and Yeh (1965) estimates. This in turn means that agricultural output must have risen significantly more than the population growth.

The main weakness of Brandt's new estimate of agricultural growth rate are, firstly, that he assumes an excessively high rate of growth of real wage for hired labour in agriculture (Richardson 1999), the empirical evidence of which is based on questionable survey data of the 1920s as discussed above. Their reliability must be questioned since the survey uses only a small sample of counties and relies on the memory of informants stretching back two or three decades.

Secondly, Brandt's growth estimate rests on the assumption that the growth of wages for farm labour can be used as a proxy for that of per capita agricultural output. This is in line with the neo-classical model's assumption of profit maximization by farm households as well as the existence of perfectly open and competitive product and factor markets. Undoubtedly, markets faced by Chinese peasants were more competitive in the early twentieth century than they had been before, due to better transport and communication and a better integration of the Chinese domestic market. The opening of China by the West had also pushed China to more integration with the international market. However, this does not mean that China's market was approximating the perfectly open and competitive market postulated in the neo-classical model. And various studies of the market institution provide ample evidence that neither the land nor the labour market in this period were as free as assumed by Brandt (Faure 1984).

The land market was restricted in that it was difficult for rural households to gain access to rented land. One reason was that villages would not generally grant cultivation rights to outsiders, especially not if they lacked the support of the lineage trust which often owned the village land, especially in South China (Faure 1984). And even if renting was allowed, outside cultivators would be given shorter leases and be subject to regular rent increases at each contract renewal.

The assumption of an open and competitive labour market for rural China in the early twentieth century is unrealistic, if not absurd, as its rigidity prevails even in the twenty-first century due to labour immobility. In traditional China it was unthinkable for elderly members of rural households, or children, or females – with bound feet – to seek off-farm employment. Most of their labour went into domestic handicrafts and

Table 8.2   Source of agricultural growth, 1890–1933

Year	Population (in million)	Cultivated area (in mill. *mu*)	Land–man ratio	Agricultural output (in mill. 1933 yuan)	Agricultural yield (1933 yuan per *mu*)
1890	380	1240[1]	3.26	14576	11.8
1913	437	1360	3.11	16769	12.3
1933	500	1534	3.07	19180	12.5

Note: 1. 1893.

Sources: Maddison (2007) and Wang (1973).

textile production anyway. Thus, in view of the above points and despite their recent challenge by Brandt, the earlier estimates by Perkins (1969) and Liu and Yeh (1965) are still widely accepted as the more realistic rate of growth of agricultural output in the second half of the nineteenth and early part of the twentieth centuries (Richardson 1999; Maddison 2007).

How was agricultural growth achieved during this period? Agricultural growth hinges on increased acreage and/or increased yield. From the 1860s, China's area under cultivation continued to expand due to the opening up of Manchuria and its settlement by Han Chinese, with a rate of growth somewhat lower than population growth: the former increasing 1.24-fold and the latter 1.32-fold. As a result the land–man ratio decreased from 3.26 in 1890 to 3.07 in 1933 (Table 8.2). In this period the continuous expansion of the cultivated area explains about three-quarters of the growth in agricultural output, with an increase in yield responsible for one-quarter. Where did the rise in agricultural yield come from? Yield can be increased by technical change, institutional change, increased multiple cropping and/or a shift to higher-yield crops. According to empirical evidence the rate of technological change during this period was limited (Faure 1984). The institutional set-up also remained largely unchanged. In the 1930s the government had tried to improve peasant work incentives with the promulgation of a land law designed to reduce the rental rate by an average of 37.5 per cent of the harvest, and to reduce the rate of interest paid by peasants, but this law was never fully implemented due to opposition by landlords (Richardson 1999).

The standard Marxist explanation is that rural China did not experience growth in agricultural output because of greater concentration of land in the hands of fewer landlords and, consequently, a greater rate of tenancy and more income inequality and poverty. Thus, they argue, in this period

Mao and his followers were able to exploit rural discontent, and using the tactics of 'surrounding the cities from the countryside' succeeded in winning the Civil War against the Nationalist government in 1949.

However, this is disputed, one of the reasons being that the rate of tenancy remained static in that period. But many scholars are divided on this issue. Huang (1985) and Myers (1970) both study the income distribution using the same survey data of the Japanese South Manchurian Railway Company (Mantetsu) in the provinces of Shandong and Hebei in the North China Plain, and reach entirely different conclusions. Huang argues that the increase in population coupled with a greater commercialization of agriculture, a greater concentration of land and rate of tenancy reduced the average income of the majority of peasants in the area under study to the level of a bare subsistence minimum or below.

Myers, on the other hand, demonstrates rather convincingly that there is no evidence of greater concentration of land ownership. He presents substantial data to show that it either remained static or became more equal. His findings are also corroborated by Brandt's (1989) study which focuses on the Yangzi and Pearl River deltas with the same results; namely, no significant increase in the rate of tenancy or landownership concentration between the 1890s and 1930s (Brandt 1989). Since he utilized a large set of survey data of 1.8 million households in 163 counties across 16 provinces, these results are more credible. The multiple cropping index decreased during this period, as Chao (1986) suggests that it reached about 1.4 in the nineteenth century and fell with the opening up of Manchuria as the climate did not allow double cropping in this area. In the 1930s the index was about 1.3 (Maddison 2007). Thus the diversifying of cropping patterns to higher-value crops other than grain on the basis of greater commercialization of China's agriculture remains the only explanation for the higher yield of farm output during the period.

In traditional China the commercialization of agriculture was severely limited with 80 per cent of cultivated area devoted to the growing of food grain to ensure self-sufficiency. After the opening to the West, spurred by up-country purchases of tea, silk, oilseeds and other farm products by Chinese and Western merchants for export, farmers started to use more land for cash crops (Hao 1986; Brandt 1989). By the 1930s the area cultivated with grain crops had decreased to 70 per cent in Jiangsu and Guangdong in the South, less than 70 per cent in the Yangzi region, and about 78 per cent in the rest of China (Faure 1984; Brandt 1989). The percentage of marketed agricultural output increased accordingly from less than 30 in the 1890s to between 45 and 50 in the mid-1930s (Brandt 1989).

This increase was triggered by the combined impact of a greater domestic and international demand, and the improved terms of trade for China's agricultural products. China's opening to the West had caused a greater demand for its products; however, agricultural exports accounted for only 4 per cent of output (Brandt 1989) and thus the role of exports was limited. The lion's share of the growth was due to the increase in domestic demand generated by the rapid growth in the non-agricultural sector as a result of industrialization and urbanization. From the 1890s on the prices of agricultural output rose substantially due to the depreciation of silver, China's monetary standard. In the same period prices for non-agricultural products, however, rose only modestly. Thus agricultural products improved their terms of trade by between 70 and 80 per cent in the period under discussion. Even though there was a setback in the early 1930s by about 35 per cent due to the onset of the Great Depression, the level of the terms of trade then was still higher than it had been in the 1890s (Brandt 1989), and it was these improved terms of trade which drove the commercialization of agriculture.

Handicraft Industry

China's traditional industries fared relatively well when faced with competition from imported and domestically manufactured goods. In contrast to Marxist assertions, these imports did not drive traditional industries to the wall and increase rural poverty, and handicrafts continued to grow because of demand and supply factors. The demand increased due to more exports and also the growing demand of modern industries for inputs and raw materials. On the supply side, traditional handicrafts remained competitive because these industries specialized in the manufacture of labour-intensive products since they had a cheap supply of rural surplus labour.

As discussed in Chapter 3, firms tend to equate i/w to mp_k/mp_l to maximize profits and since w in China was low and i high, hence i/w remained high and the productivity gap (mp_k/mp_l) between machinery and handicraft production must be very high for machine manufacturing to be more competitive than handicraft production. As a result of the prevailing prices of labour and capital, China's handicraft industries remained competitive in those areas where the productivity gap was relatively small. However, where it was relatively large, for example in cotton textile spinning, modern enterprises significantly reduced the market share of handicraft products which shrunk by one-third to one-quarter between the 1920s and the 1930s. Here the productivity gap was 40 to 1 (Richardson 1999; Huang 2002).

In contrast the productivity gap between hand and machine cloth weaving was much less, and because of its relatively high ratio of capital and labour costs China's hand loom cloth industry largely held its own, with its market share declining only slightly from 90 per cent in the early 1920s to 67 per cent in the 1930s (Richardson 1999). The silk industry saw a similar development where hand reeling of silk declined vis-à-vis the adoption of stream filature reeling in manufacturing, but where hand-woven silk output remained fairly steady as mechanization spread only slowly due to the relatively smaller productivity gap between hand and machine weaving (Richardson 1999).

IMPACT ON GROWTH

Modern industry was established in the late nineteenth and early twentieth centuries in China as the foundation for modern economic growth. However, it was not until the mid-twentieth century that the Chinese economy took off. The main reason is that the impetus of the tiny modern manufacturing sector was simply too small to generate structural change because despite its rapid growth the traditional sector of the economy remained dominant.

Table 8.3 shows the structural change of China's GDP between 1890 and 1933, and it can clearly be seen that in spite of the growth of the modern economic sector from 3 to 9 per cent in that period, agriculture and handicraft production, the main components of the traditional Chinese economy, in 1933 still contributed the lion's share with over 70 per cent of real GDP. In respect to transport and communication, which together accounted for 6 per cent of GDP, the share of the traditional component is 4 per cent. It is only with respect to finance that the share of the traditional sector had by 1933 been reduced to insignificance, since both deposits and issuing of notes were by 1936 dominated by modern banks (Rawski 1989). Hence, the traditional sectors still made up over 90 per cent of Chinese GDP in 1933 (Table 8.3).

Thus the question is whether China did experience MEG in the time from 1890 to 1933, and on this issue opinions are divided. Perkins and Yeh hold that there is no evidence of MEG since, as Table 8.4 shows, per capita GDP growth remained fairly stagnant in the period, and in the 1930s it was only 6 to 8 per cent higher than in the 1910s. A more recent estimate by Maddison (2007) puts it even lower at 3 per cent. Thus the average annual growth rates estimated by Perkins, Yeh and Maddison range from 0.4 to 0.3 and 0.2 per cent, respectively. In view of the wide margin of error of these estimates due to the crudeness of the data, the differences in the estimated annual growth rate of GDP in this period do not really matter since they agree that real per capita growth during this period was very low.

However, Rawski (1989) challenges the generally accepted view and

Table 8.3   Sectoral shares of GDP in 1933 prices, 1890–1933

Sector	1890 (%)	1913 (%)	1933 (%)
Agriculture	69	67	64
Handicraft	8	8	7
Modern manufacturing	Negl.	1	3
Mining, electricity, construction	2	2	3
Transport and communication	6	6	6
Trade	8	9	9
Government	3	3	3
Finance	Negl.	1	1
Personal services	1	1	1
Residential services	4	4	4
Total	100.0	100.0	100.0
Modern sector[1]			
Modern manufacturing	Negl.	1	3
Mining, electricity, construction	2	2	3
Modern transport and communication	Negl.	1	1.5
Modern finance	Negl.	0.5	1.0
Subtotal	3	4.5	8.5
Traditional sector	97	95.5	91.5

Note: 1. Estimates of the shares of modern sectors are explained in the text.

Source: Maddison (2007).

argues that China did experience MEG during this period. On the basis of his 'preferred estimates' (see Table 8.5) he shows that in the Republican period GDP per capita grew steadily by around 1 per cent. However, his higher estimate of per capita GDP growth is mainly due to his higher estimate of traditional sector growth.

Table 8.5 compares Yeh's and Rawski's estimates and shows that the difference between their figures for the modern sector is minimal. The weighted difference between their growth estimates (0.4% × 0.042 + 1.1% × 0.016 + 1% × 0.017 + 2.1% × 0.01 = 0.04%) for the four modern sectors of industry, construction, transport and communications, and finance is practically zero. This implies that Rawski's higher estimates

Table 8.4   Estimates of per capita GDP, 1914–18 and 1931–36

	Per capita GDP estimates	
Perkins	(1914–18)	(1933)
(US$, 1957 prices)	48	52
Yeh	(1914–18)	(1933–36)
(yuan, 1933 prices)	55	58
Maddison	(1913)	(1933–36)
(G-K$, 1990 prices)	552	570

Sources: Perkins (1975b), Yeh (1979) and Maddison (2007).

Table 8.5   Rawski's and Yeh's estimates of annual sectoral growth rates, 1914–18 and 1931–36

Sector	Terminal year weight (Yeh estimate) (%)	Yeh estimates (%)	Rawski estimates (%)	Difference
Agriculture	0.629	0.8	1.4–1.7	0.6–0.9
Modern manufact. industry incl. mining	0.042	7.7	8.1	0.4
Handicrafts	0.075	0.7	1.4	0.7
Construction	0.016	3.5	4.6	1.1
Transport and communication				
Modern sector	0.017	4.0	3.0	−1.0
Traditional sector	0.039	0.3	1.9	1.6
Trade	0.093	1.1	2.5	1.4
Finance	0.01	2.9	5.0	2.1
Government services	0.031	1.0	3.4	2.4
Personal services	0.012	0.8	1.5	0.7
Residential services	0.036	0.9	1.5	0.6
Total GDP	1.000	1.1	1.8–2.0	0.8–1.0
Population growth		0.9	0.9	0.0
GDP per capita		0.1	1.1	1.0

Source: Rawski (1989).

of GDP growth are mainly due to his estimates of growth of traditional sectors. Among the traditional sectors, due to its lion's share of the traditional economy, agriculture contributed 58 per cent, trade contributed 16 per cent, government services 9 per cent, traditional transport and communications 7 per cent, and finally handicrafts 6 per cent of the difference between the estimates of GDP growth during this period. The main weakness of Rawski's estimates is that he had to rely on many assumptions to derive them. For instance, his higher growth estimates for agriculture rest on the assumption that real wage growth of farm labour can be used as a proxy for growth of per capita output in the agricultural sector. This assumption is the same as that underlying Brandt's hypothesis which, as discussed earlier, is not reliable.

Finally, even if his assumptions underlying his 'preferred estimates' are accepted, growth during this period was the result, as mentioned earlier, of the expansion of traditional not modern sectors. This is why I have suggested that MEG did not take place until the second half of the twentieth century.

SUMMARY

Industrialization in China began with the setting up of modern manufacturing and mining enterprises in the late nineteenth century. Foreigners and gentry officials functioning as compradores played a major role in China's early drive to industrialize. Initially foreigners dominated China's modern industries, but they were soon overtaken by Chinese nationals. In the period between 1914–18 and 1931–36 the modern industrial sector grew at a very fast pace due to disruption of external supply lines in the First World War, the currency depreciation and increased tariff protection. The industrial sector was dominated by light industry and was concentrated in the two provinces of Liaoning in Manchuria and Jiangsu in the Yangzi delta. Despite its high rate of growth the contribution of modern industries to the overall growth of GDP was limited because of its insignificant share in Chinese economic output in that period. Contrary to the Marxist assertion, the rise of modern industry and increased foreign imports did not drive the traditional handicraft industries to the wall. Their output continued to expand because of the increased demand from both domestic and foreign sources. And their products remained competitive because the handicraft industries specialized in labour-intensive products and made use of the abundant supply of surplus labour.

The rise of the modern industrial sector laid the foundation for modern economic growth which, however, did not materialize until the mid-twentieth century. The main reason was that growth before this turning point was largely due to the expansion of traditional industries, for example agriculture, handicrafts and traditional service industries. Agriculture remained the mainstay of the Chinese economy and continued to expand in the transition period to modern economic growth through the late nineteenth and early twentieth centuries. Its rate of growth between 1814 and 1936 averaged about 0.6 per cent a year, according to estimates of Perkins (1969) and Liu and Yeh (1965). This growth resulted from increases in both acreage and in yield. The opening up of Manchuria for Han Chinese settlement accounted for most of the increase in acreage, and the increase in yield was mainly due to the diversifying of crop patterns to higher-value crops other than grain on the basis of greater commercialization of agriculture after the opening of China for trade by the Western powers.

9. Why Japan succeeded and China failed

This chapter examines the two major hypotheses advanced to explain China's failure to generate modern economic growth (MEG) after the opening to the West while Japan succeeded. One hypothesis is related to China's difficulties in absorbing modern technology because of its unfavourable conditions as compared to Japan (Minami 1994; Eastman 1988). The second hypothesis is related to the difference in the role of government, because in contrast to the Meiji government which took a proactive role in facilitating industrialization, neither the Qing nor the Republican government in China provided the conditions vital for the private sector to absorb Western technology and generate modern industrialization (Perkins 1967).

INITIAL ECONOMIC CONDITIONS

This section compares the level of economic development of China and Japan during their initial periods using the following key indicators: (1) per capita gross domestic product (GDP); (2) the share of the primary sector in employment and output; (3) the growth of agriculture; (4) their respective degrees of commercialization and urbanization; (5) their industrial development; and (6) the share of their transaction sectors in GDP. Japan's transition period lasted from 1868 to 1885 (Minami 1994) but since statistical data are only available for the year 1887 it is reasonable to take this as indicative of Japan's initial conditions for industrialization (Ohkawa and Shinohara 1979). China's transition was much longer and lasted, as stated previously, from 1842 to 1949.

Around 1700, Japan's GDP per capita was much lower than that of China. However, it rose by 40 per cent in the Tokugawa period (1603–1867) so that by 1887 it stood at $952 (1990 international dollars) and thus was 64 per cent higher than China's (Maddison 2001). This growth spurt of Japan's GDP in the late Tokugawa period was triggered by greater government expenditures which led to price rises, causing real wages to fall and profits to increase. These, in turn, stimulated business investments which led to greater capital accumulation (Minami 1994; Mosk 2007). And in the Meiji period growth of GDP kept accelerating due to the opening of the country to the West and to the government's economic reforms (Minami 1994).

The second factor which contributed to the rise of per capita GDP in the late Tokugawa period was the stagnant population growth (Mosk 2007). Between 1700 and 1870 the Japanese population grew from 27 million to 34 million with an annual average growth rate of only 0.1 per cent (Maddison 2007). This was mainly due to a drop in the fertility rate which was as low as 5.4 in eight selected Tokugawa villages (Mosk 2007). In contrast the fertility rate in traditional China remained relatively high and varied between a minimum of 6 and 8, or even reached 10. Thus China's population grew at a steady and much higher rate than that of Japan at almost 0.7 per cent per year (Maddison 2007).

The reason why Japanese households tended to limit their family size while the Chinese did not must be sought in the different social conditions of traditional society. In Japan, as in Europe, it was the eldest son in the family who inherited the family property. So the worry about the economic future of younger sons caused families to cut their birth rate, both male and female (Mosk 2007). Another reason is that unlike in China, Japanese families could adopt fictive heirs, and thereby secure their welfare in old age. In contrast, China strictly adhered to the lineage system which gave every family member a share in landownership and did not favour older sons over younger ones. Chinese families simply had to produce sons as insurance against poverty in old age.

China and Japan were both traditional agrarian societies but the share of Japan's agriculture in GDP was considerably lower than China's. For example, agriculture in China in 1870 still employed 80 per cent of the population while that in Japan had already fallen to 72 per cent (Minami 1994). In respect to agriculture's contribution to GDP the difference is even larger, for while in 1890 it accounted for almost 70 per cent in China, it had dropped to just 41 per cent in Japan (see Table 9.1). Thus Japan had successfully started its transition to MEG by becoming a commercial economy while China remained agrarian.

Agricultural growth is vital for modern industrial development as it contributes significantly to industrialization. According to Kuznets it does this in three ways, namely by, firstly, providing a surplus, for example a food supply for the growing industrial work force and maintaining food price stability. Secondly, it provides raw materials for industry and releases labour and capital for developing industries; and thirdly, it provides a market for industrial goods. Thus rapid agricultural growth is seen as a prerequisite for industrial development.

Table 9.1   China's and Japan's economic structure in the late nineteenth century (% share in GDP)

	China, 1890	Japan, 1874
Agriculture	68.5	41.4
Industry	15.2	9.4
Manufacturing	7.8	6.6[1]
Mining	0.2	
Construction	1.7	1.9
Transport and communication	5.5	0.9
Electricity	0.0	NA
Services	16.3	49.2
Trade	8.2	NA
Finance	0.3	NA
Government	2.8	NA
Personal services	1.1	NA
Residential services	3.9	NA
GDP	100.0	100.0

Note: 1. Including mining.

Source: Maddison (2007).

At the start of the period (1878–85) of MEG, Japan had a much higher growth rate of agricultural output than China with 1.7 per cent (Minami 1994), while in the late nineteenth century China's amounted to only 0.5 per cent. And while it increased in the following period from 1914–18 to 1931–36 to 0.8 per cent (Brandt 2000), this was still only half the growth rate of Japan's agricultural output.

Another major factor in economic development is the degree of urbanization and commercialization. The latter measures the relative responsiveness of the economy to changes in demand and supply and the effectiveness of the market mechanism. The market does not work within a self-sufficient economy. Urbanization is equally important for MEG due to the fact that city people have fewer difficulties in absorbing new technologies because they have first-hand experience with new products and technology (Rawski 1989). At the start of their MEG period Japan's economy was much more urbanized and commercialized than that of China. By the 1860s the degree of commercialization in agriculture was already as high as 80 per cent in advanced areas and 10 per cent in backward ones. The average for the whole country was probably around 60 per cent. In contrast, in the comparable period in China it was only 30 per cent, half of Japan's. And it was only in the mid-1930s that it increased to between 45 to 50 per cent (Brandt 1989).

The Qing dynasty did its best to maintain the traditional Chinese society and economy and had no reason to promote commercialization or finance. In contrast, Japan's Tokugawa period was crucial for the economic development of modern Japan, not because of its modern orientation but because of its feudal system under which *daimyo* wives and children were kept hostage in the capital city of Edo (Tokyo). Thus relatively large numbers of people resided away from their local district (*han*). In order to cover their living expenses the *daimyo* had to establish warehouses and offices in Edo or Osaka. They employed merchants and financiers to sell produce from their *han*, keep the money safe and to buy the goods needed by the hostages. The merchants also received rice allowances from the Shogunate on behalf of the *daimyo* and sold it for them (Minami 1994). This laid a great basis for the growth of commerce which further accelerated in the Meiji period with the establishment of the modern banking system. Thus Japan's commerce was far more important and developed than China's. The only respect in which China fared better was that it had more experience with foreign trade. In terms of 1990 US$ and exchange rate, Japanese exports per capita in 1870 were only US$1.5 or 39 per cent of that of China (Maddison 2007).

Japan also lagged somewhat in traditional industrial development, namely handicraft manufacturing and mining, which together had a share of 7 per cent in its GDP, whereas that of China was 8 per cent. However, the handicraft industry in Japan was much better organized since it had widely adopted the putting-out system, which was uncommon in traditional China. For example, Japanese merchants in the cotton and silk textile spinning industries would supply spinning frames, reeling machines and looms to farmers, and pay for their products at a piece rate (Minami 1994; Mosk 2007).

The share of transport in GDP in China, however, was larger than that of Japan, which is to be expected on the basis of their respective size, for in 1820 the Chinese empire covered 12 million km^2, 32 times the area of Japan. Thus China's continental economy had to rely largely on more expensive overland transport, while Japan – a relatively small island economy – was able to rely heavily on cheaper water transport. Hence, other things being equal, China's transport intensity was likely to be higher.

However, by far the most importance difference between the Japanese and Chinese traditional economies is the share of their transaction sector in GDP. According to North (2003), MEG is the result of the movement away from personal to impersonal exchanges, which allows greater

*Table 9.2   The share of transaction sectors in GDP – China, Japan and
other low-income countries (%)*

	China, 1914–18	China, 1931–36	Low-income countries, 1958	Japan, 1887
Trade	9.2	9.3	12.8	33.0[1]
Finance	0.7	1.0	0.6	
Real estate	3.7	3.6	2.4	4.0[2]
Government services	3.1	3.1	5.7[4]	4.0[3]
Total	16.7	17.0	21.5	41.0

Notes:
1. Includes finance.
2. 1874 figure.
3. Includes public administration and military investments.
4. Includes government non-transaction services.

Sources: China and low-income countries: Yeh (1979); Japan: Ohkawa and Shinohara (1979) and Maddison (2001, 2007).

specialization and division of labour with consequent economies of scale and the adoption of modern technology. However, the switch to impersonal exchange increases transaction costs because it necessitates standardization and exact measurement as well as the enforcement of agreements and contracts. These measures all together may actually inhibit further growth in impersonal exchanges and, thus, it becomes crucial for development to decrease transaction costs.

This is done by the transaction sector of the economy which, according to Wallis and North (1986), is made up of industries like finance, insurance, real estate, wholesale and retail trades in the private sector, and services such as maintenance of public order, postal services and defence in public administration. In addition it includes the services of transaction-related workers in the non-transaction industries, such as managers, clerks, accountants, lawyers and others devoted to facilitating impersonal exchanges.

Table 9.2 attempts to measure the core transactions sectors in traditional China and Japan and their relative shares in GDP. It shows that China's is relatively small, even smaller than that of other comparable low-income countries at the same stage. The contrast with Japan's transaction sector is even starker because it is nearly triple in size due to Japan's relatively highly developed trade and finance system in the Tokugawa period, and to greater spending by its government on transaction services.

SOCIAL DEVELOPMENT

Initially, Japan's social development lagged behind that of China, for at the time of the Western incursion China was a capitalist society and Japan's was feudal (Minami 1994). It was split into 260 territories, known as *han*, ruled by the *daimyo* lords which themselves were kept under close guard by the central government, the Tokugawa Shogunate. There were four classes: the samurai warriors as the elite, farmers, artisans and merchants. Unlike in China there was very little interclass or other mobility in Japan, and the reward system was based on the aristocratic principle of descent by birth rather than on individual merit or performance.

Japanese society was hierarchic and rigidly controlled. For example, farmers were not allowed to leave the land or grow crops of their choice. They had to sell their surplus produce to their lord at administratively fixed prices. After the Western intrusion in 1867 the Shogun abdicated and Imperial rule was restored a year later. The new Meiji government carried out a series of social reforms which not only abolished the social class system and restrictions on mobility, but also did away with all feudal elements. Thus by the late nineteenth century Japan had a modern capitalist society with a centralized government and was in many respects more advanced than China.

In terms of human development it was more advanced because, for instance, its rate of literacy was much higher, with 40 per cent for males. Primary education was already widespread in the Tokugawa period, which modelled education on the Chinese Confucian system and emphasized learning. Under its *terakoya* system individual classrooms were set up in ordinary people's houses where Buddhist priests and samurai taught basic reading, writing and numeracy skills (Minami 1994). Under Western influence the government introduced compulsory primary education in 1872. In contrast, the rate of literacy in China in the nineteenth century stood at only 30 per cent and remained unchanged even in the early twentieth century (Perkins 1975a). A higher rate of literacy is an indicator of readiness for MEG because it reflects the country's ability to absorb and apply modern knowledge and technology. The average traditional Japanese also seems to have been healthier than their Chinese counterparts, for by the late nineteenth century the average life expectancy at birth for the former was 30–40 years, while that for the Chinese was only 20–30 years (Mosk 2007).

China and Japan were also different in respect to the structure of traditional families, with the former having an extended family system and the latter a stem family system (Mosk 2007), a type which is much closer to the Western family structure and more conducive to MEG. The Chinese family emphasized blood ties and the lineage system and thus tended to nepotism and inefficiency in modern business operations. In contrast, blood ties were not that important in traditional Japan, and if a biological son was incompetent, Japanese families would not hesitate to adopt another male as son or consider a son-in-law as heir (Mosk 2007) in order to preserve the business enterprise.

China's and Japan's inheritance systems differed in that in China family property was equally divided among sons, whereas Japanese families favoured a single heir and successor. This is significant for MEG because it encourages capital accumulation and at the same time provides a push factor for other brothers to leave the land and employment in agriculture.

The role of merchants was also different in the two countries because in China they occupied a rather low social status (below peasants), and their activities were strictly supervised and narrowly controlled by bureaucrats. In contrast, they became the real power holders in Tokugawa Japan because they controlled the sales and finances of the *daimyo* (Minami 1994). Furthermore, unlike in China, there was no flight of human and material capital from the commercial sector into landholding because of effective restrictions on land ownership and transfer. Neither could Japanese merchants channel and apply their entrepreneurial activity to other fields, because of the impossibility of interclass mobility before the Meiji period (Levy 1955). Hence, like many overseas Chinese in the twentieth century in Southeast Asia who were barred from access to other avenues, merchants in Japan pursued success in business and they became the core of Meiji entrepreneurs (Minami 1994).

Lastly, Japan's cultural receptivity to foreign technology was much higher than that in China, because China as a large country was mainly inward-looking whereas Japan had a long history of borrowing and adapting to culture and technology from China. It had seen institutional change before, and when Western knowledge and technology came along it was relatively easy for Japan to reject old traditions and institutions of foreign origin and embrace new ones. In addition, Japan had the advantage of learning from the Chinese experience, since the defeat of China by Western powers clearly exposed the weakness of China's traditional system and values and destroyed Japan's respect for Chinese culture (Maddison 2001).

THE ROLE OF THE GOVERNMENT

The role of government is vital for MEG. The Coase theorem, for example, suggests that economic freedom is the most important factor in generating growth because rational individuals will automatically bring society close to its productive potential. The optimization of the participants in a free market eliminates any inefficiency or opportunities for supernormal returns: big banknotes are not often dropped on the pavement, and if they are, they are picked up very quickly: 'There are no big bills left on the sidewalk' (Olson 2008). Institutional economists, however, see economic freedom as a necessary but not sufficient condition for MEG and argue that society needs to provide a suitable structure of incentives to bring about the productive cooperation that would pick up the big bills (of risk-taking and higher transaction costs) by moving the economy closer to the production frontier. The structure of incentives depends on the economic policies adopted by the government in each period, and also on the long-term institutional arrangements in regard to contracts, property rights and their protection and enforcement by the legal system (Olson 2008).

For latecomers to modernization and economic development the role of government is even more crucial and demanding. As the Gerschenkron model shows, based on the experience of France, Germany and Russia, latecomers face several disadvantages because the scale of modernization is larger the longer industrialization is delayed. Thus, firstly, latecomers were forced to import modern industry and institutional patterns en masse that had been developed gradually in the more advanced economies. Secondly, the relative backwardness of the countries heightened the pressure for them to modernize rapidly because of the mounting societal tensions and the ensuing military and economic threat from the West. Thirdly, they faced large-scale problems of coordination resulting from the inevitable disadvantaging of certain groups in the transition and the protest and rebellion of these groups (Levy 1955). In conclusion, the large-scale modernization efforts required by latecomers to industrialization, together with the difficulty to mobilize investments and large-scale problems of coordination, necessitate a strong role of government in the lead up to MEG.

The Chinese and Japanese governments during the transition were completely different. Firstly, the Chinese government failed to maintain political stability, for since 1842, the time of the Western incursion, the Qing dynasty suffered internal rebellion and war. The biggest rebellions were the Taiping Rebellion (1850–64) which lasted 14 years and affected the 16 most prosperous Eastern provinces, the Nien Rebellion, and the Muslim Revolt in North China. And in times of internal strife foreign aggression intensified. There was a joint attack on China by the British and French in an attempt to expand their shipping and trading privileges, and an offensive from Russia which seized Eastern Siberia during 1858–60. Japan in 1894–95 seized Taiwan, the Descadore Islands and Liaoning peninsula on the mainland. The ensuing Treaty of Shimonoseki required China to pay an indemnity of 230 million *taels*, to Japan, about a third of the size of Japan's total GDP.

Further, eight Allied forces invaded Beijing following the Boxer Rebellion against foreigners, and in the following peace settlement China had to pay another 450 million *taels* as indemnity. This amounted to half of Japan's annual GDP at that time and China had to finance it by borrowing money from overseas.

Following the collapse of the Qing dynasty the country disintegrated into warlordism which remained rampant in the North even in the Republican period when order was restored in the South (Sheridan 1975). It was only after General Jiang Jishi staged a successful Northern Expedition in 1927 that there was a decade of relative stability, with law and order being somewhat restored. Nevertheless, many provinces remained under the rule of military leaders with varying degrees of independence, who refused to pass revenues on to the central government and spent the money on their own armies instead (Rawski 1989).

In this period Japan increased its aggression against China with the invasion of Manchuria in 1931 and attacks on Shanghai in 1932. Finally, in 1937 full-scale war between China and Japan broke out which lasted for eight years. After that the country was plunged yet again into civil war between the Communists and the Nationalist government, which led to the defeat of the latter and the birth of the People's Republic of China in 1949.

The incessant political instability had a deep impact and prevented economic growth because it disrupted normal economic activity, reduced the population and infrastructure, prevented capital accumulation by absorbing all surplus into military operations, and imposed the burden of foreign indebtedness on China. For example, the political instability disrupted trade by upsetting the planning, income and supplies of producers, consumers and merchant intermediaries (Rawski 1989). Transport was severely disrupted, and the intensity of railroad utilization was far below its potential. This directly caused a decline in farm output, because when for instance in 1942 the transport system was disrupted, farmers retreated from the market. This caused a shortage of raw cotton which forced the textile mills in Shanghai to operate at only 6 per cent of their 1936 capacity (Rawski 1989).

Political instability increases insecurity of property rights and discourages long-term productive fixed capital investment. In China's period of warlordism, for instance, the military government held the power and physical means to expropriate wealth from private citizens. Troops used to loot villages and towns, and the inhabitants were forced into compulsory labour. The military also requisitioned cars, donkeys and carts, and warlords exploited every possible source of revenue to squeeze money out for themselves (Sheridan 1975). They increased land tax, set up illegal tax stations to tax goods, in transit, introduced commodity taxes on salt and other goods and also imposed the payment of special taxes for special occasions, such as a bumper harvest tax. Nothing was beyond their reach and they collected land tax in advance or far in advance, in one instance as far as 74 years in advance (Eastman 1988). They also resorted to printing paper money and debasing the coinage in order to expropriate the private assets of citizens. In view of the insecurity of property rights, entrepreneurs had little incentive to invest in production but preferred speculative investments for immediate profit-taking.

Secondly, compared with Japan the Chinese government was inactive toward change. After the intrusion by the West, the Japanese government carried out a series of political, economic and social reforms to counter the military and economic threat from the West. As mentioned, the feudal system was abolished under the Meiji government and the feudal lands became subject to Imperial rule and tax. With the abolition of the social class and ranking system the freedom of farmers increased. They could now grow crops of their choice, leave the land or sell it, and enter commerce or industry for employment. The lifting of the traditional restrictions on travel helped to increase mobility.

At the same time the Japanese government not only introduced Western technology wholesale but also changed to Western-type institutions. Foreign experts were invited to teach the Japanese about Western methods of mining and manufacturing, and Japanese students were encouraged to study abroad to acquire Western know-how. Pilot industrial enterprises were established by the government to introduce Western technology and management into the private sector. A Western political system was introduced and a new constitution promulgated in 1889 which was based on the German model (Mosk 2007). In 1872 conscription was introduced, with a Western military system and a strong, modern army. The government not only succeeded in quelling the 1871 Satsuma Rebellion, but also fought off any external threat by abolishing the unequal treaty with the West and restoring tariff autonomy. In addition it defeated China and Russia. Further, the Western system of compulsory primary education was introduced in 1872, and Western systems of business and finance were adopted with the first joint-stock company established in 1872. Finally, a modern banking sector was developed with commercial banks and a regulating central bank.

In contrast, the Chinese government resisted change after the Western intrusion and insisted on its traditional values and methods. In the Self-Strengthening Period from 1841 to the First Word War it refused to change except by borrowing elements of Western military and industrial technology under the slogan: 'Chinese learning as essence and Western learning for practical use'. It also sent students abroad to acquire Western knowledge. However, it was only after the defeat by Japan in 1895 and by eight Western nations at the end of the Boxer Rebellion in 1900 that China's government felt the urgent need to emulate the West. In order to avoid being carved up by Western and Japanese Imperial powers it sparked the 'Save China Movement' which ran from 1905 to 1926 (Sheridan 1975).

A series of reforms was reluctantly introduced in the last few years of the Qing dynasty (Richardson 1999), one of them being the abolition of the examination system. In 1907 reforms of the political system were announced which were to replace dynastic rule with a constitutional, elected, representative government. The first step of the implementation was the election of provincial assemblies in 1908 which were supposed to have advisory functions only; however, they soon became potent centres of provincial strength. They sparked attempts to establish provincial autonomy and renewed the curse of warlordism (Sheridan 1975). However, these reform attempts were too little too late, and they did not save the Qing government from collapse in 1911.

In 1919 the Westernization movement was accelerated by the May Fourth Movement which started as a protest of Beijing University students against the Treaty of Versailles after the First World War. They were enraged at the government's failure to secure the handing-back of the former German concessions in Shandong, which were given to Japan instead. Nevertheless, the Westernization movement was largely promoted by intellectuals only and had no support from the masses. The new Republican government was weak and barely managed to unite the country or to maintain political stability. Thus the country lapsed again into warlordism. It was not until the 1927 conclusion of the Northern Expedition that there was a brief period of relative political stability, which finally allowed the government to introduce a few limited reforms.

Thus after the restoration of tariff autonomy in 1929, taxes on imports were increased to help the new domestic industries. In 1931 the government also removed the transit fees on commercial goods which had been imposed by the Qing dynasty. These were akin to an internal import tariff, and exhausted the modern economic sector which was made to pay for military expenditure and indemnity payments to Western powers. However, the government was unable to shake off the Treaty Port privileges of foreigners and their extraterritorial rights until 1943.

In 1928 a money and banking reform was launched and a new central bank was set up together with modern banks. However, these did little to finance the rural economy or newly established enterprises since they largely confined their business to the government sector (Rawski 1989). A monetary reform was carried out at the end of 1935 with the creation of a new, uniform paper currency which replaced the old silver-based one. Its objective was to eliminate the variety of multiple notes issued by provincial, domestic and foreign banks. At the same time a new standardized coinage was issued to replace the different and often debased coinages issued by provincial and national agencies.

However, despite its reform efforts the Republican government failed to provide a sound and stable monetary system because, unlike the new currency in Japan, China's new paper currency was not linked to the external standard value of gold or silver or foreign exchange. This doomed it, because in its final years the Repulican government was hard pressed to cover the increasing expenditures of the war with Japan from declining revenues. This was largely due to the loss of the coastal provinces to Japan. Therefore, it put excessive amounts of newly printed notes into circulation which fuelled hyperinflation. This contributed significantly to the collapse of the Republican government which on the whole had made significant progress to promote MEG by establishing a modern transport and communication system with the building of new roads, railways, telephone systems and so on.

The weakness of Chinese government as compared to that of Japan can be attributed partly to its lack of financial resources. As mentioned earlier, the Qing government revenue was based on land tax, the base of which was the area of land, which is income-inelastic. After the foreign intrusion the tax base was enlarged with the introduction of a transit tax and maritime customs, but they made little difference. The share of government revenues made up only 6 to 7 per cent of GDP, with that of the central government being not more than 3 per cent (Feuerwerker 1969). In the Republican period from 1932 to 1936 it was even less and only the borrowing of money helped the government to reach an amount equal to 4 per cent of GDP (Rawski 1989). Even with the inclusion of local government expenditures, the total government expenditures of the Republican government in 1931 was between 5 and 7 per cent of GDP, not much different to that of the Qing period (Rawski 1989).

In contrast, the tax base of the Tokugawa government was much larger and its fiscal levies made up between 20 and 25 per cent of GDP (Maddison 2001). The main component was, as in China, land tax. However, it was income-elastic because in the Tokugawa period it was based on land yield and in the Meiji period on land value, not as in China on the area of land (Mosk 2007). Thus the Japanese government's revenue increased in line with economic growth, which the government used to push modernization along. The bulk of the 20–25 per cent of GDP available to the government was used to pay for the pensions of the samurai who had surrendered their land after the abdication of the Tokugawa shogunate and had been disbanded as the elite. Their pensions were financed by a public bond which carried 7.7 per cent interest a year. Thus the net resources available to the government amounted to about 10 per cent of GDP, of which it used the lion's share of about 7 per cent for public investments and to pay for modernization projects such as the reform of education and assistance to industries.

In contrast, the transitional government in China had to spend most of its meagre share of revenues of the GDP on military campaigns and on paying off indemnities imposed on China by foreign powers. For instance, from 1928 to 1937 in the Republican period, each year 41 per cent of the budget was spent on the military campaign and another 31 per cent on indemnity payments (Sheridan 1975; Rawski 1989). This left the government with very little to spend on the promotion of modernization, even if it wanted to.

SUMMARY

The comparison between China and Japan on the eve of their transition to MEG shows that Japan's initial conditions were much more favourable than China's. By the late nineteenth century Japan had a higher level of social and economic development and its economy was more urbanized and commercialized. It also had a higher per capita income and a higher growth rate of the agricultural sector to support its industrialization. Its transaction sector was much more developed, which lowered Japan's transaction costs and allowed it to embrace the growing specialization and division of labour required for modern technology. Its society was also more willing to embrace modern technology due to its long history of borrowing culture and technology from China, and to adapt. The population had a higher rate of literacy and enjoyed a longer life expectancy than China's. It had a social structure had promoted the allocation of entrepreneurial activities to productive activities. It had a family system which encouraged capital accumulation and which hired labour on the basis of merit rather than blood ties.

Thus Japan was much more ready for MEG, and that is obviously one of the major reasons why its transition to a modern economy was so much faster and smoother. The other decisive reason lies in the role of the government, which is especially important for latecomers to industrialization.

But while Japan's government was strong and proactive, China's was weak and small. The former controlled between a quarter and a fifth of GDP from tax revenues, while the latter languished on only 3 per cent of GDP from revenues. And most of this had to be spent on military campaigns, foreign indemnity payments and debt servicing, so that China's transition government could do little to promote industrialization or MEG.

In contrast, the Japanese government was ready and in a position to adopt a forward-looking policy to promote industrialization. Its approach was two-pronged in that it created a favourable business environment for the private sector by maintaining political stability through maintaining law and order and repelling internal rebellion and foreign aggression. It further constructed social overhead capital in that it introduced Western institutions and established a modern banking system. In addition the government was actively involved in introducing and diffusing Western technology by way of identifying and subsidizing strategic industries.

The Chinese transitional government was weak, with its sovereignty under constant attack by foreigners and severely impaired. Thus it was unable to maintain political order and stability. Besides its reluctance to embrace the values underlying MEG, and confining itself to the borrowing of selected technology in heavy industry, the limited resource base of the Chinese government would never have enabled it to take and implement decisive steps to promote MEG. Thus its attempts of institutional and political change were late and limited in scope. It did not carry out any active industrial policy until the late 1930s, and its monetary reforms proved to be a nail in its coffin.

PART III

Modern Economic Growth under Socialism

10.   The Soviet model

THE FELDMAN GROWTH MODEL

The theory underlying the Soviet model of rapid industrialization adopted
by China in the 1950s was the Feldman model which had been formulated
in the1920s during the Great Industrialization debate by Feldman (Jones
1976). It is essentially an unbalanced growth strategy of industrialization
which emphasizes the investment in the heavy industrial sector. Contrary
to the conventional view it is not primarily aimed at 'production for production's sake' or at maximizing the speed of growth of capital goods
at the expense of the growth of consumer good production, but aims
at maximum speed of growth of consumer good production under the
assumption of a closed economy. The development of heavy industries is
only the vehicle for the accelerated growth of the downstream consumer
goods industry. Thus it is supposed not only to maximize the long-run
growth rate of the economy but also to generate quickly a maximum push
for the growth of consumption for the entire population.

Specifically, the model assumes that there are two sectors in a closed
economy, that is, sector I producing investment goods, Yi, and sector II
producing consumer goods, Yc. A further assumption is that there are two
production factors, capital, K, and labour, L, with capital as the only lim-
iting factor for growth as labour is assumed to be unlimited in supply. The
model assumes that capital stock does not depreciate and hence its rate of
change (dK/dt), in turn, equals to total investment, which, in turn, equals
the output of capital goods in sector I, that is, $dK/dt = I = Yi$. Lastly, it is
assumed that a proportion λi of capital stock is allocated to sector I and
$(1-\lambda i)$ is allocated to sector II.

Under the above assumptions it can be shown that the growth of output
of the economy, $G(Y)$ is as follows (Jones 1976):

$$G(Y) = \lambda i \, Vi \qquad (10.1)$$

where Vi is the capital productivity of sector I. From equation (10.1) it is
clear that in order to maximize growth of output in the long run the proportion of total current investment allocated to the heavy industrial sector
needs to be maximized. The same conclusion can be drawn with regard to

the long-run growth of consumer good as it can be shown that the growth of which $G(Yc)$ in the long run is as follows (Jones 1976):

$$G(Yc) = \lambda i \, Vi \qquad (10.2)$$

Equation (10.2) suggests that to maximize the long-run growth rate of consumption the proportion of total current investment allocated to the heavy industrial sector needs to be maximized.

RAPID CAPITAL FORMATION AND PRIORITY DEVELOPMENT OF HEAVY INDUSTRY

There is no doubt that in the Maoist era China consistently adopted the Feldman model of rapid growth. This is borne out by the fact that throughout this period China pursued a high rate of investment which was concentrated in the heavy industrial sector. The Chinese concept of rate of investment is known as the rate of capital accumulation, which is derived as the ratio between capital accumulation and the national income. This increased drastically after the Communist takeover: during the Republican period (1931–36) it averaged only 5 per cent a year (Yeh 1968) but it shot up to an annual average of 24 per cent in the period of the First Five-Year Plan (FFYP). Under subsequent Five-Year Plans the rate of investment was raised to an average of 33 per cent, with the single exception being the three years following the collapse of the Great Leap Forward (GLF) (1962–65) when the rate of investments fell to between 10 and 20 per cent (SSB, China Statistical Yearbook 1992).

The drastic and disproportionate increase in the rate of investment, and China's consistent efforts to keep it to nearly one-third of its annual national income, show that China in the early 1950s was an even more zealous follower of the Feldman model than the USSR. At the beginning of its industrialization drive in the early 1950s, China was much poorer than the USSR was in 1928. Its income per capita in 1955 US$ in the early 1950s was roughly US$70, compared to that of the USSR which amounted to roughly US$200–US$300. (Perkins 1975b), The USSR's grain output per capita in 1937 was also two and a half times higher than China's in 1957. Nevertheless it took the Soviet Union ten years to raise its rate of investments from 12.5 per cent in 1927 to 26 per cent in 1937 and it reached 28 per cent only in 1955. Hence, its rate of investment was comparatively much lower than China's.

Similarly, the Chinese government was determined to outdo its Russian counterparts in the sectoral allocation of state investments. Table 10.1 shows

Table 10.1   Share of state investments in industry (%)

	Heavy industry	Light industry	Total
1953–57	47	6	53
1958–62	56	5	61
1963–65	50	4	54
1966–70	61	4	65
1971–75	55	5	60
1976–78	55	7	62

Source: Ma and Sun (1987).

that in the Maoist era the heavy industrial sector received the lion's share at the expense of the light industrial and agricultural sectors. On average the industrial sector received more than 60 per cent of total state investments, of which 90 per cent were channelled into the heavy industrial sector. In contrast, the industrial sector in the Soviet Union received only 40 per cent of state investments under the first FYP up to the Second World War, with heavy industry receiving merely one-half of this (Chen and Galenson 1969).

The implementation of the Feldman model necessitates a system of state-controlled resource allocation without which resources from the rest of the economy could not be mobilized and used to finance the disproportionate investments in heavy industries. Hence, China in the early 1950s initiated the wholesale transplant of Soviet institutions and policy into the country, and in particular the system of collective agriculture, state enterprises, central planning, the administrative allocation of production factors, the use of price scissors to extract agricultural surplus to finance heavy industrial development, and the adoption of the autarky policy in international economic relations.

COLLECTIVE AGRICULTURE

The collectivization of Chinese agriculture was preceded by the land reform of 1949–52 (Ash 1976). Land and other agricultural resources were expropriated from landlords and rich peasants and distributed to poor and middle-income peasants. The major objective of the land reform was political in that it aimed at consolidating the political base of the Chinese Communist Party (CCP) in rural areas. By isolating rich peasants and eliminating landlords, and by aligning the party with middle-income peasants, the Communists attempted to transfer power to the poor peasants in the countryside. Its impact in terms of generating agricultural growth was minimal (Ash 1976) since each peasant received just over one *mu* of land (about 0.027 of a hectare).This was too small to provide farmers with the surplus essential for investment and agricultural growth. Nevertheless, it had a significant income-levelling effect. For example, Roll (1980) shows that the average income of the poorest 20 per cent of the rural population increased by nearly 90 per cent as a result of the land reform. Consequently, the income ratio between the top and the bottom 10 per cent of the population had shrunk from 10:1 in the 1930s to 4:1 in the mid-1950s.

The collectivization was launched after the land reform with the initially gradual formation of agricultural producers' co-operatives because it was thought that collective farms in China would not be viable without heavy machinery, such as tractors, which would only be available after industrialization had proceeded. Hence the collectivization of agriculture was planned to be completed in a time span of 10–15 years from 1949 on, the same time span that was envisaged for China's industrialization and the nationalization of industrial and commercial enterprises. This time frame, known as the 'general line' or development strategy in the transition period, was even written into China's 1954 constitution (Yang 2009).

The gradual collectivization of agriculture in the first half of the 1950s began with the formation of Mutual Aid Teams (MATs) comprising 5–15 households which were encouraged to pool their non-land resources in times of seasonal shortage. By 1954 more than 50 per cent of farmers participated in these MATs. Later these were encouraged to form elementary agricultural co-operatives (EACs) with an average size of 20–40 households. At first, the formation of EACs proceeded slowly and was scheduled for completion in 10–15 years, parallel to the socialization of non-agricultural enterprises. Table 10.2 shows that by 1954 only 2 per cent of China's farmers participated in them. However, in the 'high tide' of socialism in 1955, Mao attacked the gradual approach of his moderate colleagues and decided to accelerate the collectivization process (Selden 2006; Yang 2009; Liu and Wang 2006).Thus by the end of 1956, 96.3 per cent of farmers had joined the agricultural cooperatives and 87.8 per cent participated in advanced agricultural co-operatives (AACs). Thus the collectivization of China's agriculture was completed in seven years, eight years ahead of schedule.

An AAC was organized like the Soviet collective farm with an average size of 100–300 households. The difference between an EAC and an AAC was that in the former the participants retained ownership of their land, they only pooled their labour and non-land resources and the income from the co-op was distributed according to the combined contribution of land and labour of each household. In an AAC all land belonged to the co-op

Table 10.2   Development of collectivization in Chinese agriculture, 1950–58 (% of farms covered)

	MATs	EACs	AACs	Communes
1950	10.7	0.0		
1951	19.2	0.0		
1952	39.9	0.1		
1953	39.3	0.2		
1954	58.3	2.0		
1955	50.7	14.2		
1956	0.0	8.5	87.8	
1958 mid-year				30.4
1958 year end				99.1

Source: SSB (annually).

and income was distributed only according to the input of labour by each household. However, households were allowed to retain a small private plot to grow their own vegetables and to raise a pig which could be sold on the rural free market.

The acceleration of the collectivization process in the mid-1950s was triggered by the mini Leap Forward launched by Mao in the 'high tide of socialism' (Howe and Walker 1977) in order to catch up with the Western world faster; that is, within the three-FYP period, between 1955 and 1967. Thus by 1967 grain output was to be nearly doubled, that of cotton quadrupled and steel production was earmarked to be six times that of 1955 (see Table 10.3). The accelerated collectivization of agriculture was vital to the achievement of the goal of the mini Leap Forward for two reasons. Firstly, collectivization took control of agricultural surplus away from farmers and into the hands of party cadres (Walker 1966). Secondly, the government hoped that collectivization would mobilize the vast pool of underemployed labourers in rural areas for the construction of rural infrastructure, such as irrigation and labour-intensive cultivation techniques. These would increase the crop yield and boost agricultural surplus to fuel the industrialization programme (Kueh 2008).

AGRICULTURAL SURPLUS AS FUEL FOR INDUSTRIALIZATION

In the Maoist era agricultural surplus was siphoned off from farmers to fuel industrialization, in the form of various visible and invisible taxes

Table 10.3 *China's 1955 agricultural and industrial outputs and 1967 targets (in million tonnes unless otherwise stated)*

	1955 output	1967 targets	Target reached/ exceeded in year
Grain	175	300	1978
Cotton	1.5	6.0	1984
Steel	2.9	18	1970
Cement	4.5	16.8	NA
Chemical fertilizer	0.4	7.5	1964
Oil	1.0	18	1969
Electric power (billion kw/h)	12.3	7.3	1966
Tractors (in 1000)	0.0	183	1975

Sources: Howe and Walker (1977) and SSB (1986, 1989).

Table 10.4 *Farmers' tax burden (in billion current yuan)*

	1952	1978
Agricultural tax	2.7	2.8
Monopolist profit	3.4	12.0
Monopsonist profit	2.5	39.6
Subtotal	8.6	54.4
Total government expenditures	17.6	112.2
Farmers' contribution (%)	48.9	48.5

Sources: Chai and Roy (2006) and SSB, China Statistical Yearbook 1990.

which farmers had to pay under the compulsory agricultural procurement scheme introduced in 1953 (Yang 2009; Khan 1978). Table 10.4 shows the various burdens imposed on the rural sector.

The agricultural tax, which was in effect a land tax, was the most important and visible tax. It remained relatively stable between 1952 and 1978 at about 3 billion yuan a year. The invisible taxes paid by farmers included the monopolistic and monopsonistic profits of state enterprises, for in selling goods to farmers state enterprises had a monopoly of manufactured goods, the prices of which were generally much higher than their production costs. The profit mark-up plus commodity tax together accounted for an average of about 32 per cent of the prices of manufactured goods in the period 1952–78 (Perkins and Yusuf 1984). Similarly, in buying goods state enterprises acted as monopsonists under the compulsory agricultural procurement scheme which required farmers to sell a certain amount of their produce to them at a price below the market price. The difference between the state purchase price and actual market price constitutes an element of tax or monopsonist profits. An estimate of this tax of eight agricultural products for which data are available show that this invisible tax became the most important source of government revenues. Altogether the visible and invisible taxes financed nearly 50 per cent of China's government expenditures in this period.

STATE ENTERPRISES

In the non-agricultural sector the large, formerly Nationalist or foreign-owned enterprises became the first state enterprises (SOEs). And by way of the systematic buying of shares more private enterprises were gradually absorbed into the state sector (Chen and Galenson 1969) so that by 1956 the socialization of the non-agricultural sector was completed simultaneously with the collectivization of agriculture (Yang 2009). State enterprises completely dominated the industrial and commercial sector in the Maoist era with a share of almost 80 per cent of industrial output, 84 per cent of retail business, 98 per cent of transport and 64 per cent of construction in 1980, on the eve of the reforms (Chai 1997). The SOEs, like their Soviet models, featured a one-man management system with absolute authority of the director and a privileged role of specialists, such as engineers and bureaucrats. Not surprisingly, in the Cultural Revolution attempts were made to replace it with a managerial system which would allow mass participation.

CENTRAL PLANNING

As in the Soviet Union, resource allocation in the Maoist era was through central planning (Howe and Walker 1989) with the planners' preferences largely determining who produced what, how much and how. The balance between demand and supply was mainly achieved through a system of interlocking material balances with obligatory input and output targets issued to enterprises to implement the central plan. However, compared with the

Soviet Union China's planning system was less centralized, due partly to the relatively underdeveloped state of the Chinese economy and partly to the Maoist emphasis on the simultaneous development of the relations of production and productive forces towards the building of socialism.

It was also much less comprehensive than in the Soviet Union. For instance, in 1980 it covered only 180 industrial products in China, compared to over 30 000 in the Soviet Union (Gregory and Stuart 1990), and material balances were between 500 and 700 compared to over 10 000 in the Soviet Union (Rawski 1975b). Similarly, the number of obligatory targets for China's state enterprises numbered only eight (Chai 1997), versus between 20 and 30 for their Soviet counterparts (Gregory and Stuart 1990). The Chinese system of central planning was also more decentralized in that in the late 1950s and again in 1970 control over a large number of enterprises was transferred to local governments. Thus regions had more autonomy, and by the late 1970s central authorities controlled merely 2 per cent of China's industrial enterprises (Chai 1997).

In respect to the incentive system used by the government to implement its plan, China initially copied the Soviet model but later, in the times of the Great Leap Forward and the Cultural Revolution, developed its own version. There were two kinds of incentives: one for the enterprise, derived as a share in profits in proportion to the degree to which it had fulfilled its obligatory targets (Chai 1997); and one for individual staff and workers. The first fed into an enterprise fund which could be used for welfare purposes, such as the construction of a canteen or housing for workers, or for bonus payments or, in most cases, a combination of both.

The main types of incentives for workers were bonus and above-norm piecework wages (Chai 1997). Unlike the Soviet Union, China did not rely on bonus payments to motivate managers. The pay of managerial staff had no variable element and their main material reward for successful performance was promotion (Eckstein 1977). In the Great Leap Forward and the Cultural Revolution, which attempted to force the greater socialization of productive relations, the enterprise fund, bonus and other material incentives were scrapped and replaced with non-monetary awards, such as raised public status and social benefits. It was not until the late 1970s that material incentives were restored.

FACTOR ALLOCATION AND THE ROLE OF PRICE

The allocation of labour and capital in pre-reform China was largely effected through central planning. There was no labour market and mobility of labour was nearly impossible since the Labour Bureau centrally assigned labourers to each enterprise. Their demand was derived by multiplication of the given output target of an enterprise with the amount of labour required per unit of output. Once hired the labourer became tenured to the enterprise and could not be dismissed even if unsuitable or redundant (Chai 1997). Thus inter-enterprise mobility was severely restricted, as was spatial mobility which was controlled by the household registration scheme.

China did not have a capital market because the mobilization and allocation of investment funds was decided by the government through its budget. Since state enterprises had monopolistic control over all sectors of the economy due to the socialization of productive relations, the state was the main saver, with a share of 97 per cent of national savings on the eve of reform (Chai 1997). These resulted from revenues from SOE profits and budgetary revenues such as turnover tax and sales of government bonds. Hence, the government could adjust the level of government revenues by manipulating the enterprise profits, the turnover tax rate and the amount of obligatory bonds purchased by households and enterprises. For instance, in order to ensure high profits of industrial enterprises the government adopted the compulsory agricultural procurement system, which guaranteed low input prices of raw materials. It also kept wages for workers low, and used its monopolistic power to keep prices for industrial goods in rural areas artificially high, ensuring a large profit for industries and revenue for itself.

Similarly, demand for investment funds was determined by planners, who applied a capital–output norm to derive the amount of investments needed by an enterprise and then authorized the corresponding amount. While enterprises could theoretically also fund investments from their own enterprise fund, this was in practice very limited as most of the enterprise profit was siphoned off by the government through the tight control of consumer and producer prices. Thus prices in Maoist China, as in the Soviet Union, did not reflect the relative scarcity of goods and services and played a very minor role in allocation. Their major function was to serve as a unit of measurement and as a tool of revenue control and manipulation of income distribution.

CONTROL OF INFLATION

China's planners controlled inflation by balancing supply (S) and demand (D) for consumer goods:

$$D = wL + PaQa - Sa \qquad (10.3)$$

$$S = PcQc \qquad\qquad (10.4)$$

where

w = wage rate
L = number of workers
Pa = state purchase price of farm products
Qa = quantity of farm products bought by the government
Sa = household saving
Pc = price of consumer goods
Qc = quantity of consumer goods available.

In equations 10.3 and 10.4 all dependent variables are under direct control of the government. Hence, an excess demand for consumer goods can theoretically be easily be avoided. However, in practice the wage bill (wL) and/or the value of state purchase of farm products may be larger than the amount of consumer goods available. In this case the excess demand either produces inflationary pressure through the rise of consumer good prices, as it did in the famine years of the early 1960s, or it takes the form of depressed inflation with an increased accumulation of involuntary household saving deposits.

FOREIGN TRADE AND INVESTMENT

In its first 30 years the People's Republic of China (PRC) pursued an extreme policy of self-reliance with trade considered a necessary evil and its role minimized. Imports were used to end imports and exports were merely a means to pay for them. For China's leaders, a self-reliance policy with the building of a strong and comprehensive industrial base was the key to ensuring an independent military capacity and the survival of the nation and of Chinese socialism. But self-reliance was also a tool to project the superiority of the Chinese system to its population (Riskin 1987) and it was reinforced by the generally hostile international environment which China faced in the early 1950s and 1960s.

Foreign trade under China's command state trading system was centrally planned and conducted exclusively by 12 centralized national foreign trade corporations (FTCs). They had to surrender all foreign exchange earned at an artificially low exchange rate, and the use of foreign exchange to finance imports had to be authorized by the government. Chinese domestic prices were divorced from foreign prices. On the export side, the FTCs procured goods for export at internal prices set by the government and sold the exported goods at foreign market prices. Any discrepancy between converted foreign prices at the highly biased official exchange rate, and internal prices, constituted a profit or loss for the FTCs. They were absorbed in the state budget under the *Preisausgleich* practice as either profit delivery or subsidy. On the import side, FTCs procured commodities at foreign prices and sold them to domestic end users at internal prices. Again any profits or loses made by FTCs were absorbed by the state budget as either profit delivery or subsidy. As the renminbi (RMB) was overvalued during most of the period, most domestic prices for traded goods were above world market prices and consequently FTCs made profits on imports, which were used to cover losses on exports (World Bank 1988).

Foreign investments consist of foreign loans, foreign direct investment (FDI) and official unrequited transfers. China received a substantial amount of both loans and aid from the former Soviet Union which helped substantially to fill China's domestic saving and investment gap. They enabled China to run a trade deficit from 1950 to 1955 and were crucial to the establishment of China's core industrial projects in the FFYP. These included 7 iron and steel plants, 24 electric power stations and 63 machinery plants (Riskin 1987). Eckstein estimates that without Soviet loans and aid there would have been no capital good imports, as China was faced with trade embargoes from the West. And he argues that investments during the FFYP would have been cut by at least 15–20 per cent if not by 35–50 per cent, which would have reduced economic growth in that period by more than half (Eckstein 1966).

The abrupt withdrawal of Soviet aid in 1960 compounded the economic crisis due to the failure of the GLF strategy and bad harvests in the early 1960s. It made China averse to foreign investments, which were not allowed until the adoption of the open door policy in the late 1970s.

In conclusion, China largely followed the Soviet model with the collectivization of the economy, and its adoption of a system of central planning and resource allocation, tight control of production, capital and labour, its growth strategy and its foreign trade. Its system was created in the early 1950s and remained largely unchanged until the eve of the reform in the late 1970s. The only major difference was China's faster pace of collectivization of agriculture, and Mao's greater emphasis on the development of productive relations in the GLF and Cultural Revolution (CR) strategies by which he tried to force the pace of development.

11. The Great Leap Forward

THE CONCURRENT MODEL OF THE BUILDING OF SOCIALISM

The deviation of Maoist strategy from the Soviet approach can be traced back to the Sino-Soviet ideological conflict with regard to the building of socialism in the late 1950s. Marx was the only thinker in recent times who developed a comprehensive theory of social and economic change. According to him, social change results from the growing contradiction between the two basic elements: that is, the forces of production, including the dominant ones of labour, capital and technology; and the relations of production, that is, the way production is organized and, also, the distribution of goods. These two basic elements form the economic base of society which in turn, according to Marx, determines the superstructure of classes, government and the prevailing ideology.

Marx predicted the downfall of capitalism and its replacement by socialism as a process of transformation from capitalism to communism, undertaken by a society ruled by a Communist Party. Communism is defined by the following traits: (1) all people own the means of production (so there cannot be any exploitation); (2) the production process is fully socialized; (3) scarcity ceases to exist; and (4) goods are distributed according to need rather than on the basis of work or labour. Unfortunately, Marx left no road-map on how to accomplish the transition from socialism to communism and, as a result, different socialist countries developed different strategies.

The difference between the Soviet and Maoist socialist development is illustrated by the analytical framework developed by Van Ness and Raicher (1983) which is shown in Figure 11.1. The horizontal axis indicates the stage of development of the productive forces from subsistence to affluence, and the vertical axis shows the stage of development of the productive relations from a capitalist to a classless society. The northeast corner of Figure 11.1 where society is classless and affluent indicates the achievement of the ultimate goal of socialist countries, communism.

The Soviet strategy of socialist development is represented by the

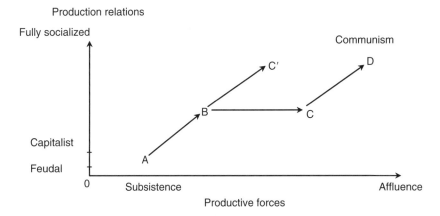

Figure 11.1   Soviet versus Maoist approach to socialist development

path ABCD which emphasizes the development of the forces of production. In the Soviet Union, there was initially a short period from
1928 and 1937 of a radical change of productive relations, with collectivization in agriculture and the nationalization of the non-agricultural
sector. After that initial period the socialization of productive relations
stopped and priority was given exclusively to the development of the
forces of production, that is, the path from point B to C in Figure 11.1.
According to Marxist theory, productive forces determine productive
relations, and in socialism at a certain stage of the development of the
former a critical mass is achieved which produces a sharp change in
the relations of production towards communism from point C to D in
Figure 11.1.

Thus the Soviet strategy assumes a sequential progression in two stages
from socialism to communism, with emphasis on the development of the
forces of production in the first, and an eventual change in productive
relations in the second. The problem with this theory is that no empirical evidence is available to support it. In contrast the Maoist strategy of
socialist development, as shaped by the Great Leap Forward (GLF) and
the Cultural Revolution (CR) can be described as a concurrent theory of
socialist development since it does not focus exclusively on the development of the forces of production. Mao believed that the rapid transformation of productive relations does not hamper, but actually facilitates
the development of the forces of production. It is represented by the path
ABC'. Hence the goal of communism can be achieved faster (see Howe
and Walker 1977; Van Ness and Raicher 1983).

THE GREAT LEAP FORWARD

The seed of Mao's GLF strategy is not to be found in his *Critique of Soviet Economics* (1977) but in his 1957 speech in Moscow to international delegates from socialist nations on the occasion of the 40th Anniversary of the October Revolution. In that speech Mao confirmed Khrushev's goal that within 15 years the then USSR would overtake the USA as the biggest producer of steel and other major industrial outputs, and announced that China would do the same in relation to the UK within the same period (Chang and Halliday 2005; Yang 2009). Subsequently the target timescale for overtaking the UK was reduced to three instead of 15 years. And Mao set the goal for China of catching up with the US within seven years (Yang 2009). In 1959 he also announced that China would achieve full-blown communism within 20 years (Yang 2009), thereby putting China in competition with the USSR for leadership of the international communist movement (Chang and Halliday 2005; Yang 2009).

In order to realize this goal the gradual development approach enshrined in the 1954 constitution was discarded. In May 1958 at the Eighth Communist Party Congress in Beijing a new development strategy, known as the 'three red flags' strategy, was announced (Yang 2009). The first red flag represents the new strategic line (*luxian*) of socialist development which is summed up by the slogan 'Go all out, aim high, achieve better and faster results'. The second flag stands for the GLF and the third represents the people's communes (Yang 2009). The gist of this strategy was to speed up socialist and economic development in China.

In order to allow China to catch up with the UK as soon as possible (Howe and Walker 1977) the bar for the achievement of major agricultural and industrial planning targets set in 1955 for 1967 was raised (see Chapter 10, Table 10.3): instead of fulfilling them within 15 years as originally planned, they were now due for fulfillment within two to five years. For example, steel output was set to double within a year from 5.4 million tonnes in 1957 to 10.7 million in 1958 (Yang 2009).

Several policies implemented in the GLF period were geared to achieve the rapid socialization and industrialization. They included: (1) the formation of people's communes; (2) the 'walking on two legs' policy; (3) the introduction of active planning; and (4) a drastic increase in the rate of investments.

THE PEOPLE'S COMMUNES

The first commune was formed in Henan in April 1958, and their formation spread like fire all over the country with the 'encouragement' of the Great Leader and the approval of the Politbureau of the Chinese Communist Party (CCP). By year's end 753 000 advanced agricultural co-operatives (AACs) had been merged into 26 576 people's communes (PCs) and the rate of peasant participation had reached 99.1 per cent (see Chapter 10, Table 10.2). With the establishment of the PCs China's collectivization had gone well beyond the Soviet model in several respects. To begin with, communes in China were much larger than the average collective farm in the USSR, because the latter normally covered all farms in a village whereas PCs covered entire townships. The average commune consisted of 4600 households with 6700 workers. In terms of labour the Chinese commune was 30 times larger than that of a Soviet collective farm and in terms of land it was four times bigger. The large size of the Chinese commune was conceived as a vital element in fast-tracking China's industrialization.

One of the prerequisites of the Soviet model of rapid industrialization is the extraction of agricultural surplus through price scissors to fuel industrialization. This was possible since on the eve of its industrialization in 1928 the country did not suffer any great pressure from the population and its per capita farmland as well as its grain output were relatively high, namely twice as high as China's in the 1950s (Chen and Galenson 1969). China was comparatively much poorer, and its farmers lived close to the margins of subsistence. Thus very little agricultural surplus was left for investment and China's drive for industrialization constantly ran up against the wall of inadequate food supplies.

In order to soften this constraint the Chinese government adopted a self-reliance approach in the promotion of agricultural development. This meant that the onus to increase agricultural output was pushed to the local level. Thus PCs had to mobilize local labour and materials themselves rather than rely on resources and investments of the central government. Communes were considered ideal tools for this since they could free especially women for participation in the labour force with the establishment of such facilities as public dinner halls, child care centres and so on (Riskin 1987). More importantly, communes could mobilize surplus labour for capital investment projects in agriculture, such as flood control and irrigation projects, and also for yet more labour-intensive cultivation techniques enshrined in Mao's eight-point agricultural constitution (see Becker 1996).

The mobilization of local rural resources, including unused or underemployed rural labour and material resources, was crucial to the policy of 'walking on two legs' (discussed below) and its aim was to enable the agricultural sector to produce its own modern industrial inputs to promote agricultural development and a greater agricultural surplus. Last but not least, it was conceived that the large size of the PC would enable Chinese agriculture to reap the benefits of more specialization, economies of scale and rapid adoption of new technology.

The commune also represents a higher form of social organization than the collective farm since it eradicates the remnant of private ownership on the part of households. Thus in the process of forming communes private plots were abolished, as was private ownership of the means of consumption, including private housing and kitchen utensils like pots and pans. Private ownership was no longer needed as the commune introduced the supply system practised in the Yenan period by giving its members ten guarantees, namely those of food, shelter, clothing, and covering the costs of maternity, weddings, education, medical care and burial as well as those of hygiene (bathing and hairdressing) and film entertainment (Riskin 1987; Yang 2009). Since communes were also established at the level of townships, the town government was merged into commune administration. Thus the major state-owned rural economic units, such as banks, commercial establishments and so on, were transferred to the commune with the result that the pattern of communal ownership was a hybrid of collective and state owned.

Communes were also more highly socialized than collectives. In terms of income distribution, this no longer followed the principle 'to each according to their labour' but was advanced to 'to each according to their needs', with the provision of the ten guarantees. Of vital importance, however, was that communes realized the CCP's goal of egalitarianism since they engaged not only in agriculture but also in a host of non-agricultural activities, such as rural-based industrialization, commerce, education, culture and government (Riskin 1987). Since communes also merged poorer and richer collectives they achieved a better income-levelling effect, because with the commune being the basic production and accounting unit the previously poorer and richer collectives now all had an equal share in income. Thus communes achieved the elimination of the three big Marxist 'contradictions' between the city and the countryside, workers and peasants, and manual and mental labour.

'WALKING ON TWO LEGS'

Soviet industrialization and choice of technology was 'walking on one leg' since it emphasized the development of large-scale, capital-intensive, urban-based industrial plants utilizing modern technology. This strategy suited the Russian factor endowment well, since unlike China on the eve of industrialization it did not suffer from population pressure. In fact, the USSR's population in 1928 was only a quarter of China's population in

1952. Thus in the 1930s, in order to recruit an industrial labour force the USSR had to coerce millions of people to move from the countryside to the cities (Chen and Galenson 1969). In contrast, China on the eve of its industrialization drive had an oversupply of labour. With the population growing at an annual average rate of 2 per cent in the 1949–52 period (Ishikawa 1983), both underemployment and unemployment were widespread in cities and the countryside (Howe 1971).

Thus the policy of 'walking on one leg' and following the Soviet model of industrialization using large-scale, capital-intensive urban-based industries as the motor of development aggravated the magnitude of China's problem of unemployment in the cities. It also neglected the development of industries in China's rural areas and increased the rural–urban divide. To address these problems the policy of 'walking on two legs' was introduced which aimed at the simultaneous development of both large-scale, capital-intensive urban industries and small-scale, labour-intensive rural industries. The latter were a means to narrow the rural–urban divide, and not only to utilize fully the large pool of rural surplus labour but also to access the widely dispersed mineral and energy resources in the countryside for the production of industrial goods to support agricultural development (Ishikawa 1972).

THE CONCEPT OF ACTIVE PLANNING

In the conventional Soviet model, planning is used to achieve a balance by matching supply and demand in order to avoid bottlenecks. The drawback of this method is that enterprises will bargain for a soft plan target and hoard materials in order to avoid penalties for failure to fulfil plan targets, or to receive a bonus for their overfulfilment. Thus production capacity in the USSR was underutilized – a luxury which China could not afford. The GLF policy tried to solve the problem by introducing the concept of active planning, which was a tool designed not to achieve a balance between demand and supply but to create an imbalance. This was perceived as a dynamic incentive for local authorities and enterprises to fulfil the very ambitious targets set by the central authority.

The way it worked was that the central administration would set deliberately unrealistic and high targets to cause imbalances and bottlenecks which pressured local authorities and enterprises to mobilize more resources and make greater efforts to overcome them. Thus communes and enterprises were constantly pushed to produce at maximum production capacity and to go beyond it via innovation. The downside of this approach is, of course, its utter neglect of the disaster effect of imbalance on an economy without a market mechanism, which might cause the economy to grind to a halt.

The method used to implement active planning was planning with 'two books', for example the use of dual targets. All authorities were required to draw up two sets of targets along the principles described in the 1958 document *Sixty Points on Working Methods* (Howe and Walker 1989). For the central government the first set of targets was publicized, mandatory and was relatively low and its fulfilment guaranteed. The second set was, however, much higher, it was not published and its fulfilment was deemed desirable. Local authorities had a parallel, dual set of targets, both based on the goals of the central authority. The first set of targets was based on the central authorities' second set of targets which was deemed the minimum mandatory for the local authorities at the lower level, and the second set was the higher output targets, which were deemed desirable by the local authorities at the higher level and remained unpublished. The trick was that the performance criteria for local authorities were based not on the first, realistic, set of targets but on the second set of ambitious, unpublished outcomes. And since the desired targets of the higher authority became, in effect, the minimum or mandatory target for the lower authority, targets were ratcheted up at every level and became increasingly inflated on their way down from Beijing to the province, to the local county and the local commune (Riskin 1987; Yang 2009).

Similarly, statistics were transformed from the neutral role of data collection to assist planners in plan formulation to an active role. Local authorities were encouraged to set inflated targets in order to motivate the achievement of higher production quotas. According to Xue Muqiao, the former Director of China's State Statistical Bureau, the latter kept two sets of figures. One was the actual figures, the other the inflated ones, and statisticians were instructed to provide those figures which the central authorities would like to receive (Yang 2009).

SPEEDING UP DEVELOPMENT

In the GLF the Feldman model was implemented to the fullest extent possible and in order to speed up development the rate of investment was drastically increased. Table 11.1 shows that it grew from 24 per cent in 1953–57 to 34 per cent in 1958, and reached its apex at 44 per cent in 1959. In 1960 the rate declined slightly but remained at 40 per cent until in 1962 it fell to 10 per cent following the collapse of the GLF. It started to climb again in 1963; however, it regained its pre-GLF level only in 1965.

Another means to speed up industrialization was that the share of

Table 11.1   China's rate of investment and its allocation in the years of the GLF (in %)

	1953–57	1958	1959	1960	1958–62
1. Rate of investment	24.2	33.8	43.8	39.6	30.8
2. Share of industries					
Heavy industries	46.5	57.0	56.7	55.3	56.0
Light industries	5.9	7.3	5.2	4.0	5.0
Total	52.4	64.3	61.9	59.3	61.0

Source: SSB, China Statistical Yearbook 1992.

investments in heavy industry was also drastically increased. Table 11.1 shows that the total investment allocated to the industrial sector had risen sharply from 52.4 per cent in the First Five-Year Plan (FFYP) period to between 59 and 64 per cent during the GLF period. And the share of heavy industry in total investments grew from the initial 47 per cent to 56 per cent in the GLF at the expense of investments in the light industries.

OUTCOME OF THE GLF

Contrary to Mao's expectation the GLF failed to achieve the anticipated great improvements in industrial and agricultural development. In fact, both sectors failed sharply after the initial spurt in 1958; however, it is hard to estimate the actual figures due to the fact that official statistics for this period are highly questionable. However, Table 10.3 in Chapter 10 shows that the major targets for grain and steel production set for 1967 were not achieved until some 13–21 years later. Worse still, the GLF led to the worst famine ever in China's as well as in world history, with a death toll of between 47.7 million and 76 million.

Estimates of the total death toll vary widely since it includes direct deaths due to malnourishment and indirect deaths due to a decline of the birth rate, for many women had stopped ovulating due to malnourishment. The lower estimate mentioned above is based on government statistics and is unreliable for two reasons. Firstly, those local cadres feared political repercussions if they reported the real birth and death rates. Secondly, under-reporting allowed them to claim more grain rations for the members of their communes (Yang 2009).

The higher estimates of the death toll are more reliable since they are derived from adjusted official death and birth rates based on the

Population Census of 1953, 1964 and 1982. For example, the renowned demographer Banister (1997) shows that the direct death toll for 1959–61 amounted to 30 million and the indirect one 31.2 million, adding up to a toll of 62 million people. This dwarfs not only the 10 million death toll of China's largest famine in 1928–30 (Yang 2009) but also that of India's 1896–97 famine with 5 million, and the 1932–33 famine in Ukraine with 7 million (Becker 1996).

China's concurrent development model of socialism was supposed to be a shortcut to the realization of communism. The great irony for Mao is, however, that it had the opposite effect and led China away from it. The famine resulting from the GLF sowed the seeds for the CR and, as will be discussed, the backlash against it precipitated the initiation of China's economic reforms and the introduction of the open door policy after Mao's death. The reforms undoubtedly boosted China's economic growth but they also constituted a retreat from socialism and the reintroduction of capitalist relations in production. Thus, Mao's GLF turned out to be really a Great Leap Backward.

12. The Great Famine

The factors responsible for China's Great Famine in the years 1959–61 are also the causes of the failure of Mao's strategy of concurrent development. While several good studies are available (see Kueh 1995; Becker 1996; Walker 1998; Riskin 1998; Lin and Yang 2000; Kung and Lin 2003) the most recent one by Yang (2009) is the most reliable and comprehensive one and this discussion largely follows it.

Prior to Sen's contribution (1977) the cause for famine was mainly attributed to the decline in food availability (FAD) as a result of either natural or man-made disasters. However, Sen argues that the more crucial factor may, in fact, have been problems with the distribution rather than the production of food, for example entitlement failure (EF). In a market economy the famine affects segments of the population who lose their entitlement to food because of the sudden loss of their possessions, or loss of the means to buy food, or because of change in the relative price structure which makes it difficult for them to acquire sufficient food. In his studies of several well-known historical famines in India he found that famines occurred even in the absence of FAD, simply because of EF.

However, in the case of China's famine at the end of the Great Leap Forward it has been shown that both factors were present: there was a significant decline in FAD and also EF on the part of the rural population (Lin and Yang 2000; Kung and Lin 2003; Yang 2009). In order to clarify the relative weight of these two factors I analyse the food availability from a national perspective to see whether the famine of the rural population could have been avoided if food grains were distributed equally without causing any EF. If it could not be avoided, FAD must be one of the causes of the famine.

Table 12.1 gives an overview of the demand and supply of the state grain department in the famine years. It shows that the main source of supply was procurement from the farmers and that grain imports were used only in the last two years as the famine deepened. The main sources of demand were the sales to the cities and resales to the countryside, with some exports continuing even in the time of the famine. In the famine years total demand outstripped total supply, causing a dwindling of reserves to only 8.59 million tonnes which finally prompted the government to import food grains.

Table 12.1   State grain balance sheet, 1957–58 to 1961–62 (husked grain in million tonnes)

	1957–58	1958–59	1959–60	1960–61	1961–62
I. Total supply	46.01	56.27	60.71	41.19	39.74
Procurement	46.01	56.27	60.71	39.04	33.96
Imports				2.15	5.78
II. Total demand	45.00	58.32	63.06	47.46	38.88
Sale to urban areas	21.12	27.32	29.63	26.25	23.39
Sale to countryside	21.00	25.25	26.35	18.10	13.45
Supply to defense force	0.62	0.62	0.66	0.61	0.62
Exports	2.09	3.65	4.33	1.20	0.88
Loss	0.17	1.48	2.09	1.30	0.54
III. Reserves	19.22	17.16	14.85	8.59	9.46

Source: Yang (2009).

The information from Table 12.1 together with data on grain output and of the population enables us to arrive at a fairly accurate picture of the per capita grain availability in the famine years nationwide and in urban and rural areas, as shown in Tables 12.2 to 12.4. Table 12.2 presents the estimates of food grain availability under the assumption that food is distributed equally, without discrimination between the city and countryside. The total national food grain availability is estimated as the sum of output minus net exports plus/minus changes in reserves. The per capita food grain availability (FGA) is obtained by dividing total FGA by the number of the total population.

Table 12.2 shows that the food grain situation was already precarious before the GLF because in 1957–58 it was only moderately above the subsistence norm of 210 kg per capita (Chang and Halliday 2005; Yang 2009). During the GLF grain output declined and per capita FGA dropped significantly below the minimum, resulting in a food grain deficit in the three famine years. Table 12.2 shows clearly that a famine could not have been avoided even if all grain had been distributed equally and without any EF.

CAUSES OF THE DECLINE IN FOOD GRAIN AVAILABILITY

From Table 12.2 it is clear that in the famine years food grain availability declined due to a decrease in grain output. In the official version of the Maoist era this was 70 per cent due to natural disasters and 30 per cent due

Table 12.2   National per capita food grain availability (FGA), 1957–58 to 1961–62 (husked grain in million metric tonnes)

Grain year	Population	Output	Net exports	Loss	Change in reserves	FGA	FGA per capita (kg)
(1)	(2)	(3)	(4)	(5)	(6)	(7)	(8)
1957–58	645.33	169.49	2.09	0.17	0.92	166.31	257.71
1958–59	659.63	160.87	3.65	1.48	−2.01	157.75	239.15
1959–60	666.54	136.30	4.33	2.09	−2.31	132.19	198.32
1960–61	663.70	126.52	−0.95	1.30	−6.27	132.44	199.55
1961–62	663.05	133.70	−4.90	0.54	0.88	137.18	206.89

Notes and sources:
(1)   Grain year begins from 1 July and ends 30 June the following year.
(2)   Moving average population of two calendar years.
(3)   Moving average of grain output of two calendar years. Source of grain output data: SSB, China Statistical Yearbook 1984. Unhusked grain output is converted to husked grain output by using a loss rate of 13 per cent as suggested by Yang (2009).
(4)   (5) and (6) from Table 12.1.
(7)   (3) minus (4), (5) and (6).
(8)   (7) divided by (2).

to policy errors. However, after the reforms the proportion of natural and human errors was the other way round.

And the latter seems closer to the truth since recent studies by Becker (1996) and Yang (2009) have busted the myth of natural disaster in the famine years. Becker (1996) suggests that the data of China's Central Metereological Bureau show that in the years 1959, 1960 and 1961 China did not experience any unusually bad weather. Yang's study (2009) largely confirms Becker's findings. He cites a study by Gao, an agro-meteorologist whose data for weather patterns in China from 1951–90 were collected from 350 weather stations across the country. She analyses climate change during this period and its impact on major agricultural outputs by comparing the average rainfall (Rs) and temperature (Tn) in the famine years (1959–61) with the long-term average (1950–90), and constructs a deviation index (D) which is calculated as follows:

$$D = (B - Y)/Y \times 100) \qquad (12.1)$$

where B is the actual monthly rainfall in millimetres or temperature measured in centigrade and Y is their long-term average. Figures 12.1 and 12.2 show that in the famine years average rainfall and temperatures did not diverge much from their long-term averages in comparison with

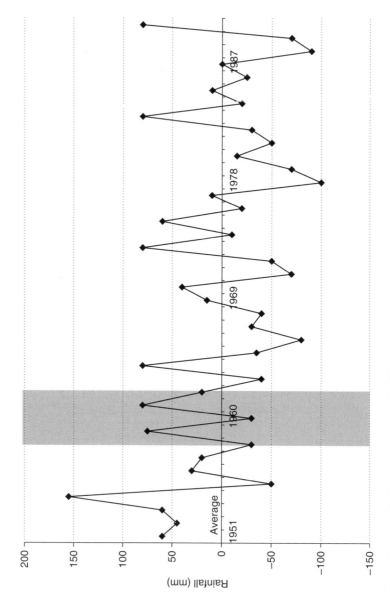

Figure 12.1   Rainfall deviation indices, 1951–90

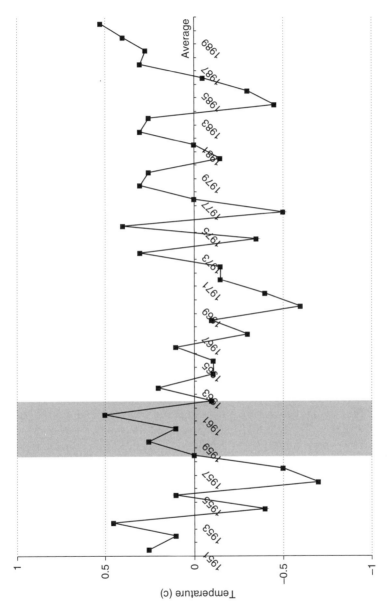

Figure 12.2   Temperature deviation indices, 1950–80

133

non-famine years. For instance, Figure 12.1 for rainfall shows that the average monthly rainfall in 1959 and 1961 was 80 per cent higher than the long-term average, indicating flooding in these two years. However, the flood intensity of these two years was comparatively less than those of the non-famine years 1954 and 1973. Similarly, the monthly average rainfall in 1960 was 30 per cent less than the long-term average, indicating the onset of drought conditions. However, the 1960 figure was less than half of the years 1955, 1963, 1966 and other years when the drought was much more intense.

In the Maoist era the Chinese government also blamed the Russians for the FAD in the famine years. China continued to export food grains and even had a spike in grain exports in 1958–59 and 1959–60 (see Table 12.1). It is a great irony that these exports went to socialist countries with a much higher standard of living than China, like the then East Germany, Hungary and Albania (Chang and Halliday 2005; Yang 2009). The then Chinese government alleged that the reason for these continued food aid exports was that the USSR government had coerced the Chinese government to repay its debts earlier than scheduled.

However, evidence available now suggests that Khrushev did not at all pressure China to repay the loan ahead of schedule (Chang and Halliday 2005; Yang 2009). In fact the opposite was the case for in 1961, in view of the spreading famine in China, the USSR offered the country an interest-free loan to import 1 million tonnes of wheat from Russia and 500 000 tonnes of sugar from Cuba, of which China accepted only the latter. Khrushev also revalued the yuan–rouble exchange rate by 78 per cent to reduce the burden of China's debt payments. Thus it was not the Russians but Mao himself who insisted that China repay its debt – famine or not – well ahead of schedule, namely 11 years earlier than planned.

Thus the official reasons given for the famine, namely bad weather and the pressure from the USSR to repay loans, do not hold. It was undoubtedly 'policy errors' fuelled by ambition, as evidenced by the early repayment of loans, that were the main factor behind the great famine. Bad policies impacted drastically on the livelihood of China's rural population. One of the major culprits was the large-scale diversion of rural labour into the building of irrigation projects, such as dams and channels. In 1958 alone one-third of the agricultural labour force or 100 million people (Yang 2009) were made to construct irrigation projects, with the result that they consumed more food (due to the heavy work) and contributed less to agricultural production. Furthermore, most dams were not built with cement but from mud and by untrained peasants, with the result that most collapsed within two years. Large dams tended to silt up quickly, like the Sanmanxia on the Yellow River, which rendered them next to useless (Becker 1996).

In the GLF labour was also diverted to steel making with the ambitious goal to overtake the UK within three years. Thus backyard iron and steel furnaces were set up in the countryside using primitive technology. By the end of 1958 several hundred thousand small blast furnaces were operating throughout the countryside and the amount of rural labour diverted to this industry was 60 million (Riskin 1987).

In addition, labour was diverted to other small-scale industrial projects, for in early 1958 the Central Committee of the CCP had resolved that within 5–7 years the value of industrial production should overtake that of agriculture in each locality. The original schedule for this had been 5–10 years (Yang 2009). Local authorities began to compete with each other in setting up small-scale rural industries which mushroomed all over China. The result was that the industrial workforce soared from 31 million in 1957 to 60 million, and the urban population increased from around 100 million in 1957 to 131 in 1960 (Yang 2009). According to one estimate the diversion of labour from agriculture into irrigation, steel making and other industrial projects was responsible for the 29 per cent decline of agricultural output in the famine years (Kung and Lin 2003).

However, rural labour (and resources) was also wasted in overly ambitious and unscientific cultivation techniques propagated by Mao in his *Eight Constitutions of Agriculture* (Howe and Walker 1989) which advocated labour-intensive deep ploughing, closer planting of seedlings and the intensive use of organic fertilizers mixed with mud as a source of manure. Some of these methods did little to increase crop yield but led instead to crop failure. For example, in South China the norm for planting rice seedlings is 1.5 million per 1.01 hectares which local authorities increased to between 6 and 7.5 million under Mao's influence. The seedlings all died because of a lack of ventilation and sunlight (Becker 1996).

Another significant factor contributing to the collapse of grain output in the GLF was Mao's '3–3' system of land use proposed in his *Eight Constitutions of Agriculture*. Fooled by the inflated grain output data submitted by local authorities, in 1958 the Chinese government had the impression that it had solved its grain problem. In December 1958 the Party's Central Committee issued a directive urging local authorities to 'sow less but produce more and aim at high yield' by adopting the '3–3' field management system. Under this system one-third of the cultivated area was to be planted with field crops, one-third with horticulture crops and one-third was to be left fallow. When local authorities followed these guidelines in 1959 the sown area declined by 10 per cent – undoubtedly one factor which contributed to the subsequent grain output collapse (Yang 2009). Walker (1984) using grain yield data from 1952–57 calculated that a 10 per cent reduction in the sown area would result in a considerable decline of grain output, namely 17 million tonnes. Hence this policy alone is responsible for 56 per cent of the 30 million tonne decline in grain output in 1959.

Last but not least, the weak incentive scheme of Chinese communes undoubtedly took its toll on grain production. In collective farms the net income available for distribution, Y, was partly based on the number of people in the household, n, and in the collective, N; and partly on the amount of labour contributed by the household, l, and by the collective, L. Thus individual household income entitlement, Yh, was determined as follows (Chai 1997):

$$Yh = Y a(n/N) + (1 - a)(l/L) \qquad (12.2)$$

where n/N and l/L are the share in population and labour of the individual household and a is the proportion of income distributed according to the number of persons in each household. If $a = 1$, the distribution is egalitarian, and if it is zero the distribution corresponds to the amount of labour contributed. All intermediate values indicate a mixed system.

Work incentives in the Chinese collective farms were already much weaker than in private farming as the relation between individual work effort and material reward tended to be tenuous and rather uncertain because part of the reward distribution was egalitarian, regardless of the work contribution of a household. Although part of the collective income was distributed according to labour contribution, if a farmer put additional effort into production he was unable to get a corresponding reward because it was shared among all co-workers due to the work point allocation system. The high transaction costs of monitoring and assessing individual work performance meant that entitlements were measured in terms of time rather than on productivity which of course gave rise to free-riders and made the relationship between effort and reward even more remote.

The communes made the work incentive problem in agriculture even worse. Since communes are a more highly socialized organization than collectives and provided free facilities and services, such as mess halls, the distribution of rewards according to work points and labour was dispensed with in 1958 and the egalitarian basis of need became the sole criterion for the distribution of rewards. However, this also removed any work incentive for the individual. Even after the demise of communal mess halls in 1961 and the restoration of the work point system, income continued to be allocated largely on the basis of need simply because this swallowed up most of the available funds, leaving little for distribution according to work point (Donnithorne 1967; Yang 2009). The disconnection between individual work effort and material rewards caused people to undersupply labour in terms of time and effort, leading to universal sloth (Chinn 1979; Yang 2009).

ENTITLEMENT FAILURE

Although the Great Famine could not have been averted, because of insufficient grain supplies, its magnitude would have been much less without the entitlement failure of the rural population which bore the brunt of the famine. Yang (2009) estimates that out of the total direct excess death toll of 16.2 million according to official statistics, only 12 per cent or 2 million occurred in the cities, whereas the countryside accounted for 88 per cent of the total direct excess deaths.

Table 12.3 shows the huge difference in the years 1955 to 1966 between rural and urban death rates. Given that the normal death rate of the rural population in the pre- and post-GLF years was 51 per cent higher than that of the urban populace, its increase to double that of their urban comrades with a rate of 28.58 per 1000 at the height of the Great Famine in 1960 reveals the extent of their entitlement failure.

The direct excess death toll in the countryside can be estimated as the difference between the total direct excess death toll and the urban direct

Table 12.3   Official statistics of the population (in million) and death rates (per 000 population)

Year	Population	Rural death rate	Urban death rate	National death rate
1955	608.66	12.60	9.30	12.28
1956	621.47	11.84	7.43	11.40
1957	637.41	11.07	8.47	10.80
1958	653.24	12.50	9.22	11.98
1959	666.01	14.61	10.92	14.59
1960	667.07	28.58	13.77	25.43
1961	660.33	14.58	11.39	14.24
1962	665.77	10.32	8.28	10.02
1963	682.34	10.49	7.13	10.04
1964	698.36	12.17	7.27	11.50
1965	715.17	10.06	5.69	9.50
1966	735.40	9.47	5.59	8.83

Source: SSB, China Statistical Yearbook 1991.

Table 12.4   *Per capita food grain availability in China's cities, 1957–58 to*
              1961–62 (husked grain, kg per year)

Year	Urban population (millions) (1)	State grain sales to cities (in million tonnes) (2)	Urban per capita grain availability (3)
1957–58	103.24	21.12	204.57
1958–59	115.29	27.32	236.97
1959–60	127.05	29.63	232.22
1960–61	128.77	26.25	203.85
1961–62	121.77	23.39	192.08

Notes and sources:
(1) Two-year moving average of the average annual population, SSB, China Statistical
     Yearbook 1991.
(2) Yang (2009).
(3) (2) / (1).

excess death toll. Following Yang's procedure the latter, Du, can be estimated as follows:

$$Du = P\,1958(Ra - Rn) \qquad (12.3)$$

Here $P\,1958$ stands for the urban population in that year and Ra and
Rn are its actual and normal death rates. In normal years (1955–57 and
1962–66) Rn stands at 7.4 per 1000 whereas it climbed to 11.3 per 1000 in
the GLF years from 1958 to 1961 resulting in a direct excess death rate of
1.966 million in those four years. Since the total direct excess death is estimated at 16.2 million by Yang (2009), using the same method, the direct
excess toll of the rural population amounted to the difference between 16.2
million and 1.966 million, or 14.23 million on average, or 88 per cent of
the total.

   Why did the rural population have to bear the brunt of the famine? The
answer lies in the inequitable distribution policy of staple food, for while
the urban populace was guaranteed its food grain rations, the rural comrades were not (Walker 1984). This policy was driven by the government's
ambition to speed up the pace of industrialization and to protect the well-
being of the urban industrial workforce. Tables 12.4 and 12.5 present a
comparison of the urban and rural per capita food grain availability. The
former is calculated as state grain sales to cities divided by the urban population, and the latter as agricultural output minus procurement by the
state plus state resale to the countryside divided by the rural population.

Table 12.5   Rural per capita food grain availability, 1957–58 to 1961–62
(husked grain, million tonnes)

	Rural population (million) (1)	Grain output (2)	Procure-ment (3)	Resale to rural areas (4)	Total FGA (5)	Rural per capita FGA (6)
1957–58	542.09	169.49	46.00	21.00	144.49	266.54
1958–59	544.34	160.87	56.25	25.25	129.87	238.58
1959–60	539.49	136.30	60.70	26.35	101.95	188.98
1960–61	534.93	126.52	39.05	18.10	105.57	197.35
1961–62	541.28	133.70	33.95	13.45	113.20	209.13

Notes and sources:
(1)   SSB, China Statistical Yearbook 1991.
(2)   Table 12.2.
(3)   and (4) Table 12.1.
(5)   (2) – (3) + (4).
(6)   (5) / (1).

Rural per capita availability is obtained by dividing the rural population by total food grain availability.

Tables 12.4 and 12.5 show the persistent discrimination of the rural population, for in the GLF the rural FGA per capita was below the norm of 210 kg for three years, but for their urban counterparts only for two. And at the height of the famine in 1959–60 the urban FGA per capita was 23 per cent higher than the rural. However, as the famine spread in 1961–62 the government had to cut grain sales to the cities back by almost 11 per cent (Table 12.1). When the famine hit the cities it had to rescind its policy of non-imports and start large-scale imports of food grain to ensure an adequate supply at least to the major cities (Yang 2009).

CAUSES OF RURAL ENTITLEMENT FAILURE

The EF of the rural population was caused by a combination of a decline in grain output in 1959–61 (see Table 12.2) and the increase in the ratio of the state net procurement to feed the urban population and for exports in spite of dwindling grain harvests. Table 12.6 shows that the ratio, measured as procurement minus state resale of food grains to rural areas divided by grain output, increased steadily during the GLF. It reached its peak in 1959–60 after which it declined again somewhat but was still higher than its pre-GLF ratio of 1957–58.

What caused the government to increase the net procurement ratio

Table 12.6   Net procurement rate of agricultural output in the GLF (%)

1953–54	1954–55	1955–56	1956–57	1957–58	1958–59	1959–60	1960–61	1961–62
NA	17.0	16.5	13.0	14.8	19.3	25.2	16.6	15.3

Source: Yang (2009).

*Table 12.7   Nominal and effective procurement ratio in Shandong
province, 1958–60 (husked grain, million tonnes)*

	1958	1959	1960
1. Grain output			
a. Announced	34.8	20.0	25.0
b. Actual	14.4	12.2	8.0
2. Procurement	3.1	3.7	1.5
3. Procurement ratio			
Nominal[1]	8.9	18.5	6.0
Actual[2]	21.5	30.3	18.8

Notes:
1.   (2) / (1a).
2.   (2) / (1b).

Source: Yang (2009).

despite the falling grain output? The reason for this unreasonable policy was the inflated output targets submitted to the central government by the cadres under the influence of the GLF slogan 'Go all out, aim high, achieve better and faster results'. A cadre who set normal or realistic output targets was in danger of being attacked as a 'rightist' and losing their job. One resulting practice was to make inflated claims, which became increasingly common and numerous '*sputnik*' fields sprung up all over the countryside. They were created by transplanting ripe crops from a number of fields into a single plot to support sky-high harvest claims (Chang and Halliday 2005). For instance, in Fengyang County in Anhui Province where the normal grain yield was only 329 kg per *mu*, the local cadre in 1958 announced a yield of 14 969 kg on that area, an increase of 4550 per cent (Becker 1996). Inflated output projections necessarily led to the setting of a still higher effective procurement ratio. How unrealistic this had become is shown by an example from Shandong province.

Table 12.7 shows that in 1959–60 local officials in Shandong inflated output by between 64 and 212 per cent, as a result of which the effective procurement ratio was double or triple the nominal one. This made it very difficult for peasants to fulfil their procurement quota and provide enough grain for sowing, their own food and feeding livestock. The government actually blamed them for hoarding food grains and often coerced them to deliver their quota. In most cases this was only a threat but sometimes force was used, resulting in deaths.

In summary, the Great Famine of 1959–61 was the result of both food availability decline and entitlement failure. The decline of food availability was triggered by the collapse of grain output, which was caused by mainly policy errors rather than bad weather. In an attempt to speed up both industrialization and socialization, unrealistic agricultural and industrial output targets had been set. To achieve these targets, huge amounts of rural labour had been diverted from agriculture to unsound rural irrigation, steel making and other rural industrial projects. Hugh amounts of labour were also wasted in unsound cultivation techniques propagated by Mao in his *Eight Constitutions of Agriculture*. The final blow to grain production came from the negative incentive effect of the excessive income levelling practised in the communes, which was seen as the bridge between socialism and communism. The magnitude of the famine would have been much less without the entitlement failure of the rural population, which bore the brunt of the famine. The entitlement failure of the rural population was caused by the inequitable distribution policy of staple foods, for while the urban populace was guaranteed its food grain ration, the rural comrades were not. Furthermore, rural cadres for fear of being attacked as 'rightists' tended to inflate local output targets, which necessarily led to a higher effective procurement ratio despite declining grain output. As a result, after the fulfilment of the procurement quota, very little was left in the hands of the famers to feed themselves, let alone for sowing and feeding their livestock.

13.   The Cultural Revolution

PRELUDE TO CULTURAL REVOLUTION: THE POLICY REVERSAL

As the famine spread the weakness of the Great Leap Forward (GLF) strategy became too obvious to ignore and forced a policy reversal. However, its implementation was rocky and, in effect prolonged the misery of the people. In the first phase from November 1958 to July 1959 the overcentralized commune structure was modified. The basic accounting unit was shifted back to the production brigade which corresponded to the advanced agricultural co-operative (AAC). Confiscated assets were returned from the commune to its production brigades, from them to the production team, and down to the household. Communal dining halls were closed, free services abandoned and the work point system was restored. There was also a significant liberalization and quasi privatization in the form of 'three freedoms and one guarantee'. The three freedoms refer, firstly, to the restoration of private plots and the permission granted to farmers to cultivate land they have privately reclaimed. However, their area was not allowed to exceed 5 per cent of total cultivated area. The second freedom refers to the reopening of rural free markets, and the third to the self-responsibility of the household for profit and loss on their farm tasks. The one guarantee refers to the responsibility farm system.

To enhance the incentive to work, various systems of contracting jobs to the households were tried out. Firstly there was the 'three guarantees and one reward system' used for contracting out farm tasks such as stock and fish breeding and irrigation works to the household, in which the collective guaranteed the capital and equipment needed, and the household underwrote the work costs, guaranteed the output target and received a bonus for its overfulfilment (Riskin 1987). Secondly, there was the responsible farm system under which land was assigned to individual households, which guaranteed the delivery of an output target to the collective. In return the collective guaranteed that the household could retain any above-quota output (Yang 2009). Another policy shift was that rural industries were closed and the redundant workers and their families were sent to the countryside to boost agricultural production.

However, the liberalization policy did not last long, for it was abruptly halted after the Lusan Conference in July 1959 which had been planned as an extended meeting of the Chinese Communist Party (CCP) Politbureau to placate concerns of the moderate party members and rectify excesses of the GLF policy. However, when Marshall Peng Dehuai, who was then the Defence Minister, after a visit to his home town in Hunan openly criticized the GLF policy, describing it as 'petty bourgeois fanaticism' (Yang 2009), Mao felt obliged to defend it, backed by Liu Shaoqi, Zhou Enlai and Lin Piao. He insisted that 90 per cent of the GLF policy was positive but admitted 'minor mistakes' (see Yang 2009).

However, Mao was so upset that he threatened that if he was opposed he would leave and 'lead the peasant armies to overthrow the government' (Yang 2009). Subsequently he launched an anti-rightist campaign and purged the party and government of all suspected 'rightists', more than 3 million in all, including Marshall Peng. The political backlash was thorough: the decollectivization and liberalization were halted and GLF policies were reinstated, including some of the more radical measures like the reopening of communal dining halls and the reintroduction of the free supply system, and practices like the 'three freedoms and one guarantee' were banned (Yang 2009).

This reinstatement of the GLF policies contributed significantly to the deepening of the crisis in 1960 when the death toll of the famine reached its peak. And it was this which finally forced the CCP in January 1961, at the 9th Plenum of the 8th Central Committee meeting, to adopt a policy of readjustment. Mao was sidelined from economic leadership and the management of the economy was conferred on Chen Yun, the director of the reinstated Finance and Economics Committee of the CCP (Riskin 1987; Yang 2009).

Thus the pre-Lusan policies were reinstated in full and the decollectivization and liberalization policies were even accelerated in the countryside. Thus the production team rather than the production brigade was again the basic accounting unit, the 'three freedoms one guarantee policy' was promoted and the responsibility farm was endorsed by Deng Xiaoping, who quipped the famous line: 'I don't care whether the cat is yellow or black. It is a good cat as long as it catches mice'. By mid-1962 responsibility farms were adopted by 20 per cent of the farmers across the nation, but in provinces like Anhui, Sichuan, Gansu and Zhejiang they were as many as 70 and 80 per cent of all farms (Yang 2009). In some production teams these farms together with private plots and privately reclaimed land even accounted for one-third to one-half of cultivated land in 1962 (Riskin 1987).

The policy reversal on the industrial front was also in full swing. The high rate of investment was brought down from 39.6 per cent in 1960 to 19.2 per cent in 1961, and again to 10.2 per cent in 1962 (Riskin 1987; Yang 2009), and the ambitious output targets for heavy industry were also reduced. For example, that for steel was lowered from 18.7 to 6 million tonnes in 1962 and that of coal from 397 to 220 million tonnes. In the early 1960s some 218 000 small industrial plants were closed, reducing the number of industrial workers by 18.3 million and the urban population by 2.6 million (Yang 2009).

In line with these changes the focus for the national resource allocation was switched back from industry to agriculture with its share in state investments increased from 13 per cent in 1960 to 18.8 per cent in 1965. Heavy industry was now required to change its production focus to produce input and tools for agricultural production. Also, valuable foreign exchange earnings were now sacrificed to pay for imports of food grains to feed the population so that the government could reduce the grain procurement quota for the farmers. In order to secure the fulfilment of the procurement quota by farmers, the prices for agricultural goods bought by the state were raised.

At the planning and management level the decentralization of control to the local level implemented in the GLF was reversed. By 1963, 87 per cent of state-owned enterprises (SOEs) transferred downwards during the GLF control were restored to central control, largely parallel to the transfer of goods and materials, of which three-quarters were returned to central control (Riskin 1987). With this came a reassertion of the role of experts, such as engineers, accountants and statisticians in the industrial management system (Riskin 1987) and, most importantly, a switch away from the use of exclusive moral incentives to material ones. Industrial wages were now largely based on a combination of piece and time rates. A bonus, limited to 30 per cent of basic wages, was permitted where the use of piece rates was not practical.

THE CULTURAL REVOLUTION

The pragmatic policy reversals of the early 1960s sowed the seeds for the Cultural Revolution (CR) which was sparked by a conflict between Mao and Liu over the 'general line' of development in those years. As mentioned earlier, Liu was a staunch supporter of Mao's ruthless industrialization policy during the Lushan Conference back in 1959. But in 1961 Liu visited his home village in Hunan and saw the famine and decided to stop Mao's strategy (Chang and Halliday 2005; Yang 2009). At the Working Conference of the Central Party Committee held on 27 January 1962, attended by 7000 cadres, he attacked not only Mao's policy but also Mao's defence of it. In his critique he argued not only that the GLF policy was a failure, but also that it was due neither to natural disasters (as claimed by Mao) nor to the failure of local cadres but to the Party Centre itself (Yang 2009). Lin Piao, of course, defended Mao's line. However, Liu's points found some resonance and half a year later, in July 1962, while Mao was travelling, a meeting was held in Beijing which resolved to stage a reversal of the GLF strategy.

When Liu briefed Mao after his return on the meeting, Mao was furious and questioned why Liu had not stood firm to defend his policy. Liu replied that his and Mao's name would be associated with cannibalism in the historical records because so many people had died (Yang 2009). Mao replied, outraged and childishly: 'Three flags were down, land was divided. If you did not stand firm, what would happen to me if I died?' Mao was not ready to give in, and in September 1962 at the Tenth Plenum of the Eighth Central Committee he used his speech as Party Chairman to stop what he saw as a retreat from socialism. He urged members never to forget the class struggle and maintained that 30 per cent of rural party cadres were not genuine communists. A mass campaign was needed to 'clean up' the countryside and take power away from corrupted cadres 'who took the capitalist road'.

As a result the Socialist Education Movement and the 'Four Clean-Up' campaign were launched (Riskin 1987; Yang 2009) under the leadership of Liu. However, he argued with Mao over the method and target of the 'Four Clean-Up Campaign' and committed the mistake of cutting short Mao's speech at a subsequent meeting which was to have resolved these issues. Mao did not take it kindly and told Liu that: 'I can wag my little finger and there would be no more you' (Yang 2009). Subsequently, Mao and his closest ally, Lin Piao, conspired to purge Liu from the Party and in May 1966 the Cultural Revolution Small Group headed by Madam Mao was set up to help run the purge. The Cultural Revolution had begun.

In the first phase of the CR, Red Guards were formed with the children of cadres and used to attack traditional Chinese culture and prominent cultural figures. In August and September 1966 in Beijing alone 33 695 homes were raided by them, 1772 people were tortured to death and 4922 out of 6843 old monuments were destroyed (Chang and Halliday 2005). Even the home of Confucius in Shandong was not spared. During the second phase of the CR, new groups of Red Guards known as Rebel Groups were formed and their target was not traditional Chinese culture and its bearers but party officials branded as 'capitalist roaders'. They had been ordered by Mao to seize power from the party bosses and after torture they would usually be sent to labour camps known as May Seventh

Cadre Schools. The first prominent Party member to fall was Liu, who in August 1966 was branded a capitalist roader, expelled from the Party and put under house arrest. Deng Xiaoping followed a year later as 'Capitalist Roader No. 2'.

As more rebel groups were formed, the country in the third phase of the CR descended into something resembling civil war with factional fighting between rightists and leftists. One of the most prominent leftist groups was the Shanghai group led by the most prominent figure of the Gang of Four, Wang Hongwen. Finally Mao had to send in the People's Liberation Army (PLA) to restore order and to disband rebel groups. The scale of the CR can be seen from the fact that at its ending some 16 million urban youth, former Red Guards, were sent to villages for re-education (Chang and Halliday 2005).

In April 1969 the Party Congess met again for the first time after 13 years and apointed Lin Piao as Mao's successor and made Madam Mao a member of the Politbureau. She and her closest allies, Wang Hongwen, Zhang Chunqiao and Yao Wenyuan – the Gang of Four – dominated the Politbureau. Through their writings the latter two were largely responsible for the misleading conceptions about the nature of the CR in the West (Riskin 1987). However, Mao's alliance with Lin Piao did not last long because in August 1970 at the Lushan Conference they fell out over the presidency. Mao wanted to abolish the position altogether, whereas Lin insisted that Mao should be President and he the Vice-President.

Mao was not known to tolerate dissent. Lin's son, nicknamed 'Tiger', plotted to assassinate Mao but was betrayed by his own sister who had been successfully indoctrinated by Mao's thought. Pursued by Mao's henchmen, Lin Piao attempted to flee but lacked time to refuel his plane. He and all aboard crashed in September 1971 in the Mongolian desert (Chang and Halliday 2005).

During the CR, Mao rolled back most of the more pragmatic policies that had been adopted after the failure of the GLF. Mao's radical policies were reinstated in agriculture. The practice of 'three freedoms and one guarantee' was denounced and the responsibility farm system was banned again. In 1964 the Learn from Dazhai Campaign was launched with the objectives of, firstly, increasing the degree of socialism and control over production, and secondly, enhancing the government's ability to extract agricultural surplus. Thus ownership of the means of production and income distribution decisions were again shifted to a higher collective level with the transfer of the basic accounting unit back to the level of the production brigade (Zweig 1991). At the same time, in order to speed up industrial development, the transfer of resources to the agricultural sector was drastically cut back and rural industries were made to rely once again on local resources and self-finance. Labour was again mobilized for the construction of rural infrastructure and irrigation projects, and moral incentives were emphasized again.

While the work point system was retained, it was changed into a tool for the mobilization of peasant support for socialist values and policies and as a means to achieve income levelling. For example, the Dazhai work point system was a proposition of an individual's entitlement on the basis of self-assessment and a discussion by workmates. The final work point awarded would also take into account such criteria as the comrade's work attitudes, helpfulness to others, political orientation and contribution to promoting the Thought of the Great Chairman.

In addition, self-sufficiency in grain production and capital accumulation was pushed within the communes. To minimize resources transfer to agriculture, moral incentives were once again promoted. There was a similar reversal in respect to management for central planning was again out of fashion and severely weakened. Thus between 1970 and 1973 the management of the most important SOEs was transferred to the local authorities, including the famous Anshan Steel Factory and Daqing oil fields (Riskin 1987). Also, in 1972 the number of centrally allocated products was reduced by 30 per cent.

In management, expertise was again renounced in favour of 'redness'. And in order to eliminate the key source of alienation, the social division of labour between intellectual and manual labour, a system of mass participation in management was introduced. This was known as 'two participations, one reform and triple combination' or the '2-1-3 system of management' (Andors 1977). 'Two participations' refers to the participation of workers in management and of the cadres in manual labour; 'one reform' refers to doing away with red tape and reforming irrational rules; and 'triple combination' refers to the forming of teams for technical innovation consisting of workers, technicians and cadres.

One key element in this radical policy was the promotion of the principle of self-reliance which essentially implies the establishment of a comprehensive, independent economic system not only in the nation, but at the regional and local levels as well, even down to that of the commune and the individual enterprise. This policy had disastrous consequences for economic growth because it totally neglected the basic economic principles of comparative advantage, namely specialization and economies of scale. Furthermore, it exacerbated interregional and inter-enterprise income inequality (Donnithorne 1972).

The motives for Mao's self-reliance policy were complex. Obviously the ideological goal of diminishing or even eliminating the 'three big differences' between town and country, industry and agriculture, and mental and manual labour were important in the shaping of the self-reliance policy. However, the growing isolation of China in the world and the perceived military threat from the USSR on the one hand, and the Vietnam–American war on the other, also played a role (Joseph et al. 1991). China faced the imminent threat of air strikes on its nuclear facilities and its heavy industries along its coasts and border areas, known as the 'first front'. In order to create an alternative industrial base to allow it to keep up industrial production in case of fighting, China began a massive industrial investment in the remote areas of Southwest and West China known as the 'third front' (Chen 2009).

Initially six provinces and one autonomous region, namely Sichuan, Guizhou, Yunan, Shanxi, Gansu, Qinghai and Ningxia, were chosen for this as were the western areas of Shaanxi, Henan, Hubei and Hunan. Later, parts of Guangdong, Guangxi and Hebei were also included and Ningxia was excluded again (Chen 2009). The area between the first and third front was known as the 'second front'. The third front was launched in 1964 with the relocation of 1100 large industrial enterprises to these areas (Chang and Hallday 2005). In 1965, what was known as the 'minor third-front construction' was launched by Mao in each province in the first and second front, which centred on the construction of mainly small-scale military industries and self-contained industrial steel plants in mountainous areas (Chen 2009). The objective of the minor third-front construction was to enable these regions to fight a war without the help of the central government. The major and minor third-front construction costs swallowed a huge amount of China's investment resources and contributed significantly to its stagnant industrial productivity in this period.

14. Socialist modern economic growth: the outcome

RAPID INDUSTRIALIZATION

What were the results of three decades of socialist modernization in China? The results were mixed. On the one hand, the achievement in economic modernization was impressive. In terms of industrialization, according to official statistics Chinese industries, including manufacturing, mining as well as utilities, grew at a rate of 11.5 per cent over the quarter century from 1952 to 1978, that is, at one of the highest rates in the fast-growing East Asian region (Maddison 2007). However, the official Chinese growth rate of industry has several weaknesses and overestimates the real growth rate (Field 1996). Maddison and Wu, using constant 1987 prices, estimate the rate of growth of industrial gross value-added at 10.1 per cent a year for the same period (Maddison 2007). However, even at this lower rate the growth of China's industries was impressive when compared with the 1.7 per cent growth rate in the period from 1890 to 1952. As a result the share of industry in China's gross domestic product (GDP) shot up from 10 per cent in 1952 to 37 per cent in 1978 (Maddison 2007).

In terms of share of manufacturing in GDP, an international comparison by the World Bank (1983) shows that China's share was exceptionally high. As Table 14.1 shows, the manufacturing sector accounted for 24.5 per cent of China's GDP in 1981 as compared to 18.1 per cent for India and the 13 per cent estimated for large low-income countries. In fact, the size of China's manufacturing sector at that time was more akin to that expected for large upper-middle income countries.

In addition to its relatively large size the structure of China's manufacturing sector was also different from that of comparable countries. Its share of heavy industry was more comparable to that of Korea – which at that time had an income level five times higher than China – than to other large low-income countries like India and Indonesia (see Table 14.2). Even more striking is that machinery, with 10.8 per cent of GDP, even exceeded South Korea's figures and was roughly at the same level as that of Japan in 1965. However, some caution is in order since the dubious nature of Chinese machinery prices, which were set at a very high level by international

Table 14.1   International comparison of China's share of manufacturing in GDP

	%
China, 1981	24.5
India, 1979–80	18.1
Predicted value for large	
lower-income countries	13.0
middle-income countries	19.0
upper-middle income countries	25.0

Source: World Bank (1983).

Table 14.2   International comparison of the share of heavy and machinery industry in GDP

	Heavy industry %	Machinery %
China, 1981	16.4	10.8
India, 1979–80	9.6	3.1
Indonesia, 1980	4.5	2.2
South Korea, 1980	15.9	6.1
Japan, 1965	20.4	11.7

Source: World Bank (1983).

standards, may have exaggerated the share of China's machinery sector in GDP. Nevertheless, as Table 14.2 shows, given China's level of development this sector made an exceptionally large contribution to GDP.

However, in terms of technology China's industrial performance at that time was poor. This is evidenced by the widening technological gap between China's and international industries, which by the late 1970s generally was 10–20 years but in some fields was as wide as 20–40 years (Ma and Sun 1987; Harding 1987). When World Bank delegates visited China in the early 1980s they observed that China's industrial equipment tended to be 20–30 years out of date (World Bank 1983).

MODERN ECONOMIC GROWTH

Another great achievement of China during this period was modern economic growth (MEG). As mentioned in Chapter 8, China had never

Table 14.3   Estimates of China's economic growth rates, 1952–78

	%
Official statistics	6.1
Maddison	4.4
Perkins and Rawski	4.4

Sources: Maddison (2007) and Perkins and Rawski (2008).

achieved this before, for even in the golden Republican years (1914–33) the economy never achieved enough momentum to propel itself sufficiently into the modern era. Its growth rate remained at a respectable but feeble 2 per cent. The exact rate of China's economic growth during this period is, however, hard to pinpoint. Table 14.3 shows the three different estimates of China's growth for the 1952 to 1978 period from the major sources, for example China's official statistics, Maddison (2007) and Perkins and Rawski (2008). The problem with China's official statistics is that they tend to overestimate the real rate of growth due to the distorted structure of relative prices between industrial and agricultural products. As mentioned previously, the former were set too high and the latter too low in order to extract agricultural surplus from the rural sector. When the industry grows at a faster rate than agriculture the exaggerated relative price for manufactured goods leads to a greater overestimation of the real growth of GDP (Perkins and Rawski 2008).

Therefore, alternative estimates by the major Western economists try to correct this error. Perkins and Rawski base their estimate on official data but use 2000 prices to recalculate the GDP in order to remove the price distortion effect. Maddison's estimate is based on the adjusted official figures and 1987 prices. He goes one step further in that he also converts Chinese GDP in yuan into 'international dollars' which makes the figures more comparable internationally. Though they use different methods, these authors come to a much lower figure than the official data and are in remarkable agreement, coming up with an identical figure of 4.4 per cent instead of the official 6.1 per cent growth rate. Yet the performance of the Chinese economy is impressive even with the lower growth estimate, as can be seen from Table 14.4 which compares the growth in the pre-liberation period (1890–1949) with that of the Maoist era (1952–78). It shows that per capita GDP, while stagnant in the pre-liberation period, increased by 2.3 per cent during the Mao period. Hence, Mao should be credited with starting MEG in China.

Yet China's growth rate would still have been higher if not for the

Table 14.4   Growth of China's GDP and GDP per capita, 1890–1978 (annual average compound growth rate)

	1890–1952	1952–78
GDP	0.6	4.4
Per capital GDP	0.0	2.3

Source: Maddison (2007).

disturbances of the Great Leap Forward (GLF) and the Cultural Revolution (CR). For example, based on official statistics, Chow (1993) estimates that the GLF cost China almost one-third of total output and the CR another 12–23 per cent. Thus China's official growth rate could have reached 7.6 per cent a year, or could have been 1.6 percentage points higher.

STANDARD OF LIVING

Despite the significant improvement in China's rate of growth, Mao failed to make the Chinese people richer or achieve better welfare. Material welfare can be measured in terms of per capita income and per capita consumption. In terms of per capita GDP, China's growth rate is significantly lower than that of its Southeast Asian neighbours. In the period from 1952 to 1978 per capita GDP adjusted for international differences in purchasing power parity (PPP) grew at an annual compounded rate of 5.8 per cent in the four Asian 'little dragons'. In contrast, the Chinese growth was less than 40 per cent of that (Table 14.5). And the comparison with Japan is worse, for the latter's growth rate was three times that of China, as Table 14.5 shows. As a result, the income gap between China and its Asian neighbours widened significantly. According to Maddison (2001), China's per capita income in 1952 stood at $537 in 1990 international dollars, which was about one-third of that of the four Asian 'little dragons' ($1618.8) and 23 per cent of Japan's ($2341). Twenty-six years later in 1978, this amounted to less than 15 per cent of that of the four Asian 'little dragons' and to less than 8 per cent of Japan.

In terms of consumption standard, China lagged even further behind its neighbours. For while it grew in Taiwan, Hong Kong and Singapore at an average rate of between 6 and 9 per cent (World Bank *World Development Report* 1980), China's corresponding rate during the period 1957–78 grew at only 1.3 per cent in real terms (Lardy 1984). Worse still, most of the growth in China's consumption standard was due to the growth in public

Table 14.5   *Comparative growth rates of GDP per capita: China versus East Asian countries, 1952–78 (annual average compound growth rates)*

	GDP growth rate
China	2.3
Asian 'Four Little Dragons'	5.8
Hong Kong	5.4
Singapore	4.8
Taiwan	6.6
South Korea	6.3
Japan	6.7

Source: Maddison (2007).

consumption, while the rate of private consumption actually declined. This is evident from the facts, for both the real average wage of workers and the real average income of farmers declined during 1957–78 (Liu 1984). It is also evident from Lardy's (1984) finding that per capita consumption of grain, vegetable oil and cotton in 1978 was actually lower than the 1957 consumption level. In a similar vein, urban per capita housing space in 1978 was 20 per cent less than it had been in 1952 (Walder 1987).

The main reason why standard of living growth failed to match the growth of GDP lies in the inherent weakness of the development strategy adopted during this period, which emphasized resources mobilization for growth rather than increased efficiency. A good indicator of the efficient use of resources in the economy is the total factor productivity (TFP). During the First Five-Year Plan (FFYP) (1952–57) China experienced a rapid increase in TFP of almost 5 per cent per year (see Table 14.6). This was mainly due to one-off effects, such as the recovery from wars. From 1957 on China's growth rate slowed down significantly with the TFP turning negative. In such circumstances the tempo of economic growth can only be maintained with ever increasing inputs of labour and capital. But since capital can only be expanded at the expense of consumption, and labour only at the cost of declining leisure, the economic growth during the Maoist period was mainly sustained at the cost of consumer welfare.

HUMAN DEVELOPMENT

However, China's performance excels in respect to human development. The UN Development Programme has developed an index to measure the

Table 14.6   Sources of growth of China's GDP, 1952–78 (annual average growth rates)

	1952–57	1957–78	1952–78
1. GDP			
Maddison			4.4
Perkins and Rawski	6.5	3.9	4.4
2. Fixed capital			
Maddison			7.7
Perkins and Rawski	1.9	6.7	5.8
3. Education enhanced labour			
Maddison			4.9
Perkins and Rawski	1.7	2.7	2.5
4. TFP			
Maddison			−1.4
Perkins and Rawski	4.7	−0.5	0.5

Note: Maddison's figures are based on the average annual compound growth rate whereas those of Perkins and Rawski are based on average annual growth rates.

Sources: Maddison (2007) and Perkins and Rawski (2008).

improvement in the physical quality of life (UNDP 1990). Its major indicators are relative improvements in people's lives in terms of longevity (for example life expectancy at birth), the literacy rate and per capita income. According to the UNDP report (1990) China's human development index in 1978 approached the level of developed countries which have a much higher per capita income. This was achieved through the egalitarian system of the provision of basic goods and services, including access to education and health care. That way China succeeded in reducing mortality, morbidity and malnutrition (World Bank 1983). This is reflected in the dramatic increase in the average life expectancy which rose from 36 years in the 1940s to 64 years in 1979. In the same period the adult literacy rate rose from 20 to 66 per cent (Chai and Roy 2006).

INCOME EQUALITY

In terms of income levelling China actually made significant gains in maintaining interpersonal income inequality low in both the rural and the urban sectors. Compared to other low-income countries urban inequality in China was far lower than theirs. The Gini coefficient for China's urban households in 1981 was only 0.16 while that of other low-income countries

Table 14.7   Income inequality in China and South Asia (Gini coefficient)

Urban households		Rural households		All households	
China	South Asia	China	South Asia	China	South Asia
(1979)	India	(1981)	India	(1979)	India
	1975–76		1975–76		1975–76
	Pakistan		Pakistan		Pakistan
	1970–71		1970–71		1970–71
	Sri lanka		Sri Lanka		Sri Lanka
	1969–70		1969–70		1969–70
	Bangladesh		Bangladesh		Bangladesh
	1966–67		1966–67		1966–67
0.16	0.40	0.26	0.30–0.35	0.330	0.345

Sources: Riskin (1987) and World Bank (1985).

was around 0.40, as can be seen in Table 14.7. Rural inequality in China in 1979 was also among the lowest in the world. The Gini coefficient of rural interpersonal income distribution was only 0.26 as compared to an average of between 0.30 and 0.35 in other South Asian countries.

But in terms of eliminating the 'three great differences' between white-collar and blue-collar workers, between industry and agriculture and between town and country, Mao's success was limited. Superficially he succeeded in erasing the differences between mental and manual workers with the introduction of the 3-in-one system under which cadres were supposed to participate in actual production and workers in management. While this strategy helped to change the image of workers and reduce status differences, it was only implemented in the more socialist periods of the GLF and the CR and its long-term impact is questionable.

However, more seriously, Mao's ambition to develop China as fast as possible led him to adopt policies which actually widened the urban–rural divide because of his squeezing of agriculture to force the speed of industrialization and heavy industrial development. The widening rural–urban income gap can be inferred from the gap in consumption. Riskin (1987) and Parish (1981) show that the real consumption per capita of the agricultural and non-agricultural population widened from 2.4 to 1 in 1952, to 3.1 to 1 in 1979. However, this ratio of 3 to 1 still underestimates the urban–rural income divide because of the huge amount of subsidies received by urban residents for housing, transport, utilities, food, medical services, child care and pensions. In addition urban residents also had access to a much higher quality of medical care and education and enjoyed better employment opportunities for relatives than their rural counterparts could ever hope for (Rawski 1982). With the inclusion of these subsidies the urban–rural divide would widen to a ratio of almost 6 to 1 according to Rawski (1982). And this is significantly higher than the average of South Asian countries (World Bank 1983).

Taking this large urban–rural income difference into account increases China's overall Gini coefficient in 1979 to 0.33, which does not differ substantially from the 0.345 level of other low-income South Asian countries, as Table 14.7 shows. In conclusion, Mao failed to eradicate class differences in terms of status and privilege; he only shifted the gap away from mental and manual workers towards industrial and rural workers.

STRATIFICATION

One of Mao major goals was to establish a classless, socialist society by way of income levelling and the thorough elimination of status privileges and differences between classes. The question is whether he achieved this during his lifetime. Mao failed to eradicate the status and privilege differences not only between the main classes but also within them. It can actually be argued that while he changed the structure of Chinese society from one based on classes to one based on ideology, his socialist structure was much more clearly delineated and rigid than the old class structure, even though class and status differences were less visible.

After the purge of landlords, capitalists and the professional class, China's social pyramid was much flatter in shape and under Mao China's social structure was simplified and consisted of only two parts, the elite and the masses. The former were the political cadres and professionals, the latter the workers and peasants. Theoretically the ownership system in a socialist or communist society, through either the state or collective organizations, eliminates classes and class differences. However, in practice, cadres are the new ruling class in a communist or socialist society (Djilas 1957; King and Szeleni 2004), and China was no exception. Party cadres, because of their control over political power and the nation's reward and promotion system, gained quasi property rights not only to command the production of material goods but also to use and to enjoy them and to pass them on to the next generation (King and Szeleni 2004; Yang 2009).

Cadres were divided into three classes, the first (ranks 1–13), second (ranks 14–17) and third (ranks 18–25). The first class included all top party and government officials from Mao Zedong down to the heads of counties in rural areas. The second class was made up of department chiefs, section

Table 14.8   Categories of Chinese workers, 1981

Type	%
1. Urban permanent workers in state enterprises	37.8
2. Urban workers in collective enterprises	19.5
3. Urban temporary workers	5.2
4. Rural temporary workers in urban collective and state enterprises	11.8
5. Rural workers in collective enterprises	25.8

Source: Walder (1987).

members down to bureau chiefs in county government level (Kraus 1981; Li 1994). The third class included most of the section members as well as office workers in central, provincial and county governments.

The three classes of cadres were carefully stratified with differential status and privileges. For instance, they had different access to information and received different amounts of food rations (Becker 1996; Li 1994). There existed a parallel, carefully differentiated hierarchy of ranks for professionals with educational administrators divided into 25 grades, with 12 grades for professors, 8 for engineers, and 5 for technicians. Strangely, writers, actors and opera singers were graded like party cadres (Kraus 1981). And in Mao's socialist paradise the delineation of ranks and privileges extended all the way down to the masses of workers. For example workers were divided into eight grades based on their skills and experience. The main class of workers was divided into five different categories with status, privileges and income differentiated accordingly. However, this also largely depended, on the one hand, on their work unit (*danwei*), for example whether it was rural or urban, state or collective; and on the other hand, on their contract, for example whether it was temporary or permanent (see Table 14.8).

In the top rank of workers were urban permanent industrial workers in state-owned enterprises (SOEs) with lifetime tenure. As the proletarian showcase class their average income of 854 yuan was significantly higher than that of their counterparts in collective enterprises, and double that of urban or rural temporary workers (Walder 1987). In addition, their fringe benefits included subsidies, allowances and regional supplements, such as transport supplement, to compensate workers for the high cost of living. They further enjoyed fringe benefits in the form of welfare insurance (health, age and so on), and free access to housing, medical care, child care and meal halls as well as preferential access to education and employment opportunities for their relatives (Walder 1987). The cash value of all these benefits was estimated to as be much as 526 yuan in 1978, which is equivalent to 82 per cent of the average wage of workers (Walder 1987).

The differentiation of fringe benefits allowed an invisible but important stratification even within the ranks of permanent urban workers. In general, workers in large SOEs run by ministries of the central, state, provincial and city governments enjoyed more benefits than did workers employed by small enterprises run by various levels of local government.

On the whole, China's rural population was the bottom class with the lowest pay and hardly any access to the privileges enjoyed by many of their urban counterparts. Nevertheless, there was a huge intra-class stratification among the peasants depending on where they lived. For example, in 1979 the ratio of net income per capita between the richest and the poorest production brigades was as high as 26 to 1. This was partly due to Mao's policy of making peasants rely solely on local resources, which varied considerably in respect to factors such as the fertility of land, availability of water, access and closeness to urban markets and industrial inputs (Riskin 1987). The fact that Chinese citizens were not allowed to migrate to other places in the country trapped many of them in poverty. As proletarians they were powerless and were left to starve to death when the inevitable food shortages developed.

Despite all of Mao's policies which aimed at driving China towards a classless socialist society, society actually became more stratified under Mao than it had been before and degenerated into a one resembling the feudal system. To begin with, from the description above it can be seen that China had a rank and status hierarchy as clearly defined and rigid as any feudal system, even if the spoils of rank were not as obvious and the system as a whole was less transparent. Secondly, it was also a closed society, and Chinese farmers under Mao had as little freedom as their counterparts in traditional society. Their lot was more akin to that of Japanese farmers in the Tokugawa period than that of free peasants in a capitalist society, for they had no authority to make decisions on what crops to plant or where or how much. Neither had they control over their produce, or decisions about savings and investments. In addition, the household registration system together with the rationing of basic necessities tied farmers closely to the land, which they were not allowed to leave without permission. Thus it was virtually impossible for them to improve their lot in any way or to join the ranks of the urban population.

Though better off, workers did not have much freedom either: they had their jobs and work units assigned to them by bureaucrats, and once assigned they tended to remain in the same job for the duration of their working life. This meant that married couples were often separated for life and were allowed to meet for only 12 days a year. Theoretically, vertical mobility in the urban sector was open, with the only requirement for admission to elite administrative posts being a good education, Party membership and demonstrated loyalty to the Party (Walder et al. 2000). In practice, however, there were strong barriers to upward mobility for members of the traditional middle class or elite, especially when they were related to people of 'bad class origin' such as counter-revolutionaries, landlords, capitalists and political 'rightists'. At the same time permanent workers in state enterprises were given the privilege of assigning a son or daughter to replace them at retirement (Walder 1987). Similarly, the children of party cadres enjoyed a definite advantage in access to and advancement in education and occupation (Parish 1981).

Last but not least, the system of distribution of goods and services among the population also resembled that of a feudal society, for it was institutions, not markets, that were the primary distribution mechanism. And the primary determinant of the individual's standard of living and future life chances was the institution of the work unit (*danwei*) to which they belonged. The worker's rank within the work unit was only the secondary determinant of their entitlement to privileges and rewards (Walder 1987).

SUMMARY

The outcome of three decades of socialist modernization under Mao was mixed. Economic change was impressive, for in this period China achieved rapid industrialization and started modern economic growth. But these results were achieved at an enormous loss of human lives and output. A whole generation of China's rural population was sacrificed and driven to achieve ever higher production outputs without being given adequate resources, inputs or material rewards. Their standard of living suffered badly and they were trapped in poverty and malnourishment. At the time of Mao's death, China's standard of living was among the poorest in the East Asian region. The policy mistake of the Great Leap Forward produced one of the largest famines in world history.

The results of Mao's social change agenda were equally mixed. On the one hand, China achieved excellent results in terms of human development with a dramatic rise in the population's longevity and literacy. On the other hand, Mao failed to create an egalitarian society. Though he succeeded in keeping the interpersonal income inequality in both rural and urban sectors low, he failed to narrow the urban–rural income gap.

And though he dismantled the traditional class structure successfully, the stratification in 'socialist' China was no less pronounced and rigid than it had been before. Vertical mobility was impossible for most people, even though it theoretically depended on little more than 'redness', that is, Party loyalty. And since the major distribution mechanism was not the market but worked through the allocation of rewards and privileges by work units and party cadres, it was clearly defined and strictly controlled by institutions. The opportunity structure for education and jobs was rigidly fixed and choices were so limited that everyone was virtually frozen in their rank through the *danwei* and household registration system. Whatever opportunities for improving one's life chances were available were allocated in small increments with great ideological fanfare. Thus while the stratification was less visible in Maoist China, it was definitely more pronounced and rigid than it had been before, and in substance it was more akin to that of Tokugawa Japan than to a modern socialist society.

PART IV

Reform and Growth Acceleration

15. The reforms

EVOLUTION OF THE REFORM STRATEGY

Mao's death in 1976 sparked an intense succession crisis in the Chinese Communist Party (CCP) because three factions fielded candidates who hoped to succeed the Chairman (Harding 1987). On the far left were the revolutionary Maoists known as the Gang of Four, headed by Mao's wife, Jiang Qing. They sought to preserve the legacy of the Cultural Revolution (CR). They were opposed by the right-wing coalition of reformers led by Deng Xiaoping; and the centre, known as the restorationists, fielded Hua Guofeng as claimant to the Chairman's vacancy. This faction aimed at restoring the pre-Great Leap Forward (GLF) and CR political and economic institutions. Initially, Hua Guofeng defeated the revolutionary Maoists, arrested them and governed China.

His principles were the 'two whatever-isms', which stood for 'whatever decisions were made by Mao we support and whatever instructions were given by Mao we follow'. Under Hua's leadership China launched another Great Leap Forward known as the Great Leap Outward. Under this programme a grandiose Ten-Year Plan for the period 1975–85 envisaged China's modernization in four key areas, namely in industry, science, technology and defence. To achieve the vision China embarked upon a massive programme of importing foreign plant and technology, financed with the help of foreign loans.

However, Hua had only a limited power base within the Party and was soon replaced by Deng Xiaoping as paramount leader. Deng boldly cast off much of the Maoist ideological baggage of class struggle and in the Third Plenum Meeting of the Central Committee of the CCP in December 1978 set China on course for economic modernization by way of pragmatic reform and an open door strategy.

China's long march towards a market economy can be divided into three stages (Chai 1997; Clark et al. 2008). In stage one (1979–84) China's reforms were fairly low-key and restricted because Deng Xiaoping and his reform strategist Zhao Ziyang were restrained by party elders like Chen Yun and Li Xiannian who were in charge of the economy after the collapse of the GLF (Zhao 2009). They much preferred central planning and moderate reforms. In fact Chen Yun is well known for his theory of the 'bird cage economy', where the economy is the bird and the plan is the cage. If the cage is too small, the bird will die, but if there is no cage at all the bird is unrestrained and will fly away. The compromise between these two views lay in the introduction of some carefully selected aspects of the market economy in order to enliven and support the dominant planned economy. Reforms at this stage were mainly focused on the rural sector, aiming at the improvement of incentives for peasants. This was achieved through the reintroduction of the household responsibility system (HRS), the abolition of communes and a rise in the agricultural purchase price (Ash 1993).

In contrast, reforms in the urban sector were very limited in this period. New measures were largely confined to the administrative streamlining of the industrial system and the experimental reform of state-owned enterprises (SOEs) in the form of an expanded enterprise autonomy and enhanced financial incentives. Externally, the open door policy was introduced to increase trade and attract foreign investments. The fear of many leading party officials that this might invite negative Western influences to penetrate China accounted for the rigid investment regime and the strict geographical limitation of the open door policy to four Special Economic Zones (SEZs) and 14 coastal cities only.

In the second stage of the reforms (1985–89) Zhao finally got the 13th Plenary session of the CCP in October 1987 to accept that the goal of the reforms would be to make the market the dominant resource allocation mechanism in China, and that the government would exercise control over the economy only indirectly. Thus a package of comprehensive urban reform measures was planned. However, only parts of the measures were implemented due to the ongoing conflict between Chen Yun and Zhao (Zhao 2009). This period also saw the rise of non-state enterprises (NSEs) and the introduction of a dual pricing system.

However, China's reform movement suffered a serious setback in 1989–91 triggered by student unrest in June 1989 centred on Tiananmen Square. The students demanded that the government better control inflation, curb the then rampant corruption, and speed up political reforms. Corruption was certainly rampant since the earlier dual price system had created too large a grey area and thereby had fuelled corruption and inflation, as will be discussed later. The government planned the wholesale price reform in late 1988 which aimed at eliminating the dual price structure by adjusting the fixed state-set prices to the level of the higher market prices. However, the premature announcement of the reform (Zhao 2009) raised the population's fears of rising inflation. They thus withdrew their saving deposits from banks and made advance purchases in order to stave off the worst impact. The banks responded to the run by issuing more bank notes which in turn led to an increase in money supply and rampant inflation (Zhao 2009).

The last demand of students, namely that for political reform, had been encouraged by the rise of Hu Yaobang, who was Deng's designated successor as Chairman of the CCP. However, Hu was just a bit too liberal-minded for the more conservative party elders. And there was even some tension with Deng who, in spite of driving the reforms forward, still insisted that China adhere to the four principles of socialism; dictatorship of the proletariat; leadership of the Communist Party; and Marxism, Leninism and Maoism (Zhao 2009). The fallout between the two forced Hu to resign as party leader in 1987 and he died shortly after that in April 1989.

When the students gathered in Tiananmen Square in 1989 it was to remember Hu's death. However, inflation had put many people on edge and corruption and the resulting economic inequality had become too obvious for a generation imbued with China's egalitarian brand of socialism. Thus the memorial gathering strengthened into a long and volatile political protest against political crackdowns, inflation and corruption. The students' unrest lasted 50 days until 4 June, when Deng ordered the People's Liberation Army (PLA) to clear the square. Zhao sided with the students and was subsequently put under house arrest until his death in 2005. The image of heavy tanks advancing towards the square with one lone person daring to stand in their way is well known around the world. The place was cleared, not without bloodshed, and many student activists subsequently fled the country, went underground or were sent for 're-education'.

Following that tragedy a three-year austerity programme was introduced to curb the overheated economy, and many of the reform measures were rolled back (Zhao 2009). In the third stage of the reforms, starting from 1992 (and continuing at the time of writing in 2010) China's economic reforms resumed and even accelerated after the famous Southern tour of Deng Xiaoping in 1992. On that trip he called upon local authorities to open China further to the West and to deepen the reforms. The reason for the renewed reform vigour stems from three sources, one of which was the slow but steady passing-away of the older conservative party elite which had felt uneasy about the reform movement. With that block removed, China's post-war third generation of leaders under Jiang Zemin and Zhu Rongji could push the reform movement ahead (Naughton 2008).

The second reason was the collapse of communism in the late 1980s which sent a strong signal that the old system was unworkable. The third reason is that China wished to rejoin the World Trade Organization (WTO) which was, however, only possible if China opened the economy wider to international trade and standards. As a result the 14th Party Congress in 1992 resolved finally to cast off the framework of the planned economy. It proclaimed the establishment of a full-fledged market economy as the country's final reform objective. To achieve the goal, a subsequent third plenum of the 14th Party Congress in 1993 adopted (for the second time) a comprehensive reform programme which was very similar to that which had been announced by Zhao Ziyang in 1987 (Naughton 2008).

From then on reform measures were implemented sequentially and systematically. One of the first steps was to phase out material balance planning, and the dual price system was abolished in 1993. By 1994 new market-based fiscal and foreign trade systems were introduced and a new company law was enacted, providing the institutional framework for the market economy. In the same year reforms of the SOEs were accelerated, with the privatization of the smaller ones (Chai 2003; Cai et al. 2008), which was followed in 1997 with a massive restructuring of the larger ones. The large-scale laying-off of workers signalled the end of the 'iron rice bowl' of guaranteed employment and benefits for urban workers (Cai et al. 2008). The industrial ministries which had formed the core of the planned economy were abolished in 2003 and, finally, in 2007 a new property law was passed to protect property in the rapidly expanding private sector.

In this period China also opened up further to world trade and became more integrated into the world economy. The open door policy was extended to China's interior with another 28 cities and eight prefectures along the Yangzi River and 13 border cities in the Northeastern, Southwestern and Northwestern regions (Chai and Roy 2006). In preparation for its membership in the WTO, China also increased the pace of import liberalization with the cutting of import tariffs on 225 commodities in 1992. This reduced the average tariff from 38.4 per cent in 1986 to only 7.3 per cent in 1992 (Chai and Roy 2006).

In 1994 the renminbi (RMB) was sharply devalued and adjusted to the market rate, so that the Chinese currency became convertible on the current account. And after nearly 15 years of protracted negotiations China was finally admitted to the WTO in 2001. As a member, China is committed to continue its open door policy, to extend it to all of its territory and to significantly reduce all tariff and other barriers to foreign imports. Furthermore, in compliance with the Agreement on Trade Related Investment Measures (TRIM) China is required to treat foreign-invested enterprises (FIEs) equally to domestic enterprises, and cannot discriminate against them by way of imposing restrictions on their activities and operations in any way. That is, China can no longer bar them from entering certain sectors of the economy, or impose requirements of export quotas or of foreign exchange balancing, local content and so on.

CHINA'S APPROACH TO REFORMS

Various authors have tried to capture the essence of China's approach to reforms in various names, for example, Srinivasan (1990) has labelled it the 'two steps forward, one step backward' strategy. Naughton (1995) called it more pragmatically the 'growing out of the plan', Lau et al. (2001) call it 'reform without losers' and Chai (2003) and Walter and Howie (2003) simply label it 'Chinese-style privatization'. All these names focus on only one aspect of China's approach. To many Chinese economists, the Chinese approach is simply a gradual strategy aiming at minimizing political, social and economic instability. This is, of course, in stark contrast to the 'big bang' approach of other European transitional economies.

The Chinese leadership was far-sighted enough to introduce and try out reforms first in sectors where resistance was weakest. Only then were they introduced to other sectors, often hesitantly, and if they were too unpopular they often got weakened or withdrawn for a while. In contrast to the Eastern European transitional economies which started with political reform and drastic economic change, China postponed political reforms and introduced economic reforms softly, first in the rural sector – which was economically so depressed that any reform was welcome – and later in the more politically sensitive urban sector. This had relatively more to lose through reforms because the urban industrial sector had been pampered by Mao's strategies. Thus urban reforms, significantly, started not with ownership changes but with autonomy and changes to the structure of incentives. Changes in ownership and institutional reforms for the market economy came only later when the Maoist ideological mould was sufficiently perforated by visible examples of economic success in the cities and the promise of a better standard of living for the population.

IMPLEMENTATION OF THE REFORMS AND ITS PROGRESS

The transformation of a planned into a market economy involves not only privatization of property and marketization but also, simultaneously, control of macro stability/instability and the avoidance of the reform trap. In the following I review the methods of the Chinese reforms in these four main areas, and assess their progress.

Privatization

China has made significant progress in the development of the private sector. At the time of writing in 2010 the output share of the NSEs amounted to 72 per cent (Fan Gang 2010). In terms of employment their share is even higher, with 93 per cent of total non-agricultural employment (OECD 2010). And in terms of assets, the NSEs now have a bigger asset base than the state sector (OECD 2010). Similarly, in terms of exports the share of NSEs in 2007 had reached 85 per cent (OECD 2010).

In order to minimize social, political or economic disturbances China developed a unique approach to privatization for it did not want to engage in the outright sale of state and collective properties. In the agricultural sector, the way to privatization was filtered through a contracting-out system. Thus, under the HRS the collectively owned land, together with farm animals and tools, was contracted out to farmers. They, in turn, were obliged to meet certain grain delivery quotas and fulfil given tax obligations. Otherwise they had the exclusive right over the land, which was allocated to them on the egalitarian principle of number of persons per household.

The objective of the allocation was to ensure that each household could grow enough produce to satisfy their own needs. The egalitarian distribution of farmland and other productive assets into the hands of individual peasants involved most of the transfer of collective assets in agriculture. For example, in 1978 collectives owned 93.5 per cent of all productive assets in China's agriculture, with private assets limited to only 6.5 per cent. By 1985 the situation was reversed with Chinese peasants now owning more than 92 per cent of total agricultural assets (Chai and Roy 2006).

In spite of the redistribution of assets in agriculture, collectives retained certain residual control, income and transfer rights over the properties. Firstly, the ownership title of the land belonged to the village, not to farmers. Secondly, as mentioned before, farmers had to fulfil certain obligatory deliveries. However, in recent years the burden of the obligations for farmers has been significantly reduced with the dismantling of central planning in agricultural production and the abolition of the agricultural tax in 2004–05. Currently, they are still obliged to contribute to local infrastructure, such as the building and maintenance of roads and irrigation works, as well as providing education. Thirdly, the village holds the right to reallocate land between households periodically in accordance with demographic changes. Fourthly, farmers are allowed to keep the land for only a limited period, presently set at 30 years. And fifthly, the land assigned to farmers cannot be sold, with only the user rights being allowed to be transferred through subletting.

In the non-agricultural sector China, too, took a unique path and paved the way for privatization not by means of the divestiture of existing SOEs, as its Eastern European counterparts did, but by means of the development of NSEs. Traditional Chinese NSEs consisted of collective, township, village and private enterprises. Of late, NSEs also include foreign-invested enterprises (FIEs) and non-wholly state-funded shareholding firms. Among these various types of NSEs, it is the township- and village-owned enterprises (TVEs) and FIEs which in recent years have emerged as the main contributors to China's rapid economic growth. Initially the development of TVEs was promoted by the government to soak up the surplus labour generated by the higher productivity which had resulted from the introduction of the HRS in the countryside. Later on they were promoted because they provided a competition to SOEs.

However, China classifies both rural collective and private enterprises as TVEs. The distinction between them is often blurred, as many private enterprises like to disguise themselves as collective ones for fear of persecution, or in order to benefit from tax concessions. Initially, collective ownership was dominant but since the 1990s many have been converted to private ownership status. For example, in 1985 the latter accounted for 27 per cent of value-added and 41 per cent of employment in the TVE sector, but by 2002 their contributions had soared to 63 and 71 per cent respectively (Heston and Sicular 2008). By 2003, all rural enterprises were, in essence, privately owned (OECD 2010).

With the extension of the open door policy from the initial four Special Economic Zones to the rest of China, the FIEs gained a growing significance in the non-agricultural sector. In the industrial sector alone FIEs now employ more workers than the combined total of state and collective enterprises (Brandt et al. 2008) and they contribute more than 50 per cent of industry sales and nearly 70 per cent of exports in the most important sectors of China's manufacturing industries (Brandt et al. 2008).

The state sector, too, was privatized to some extent in the form of a contracting-out system for medium-sized and larger SOEs, and the divestiture of smaller ones, of which 80 per cent had been privatized by 2002 (Chai and Roy 2006). The partial divestiture of the larger and medium-sized SOEs (LMSOEs) was implemented between 1980 and 1994 along the same pattern that had previously been tried in the agricultural sector. Thus the management of an enterprise was contracted out to either the manager and/or a group of workers of the SOEs, who were obliged to fulfil a certain quota of profit and meet set plan targets. In return, they were allowed to retain all excess profits which could be used to finance bonus payments or housing construction and so on for the benefit of workers and staff (Chai 2003).

Table 15.1   *The proportion of state-owned shares in the capital structure*
                of China's listed companies (%, year end figures)

Year	Share	Year	Share
1992	65	2000	61
1993	69	2001	64
1994	65	2002	64
1995	62	2003	63
1996	61	2004	62
1997	61	2005	55
1998	61	2006	35
1999	61	2007	30

Source: Ma (2010).

With the end of material balance planning in 1993 and the fiscal reform in 1994, the planned elements of the management contract system, namely profit delivery and planned targets, became obsolete and were scrapped (Naughton 2007). Thus LMSOEs were converted into shareholding companies in which the state still held and controlled the majority of shares, but with some shares sold to institutions and private or foreign investors.

State ownership in the newly incorporated shareholding companies can be in the form of sole, majority or minority ownership depending on the relevance and competitiveness of the industry. For those of strategic value or those holding a natural monopoly, the state retains sole or majority ownership, whereas it was much more easy-going on companies in competitive industries where a minority share was deemed sufficient.

Thus the move towards corporatization led to the diluting of state ownership and control which were further eroded by subsequent developments such as the sale of state shares in the parallel market. While initially the state shares were declared non-transferrable to safeguard the state's control of a company, state shares nevertheless changed hands since 1994. This happened either over the counter or through direct negotiations in parallel markets, and often the shares were discounted by up to 80 per cent of their market price (Ma 2010). The 2005 share conversion programme also helped to make state-owned shares more tradable and together they led to the accelerated decline of state ownership in the old SOE sector. Table 15.1 shows the proportion of state-owned shares in the capital of companies listed on China's stock market. It shows that the state-owned share in capital declined sharply from 65 per cent in 1992 to 30 per cent in 2007.

It is worth noting that though corporatization has diluted the state's share of SOEs it has done little to improve their corporate governance.

Few board members are independent and the power of the board of directors is very limited, since the manager is not appointed by the board but by local authorities or the SOE's holding company which controls the listed companies.

Despite the rise of the private sector in recent years, the development of this sector is still subject to a number of restrictions. To begin with, China lacked a systematic law of property rights (Clark et al. 2008). This was addressed only in 2007 with the promulgation of a new property law; however, it remains to be seen to what extent it will be enforced. Second, private enterprises are still very much discriminated against in terms of finance and entry. In finance the situation was that while SOEs were the dominant recipients of bank loans and had the greatest share in investment spending, private firms often had to rely on the informal financial market for finance (Haggard and Huang 2008). In the area of entry, private companies remain barred from entry into the so-called strategic and pillar industries in spite of the government's 2005 declaration that it wanted to encourage actively the development of private enterprises. Currently private domestic enterprises are only allowed to operate in 41 of the more than 80 different industrial branches (caijing.com.cn, accessed 24 May 2010).

In May 2010 the government renewed its efforts to promote private enterprises with two new policy directives. The first was to allow them entry into industrial sectors from which they had been barred hitherto, such as transport, electricity, telecommunication, petroleum and the defence industry as well as high-tech industries and important service industries, such as finance, real estate, culture, education, sport, medical care and social welfare. The other move was that in order to ease the financial problems of private enterprises the government undertook to provide more small- and medium-scale financial institutions and, simultaneously, to instruct state banks to increase their lending to private enterprises.

Marketization

The marketization of a planed economy involves: (1) substitution of the planning by the market mechanism for the distribution of goods and services; (2) the liberalization of prices; and (3) the development and strengthening of the market institution. While China has made significant progress in respect to the first two criteria, the strengthening of the market institution still leaves a lot to be desired. As mentioned before, mandatory planning was abolished in 1993 and in 2010 90 per cent of all prices were completely determined by demand and supply. Only some energy and utility prices remain regulated, as is the price of tobacco and grains by the government (Geiger 2008; OECD 2010).

*Table 15.2   The dual price system in China's industries, 1978–92
                (coverage of manufacturing sales)*

	1978	1987	1990	1992
Producer goods				
Fixed prices	97.0	64.0	45.0	20.0
Market and floating prices	3.0	36.0	55.0	80.0
Consumer goods				
Fixed prices	100.0	50.0	30.0	10.0
Market and floating prices	0.0	50.0	70.0	90.0

Source: Chai (1997).

As discussed, marketization was achieved in China through the introduction of the dual-track system where the two modes of allocation, plan and market, existed side by side together with their respective sets of prices for one product (Table 15.2). According to Zhao (2009) this dual-track system was introduced in the second phase of the reforms to enable the growing number of NSEs to purchase their inputs and sell their products, while the planning system remained intact for the state sector. Thus enterprises were allowed to sell on the market on their own behalf surplus over and above the mandatory quota at market prices.

The coexistence of a significantly higher market price with a lower planned fixed price for a single product created a potential for non-exclusive rental income. This proved such a great temptation for producers that they diverted ever more goods destined for planned delivery to market sales instead, so that most goods eventually ended up being sold on the market for substantially higher prices (Chai 1997).

In 1988, the state tried to correct the dysfunctional mechanisms by aligning the state set prices upward to the market prices (Zhao 2009). However, since the premature announcement of this measure led to inflation and a run on banks, which also contributed to the Tiananmen disaster in 1989, the government abandoned the price reform and did not eliminate the dual-track system until the third phase of the reforms.

In respect to developing markets and their supporting institutions, progress in China is uneven and results are mixed. It has made substantial strides with product markets with the exit of SOEs and the growth of NSEs generating much more competitive product markets. For example, the number of industries deemed to be concentrated fell from just over one in four in 1998 to around one in eight by 2007 (OECD 2010). Yet, in spite of 30 years of economic liberalization government intervention in business

Table 15.3   Product market regulation in China, international comparison

	China	Russia	OECD average	Emerging markets[1]	Eastern Europe[2]
Overall index	3.296601	3.295532	1.340397	1.830717	1.725142
State control	4.63166	4.390856	2.027465	2.5385876	2.666524
Barriers to:					
Entrepreneurship	2.887586	2.383329	1.40579	1.914332	1.236254
International trade and investment	2.370555	3.112409	0.587936	1.0392324	0.184543

Notes:
1. Czech Republic, Hungary, Korea, Mexico, Poland, Turkey.
2. Czech Republic, Estonia, Slovenia, Turkey.

Source: OECD (2010).

remains heavy handed. The Organisation for Economic Co-operation and Development (OECD) has constructed a product market regulation (PMR) index based on rules and regulations covering three broad areas: state control, barriers to entrepreneurship, and barriers to international trade and investment. Its scale ranges from 0, the least restrictive, to 6. In Table 15.3 the PMR index in 2008 for China is compared to those of the Eastern European states and Russia, revealing that despite having started its liberalization well before the others, China's overall index is similar to that of Russia and significantly behind not only other economies in transition but also behind emerging market economies in the OECD area.

The labour market
China's factor markets, especially the labour market, remain underdeveloped because of lacking labour mobility. In spite of the increased rate of rural labour migration between sectors, villages, towns and cities (Cai et al. 2008), mobility is still very constrained by administrative and institutional barriers. The household registration system, which stipulates that all households in cities need registration permits, is the biggest of them. Even though its enforcement has been relaxed over the past few years and even though the development of urban markets for food, housing and other necessities has enabled migrants to meet most of their need without enjoying urban resident status, migrating incurs high opportunity costs.

Thus mobility is only temporary and only for an individual because they need to leave their family behind in order to ensure their access to housing, education, medical care and welfare. Nevertheless, the opportunity for upward mobility is attractive for the rural population that has been kept at the bare level of survival for a generation. Many people migrate in spite of the risks involved, and make up the 'floating population'. According to a government survey in 2005 it comprised 74 million people and accounted for 23 per cent of the urban population and labour force (OECD 2010). Recently new laws have been enacted in order to eliminate some of the structural discrimination. For example, local governments are now prevented from demanding fees for temporary urban resident permits, and urban schools have to enrol children of temporary residents (Cai et al. 2008). However, regional migration within rural areas remains highly restricted because of the local protection policy. This means that a rural enterprise is not allowed to recruit labour from other rural areas unless it can convince the relevant authorities that local labour cannot meet their demand, either quantitatively or in terms of skills (OECD 2002).

In urban areas the informal labour market is very active while the formal sector, especially for the SOE sector, remains rather restricted. This is evidenced by the low rate of labour mobility (OECD 2002; Cai et al. 2008), which is due to the following factors. First, the SOEs' right to hire and fire workers is still rather limited as the majority of workers are still assigned by the state or jobs are even 'inherited' as in the old system (Chai 1997; OECD 2002). That the management cannot fire workers as they like is evidenced by the fact that in spite of massive job lay-offs in the late 1990s, a significant percentage of labour was still considered redundant by managers in the early 2000s (Cai et al. 2008). The difficulty enterprises have in getting rid of workers is due to the fact that firing needs official sanctioning and that the enterprise has to provide assurance of special assistance to the workers that are laid off.

Another factor restricting urban worker mobility was that China's welfare system was enterprise based, for example workers were reluctant to quit jobs that guaranteed them pension entitlements, unemployment benefits, medical care and other welfare benefits. It was only in the late 1990s that a government-sponsored unemployment insurance was established in the form of a modest minimum living standard programme (MLSP) which was intended to provide enough subsidies to needy households to raise their per capita income above the poverty line (Cai et al. 2008). However, access to these subsidies remains very limited, especially for the urban poor. Of late the government has also introduced other social welfare benefits schemes, including a pension and health care insurance system for both the rural and urban populations. However, since they are financed and carried by local institutions, benefits show strong regional differences. And since the benefits are not portable across administrative borders the effect of these insurances on easing poverty is rather limited (OECD 2010).

The capital market

Three decades of ongoing 'two steps forward, one step backward' reforms have changed China's financial system from a closed and centralized one into an open market-oriented system. Yet it still has a long way to go towards developing a fully fledged capital market, for the thrust of the reforms was aimed at developing a financial market and reforming banks (Chai 1997; Allen et al. 2008). The main objective of the banking reform was to increase the efficiency of the institutions, improving their management and increasing competition. For that purpose new banks and non-bank financial institutions were established, foreign banks were in China, and the monopoly of the state bank was broken with the central banking function separated from commercial banking activity.

In spite of these changes and ongoing reforms (Lardy 1998; Laurenceson and Chai 2003) the Chinese banking system is still dominated by state banks whose share of total assets remains above 50 per cent (OECD 2010), and the big four state banks are responsible for three-quarters of all loans. Thus loans in China are still offered in line with government rather than market principles (OECD 2010) and policy loans continue to dominate loan portfolios. As a result the bulk of savings in state banks is used to finance SOEs and government investment projects. As the SOEs' profitability deteriorated due to increased competition from NSEs, the non-performing loans (NPLs) of the state bank soared and put China at risk of a financial crisis (OECD 2002; Allen et al. 2008). The government recognized this and subsequently cleaned up the stock of NPLs, reducing the ratio of NPLs of the commercial banks from 17.4 per cent at the end of 2003 to only 1.8 per cent in mid-2009 (OECD 2010). This enabled China to weather the onslaught of the storm of the global financial crisis (GFC) in 2008.

The financial market was reopened in China in 1979 in the first phase of reforms, with the introduction of new Treasury bonds. In the second phase, broader and more varied measures were added, such as enterprise bonds and shares (Chai 1997). However, China's financial market remained narrowly based and was dominated to 97 per cent by government bonds in terms of total securities issued (Table 15.4). The issuing, transfer and pricing of enterprise shares remains strictly controlled. And as a rule only SOEs and listed companies can issue shares. Thus most of the NSEs, which account for two-thirds of the economy, remain at present largely excluded from the formal financial market and have to rely on internal and/or informal financing. The latter usually involves funds raised

Table 15.4 Composition and value of securities issued (in million RMB)

	Government bonds	Policy bank bonds	Enterprise bonds	Enterprise shares
1990	19.7	6.4	12.4	NA
1991	28.1	6.7	24.9	0.5
1992	46.1	5.5	68.4	9.4
1993	38.1	0.0	23.6	37.6
1994	113.8	0.0	16.2	32.7
1995	151.1	NA	30.1	15.0
1996	184.8	105.6	26.9	42.5
1997	241.2	143.2	25.5	129.4
1998	380.9	195.0	15.0	84.2
1999	401.5	180.1	15.8	94.5
2000	465.7	164.5	8.3	210.3
2001	488.4	259.0	14.7	125.2
2002	593.4	307.5	32.5	96.2
2003	628.0	456.1	35.8	135.8
2004	692.4	414.8	32.7	151.1
2005	704.2	711.7	204.7	188.3
2006	888.3	908.0	393.8	559.4
2007	2 313.9	NA	505.8	868.0
2008	8 558.2	NA	843.5	385.2

Sources: Allen et al. (2008) and SSB, China Statistical Yearbook (various issues).

from friends and family as well as from unlicensed banks, based on trust, reputation, relationship and competition. In order to improve the access of private companies to the capital market the government in 2005 gave permission to a number of small and medium-sized companies to list their shares on the second and third board of the Shenzhen stock exchange (OECD 2010).

The land market
Theoretically, land in rural areas is owned collectively by the farmers; however, it is run by the local government office, for example the village committee. Under the HRS farmers received the right to use a certain piece of land for 30 years, and that right can be transferred. However, land can not be mortgaged. Transactions of land user rights first occurred in the second phase of reforms, but developed only slowly in the 1990s.

Restrictions on both the demand and supply sides were responsible for keeping a tight cap on the market. On the demand side, the right transferred was strictly regulated by the authorities. And since the rented land could only be used for grain crops which had a relatively low price compared to other produce, there was little demand. On the supply side an increased number of farmers found more profitable employment elsewhere. However, they were reluctant to part with their contracted land due to the fact that land entitlement is considered a principal element of social security in rural areas. But this was also partly due to the fact that the village authority retains ownership of the land and that they would from time to time carry out administrative reallocation of land in response to demographic changes, even within the specified contract period of 30 years (Krusekopf 2002). Thus farmers were afraid that they might lose their right to the land if they rented it.

In 2006 the government introduced remedial measures to speed up the transfer of land rights (caijing.com.cn, accessed 16 April 2010). These comprised the abolition of the agricultural tax and the introduction of farming subsidies to improve farm profitability in order to stimulate the demand for rented land. Another measure, as mentioned before, was the introduction of a collective medical and pension insurance scheme for rural areas which was designed to encourage the 'floating population' to part with their contracted land in the countryside. The government also relaxed its control over the use of the contracted land. The demand soared in response to these measures and most rented land was now used to grow vegetables and other horticultural products as well as for fish farming.

Most recently, however, the ambiguity of property rights sparked a land grab which became a major source of grievances in the countryside. Theoretically, village officials and township cadres cannot convert or lease farmland for other purposes without the majority consent of their villagers. In practice, however, to boost the local government revenues, land was often leased to factories or converted to other purposes without due process and then sold to property developers at inflated prices (caijin.com.cn, accessed 25 May 2010).

In urban areas the situation is similar in that land is owned by the state, but use rights can be transferred for up to 70 years for residential and 50 years for commercial land. However, in contrast to the rural areas these user rights can be mortgaged and sold. The assignment can be done either by way of auction or through administrative allocation. The latter is so far used in most of China's major cities with the exception of Guangdong province (Li 2003). But land seizures have become a source of unrest in the cities as well, for government officials tend to work in collusion with developers to convert old town centres into new development opportunities without paying proper compensation to sitting tenants. This is a great problem because the latter possess *de jure* development rights and often were able to make residual claims over new development projects as the land was initially allocated to them prior to the reforms (Zhu 2004).

Macro Stabilization

Inflation is a key issue in a transitional economy, especially when enterprise reforms remain incomplete and enterprise budget constraints remain weak, and when economic liberalization generates an explosion in investment and wage expenditures. Such inflation can only be controlled by way of direct administrative means since the effective indirect monetary and fiscal control mechanisms have yet to be fully developed. However, the reassertion of such direct administrative controls can quickly lead back to state intervention in enterprise behaviour, and stop liberalization in its tracks. Thus, once inflation is under control the government needs to loosen the control measures again and restart the reform process until the next wave of inflation emerges. Thus a cyclical pattern of macro stability and waves of stop-and-go growth in prices and output are generated. In the following I will discuss the experiments of China with these monetary and fiscal control mechanisms through the 30-year reform and transition period.

Monetary policy

Compared with other transitional economies China has been rather successful in achieving price stability, as Table 15.5 shows. Unlike its Eastern European counterparts it was able to avoid huge surges of inflation with their associated unrest in its initial transition phase, and it has been able to maintain a relatively low rate of inflation in recent years. Its success in maintaining relative price stability is due to the use of a mixture of direct and indirect monetary control instruments.

China's monetary policy in the transition can be divided into two distinctive phases. In the first, from 1979 to 1997, China experimented with indirect monetary controls by way of regulating the amount of credit supplied to banks and by varying their reserve ratio and the use of interest that the Central Bank charges on its loans to commercial banks as a tool of monetary control (Chai 1997). However, the effectiveness of these two indirect monetary control instruments proved limited for two reasons. Firstly, the reserve requirement proved ineffective in containing the growing liquidity of banks and their lending in this period, as the banks held significant amounts of excess reserves at the Central Bank (Chai 1997). This excess reserve was induced by the fact that budget constraints by the state banks remained rather soft as they were not yet fully

Table 15.5   Rate of growth of China's GDP and the consumer price index, 1979–2009

Year	GDP (%)	Price (%)
1979	7.6	2.0
1980	7.8	6.0
1981	5.2	2.4
1982	9.3	1.9
1983	11.1	1.5
1984	15.3	2.8
1985	13.2	8.8
1986	8.5	6.0
1987	11.5	7.3
1988	11.3	18.5
1989	4.2	17.8
1990	4.2	2.1
1991	9.1	2.9
1992	14.1	5.4
1993	13.1	13.2
1994	12.6	21.7
1995	9.0	14.8
1996	9.8	6.1
1997	9.3	0.8
1998	7.8	−0.6
1999	7.6	0.7
2000	8.4	0.4
2001	8.3	0.7
2002	9.1	−0.8
2003	10.0	1.2
2004	10.1	3.9
2005	10.4	1.8
2006	11.6	1.5
2007	13.0	4.8
2008	9.0	5.9
2009	8.3	−1.1

Source: SSB, China Statistical Yearbook (various issues).

responsible for profits and losses in that period. Secondly, the use of interest rates to discourage commercial banks from borrowing funds from the Central Bank was not effective because of the low elasticity of loans with respective to interest rate change during the period, because local governments could put pressure on their People's Bank of China (PBC) branches to extend credits to commercial banks to enable them to meet regional needs (Blejer et al. 1991).

The ineffectiveness of the indirect monetary control measures in curbing inflation forced the central government to continue to rely on the direct administrative credit quota, which in turn resulted in the cyclical pattern of stop-and-go growth in output and prices. Altogether four cycles can be clearly detected in the last two decades of the twentieth century, namely: phase 1 from 1979 to 1981; phase 2 from 1983 to 1986; phase 3 from 1987 to 1990; and phase 4 from 1992 to 1996 (see Table 15.5).

In the second stage of reforms (from 1998 up to the time of writing in 2010) the Central Bank scrapped the credit quota system and instead relied more on a mixture of direct and indirect control instruments to maintain price stability with the result that the stop-and-go growth of China's output and prices largely disappeared, as evidenced in Table 15.5. In the period from 1997 to 2010 China managed to stabilize GDP growth to around 10 per cent a year, and the rate of inflation was reduced to less than 2 per cent. This has happened against the backdrop of such destabilizing factors as the onset of the Asian crisis in 1997, the subsequent severe acute respiratory syndrome (SARS) crisis and the GFC crisis which started in 2008.

China's main challenge in maintaining price stability since 1998 has been the 'impossible trinity' of simultaneously maintaining a fixed exchange rate and free capital flows and conducting an independent monetary policy. China's answer to these problems is to constrain capital mobility in order to achieve a fixed exchange rate regime against other currencies, which still allows an independent monetary policy. However, capital account controls can never be watertight and a certain amount of leakage is bound to occur. Thus in the period from 1994 to 2006 money worth US$200 billion was able to cross the Chinese border, which appears as 'errors and omissions' in China's balance-of-payments statistics. Three-quarters of this amount was outflow and only one-quarter constituted inflow (Geiger 2008).

Furthermore, foreign capital inflow in the form of foreign direct investment (FDI) is not controlled. According to Glick and Hutchison (2008) the huge FDI inflow together with the even larger amount of current account surplus induced by the undervalued renminbi (RMB) swelled China's foreign exchange reserves from US$140 billion in 1997 (equal to 15 per cent of GDP) to over US$1.5 trillion at the end of 2007 (more than 45 per cent of GDP). The growing foreign exchange reserve increased the reserve money base and built up inflationary pressure.

China used two measures to dampen its effects on the monetary base (Geiger 2008). The first was the use of the open market mechanism by issuing domestic securities by the PBC in its own name, for example Central Bank bills. The other was to introduce changes to the reserve requirements of commercial banks to soak up excess liquidity held by them and other domestic agents. The stabilization incurred some cost since the PBCs who sold the Central Bank bills had to offer an increasingly higher yield to convince domestic agents to hold them. Hence the cost of sterilization is given by the difference between the domestic and foreign interest rate differential. Several studies show that the sterilization cost was relatively low and even negative, as the level of domestic interest rates was relatively low compared to that of the US (OECD 2010).

Another measure China used to offset the effects of growing foreign reserves on the monetary base was to increase the outflow of capital from China to balance the inflow (Geiger 2008). This was achieved by promoting outward direct investment (ODI) since 2001, and the introduction of a qualified institutional investor scheme in 2006. Under its umbrella Chinese institutions and individual investors were allowed to invest offshore and to hold US dollar and RMB deposits in offshore markets (OECD 2010).

Despite China's shift in recent years to the greater use of open market operations and other indirect monetary control instruments, such as reserve requirements, interest rate policy is still of limited use for several reasons. Firstly, the PBC has only a limited flexibility in controlling the interest rate because any change has to be approved by the State Council. Secondly, under the pegged exchange rate system the Central Bank cannot rely on the change in interest rate to manage aggregate demand, given that the monetary tightening may result in a larger capital inflow and thus thwart an independent monetary policy. Lastly, state-owned banks are not profit driven and, hence, may not be responsive to a change in the interest rate. This is also evident from the relatively large excess reserves in China's banking system (OECD 2010).

In view of the limited role of the interest rate policy, the Central Bank has to rely largely on quantity-based direct monetary control instruments, the major ones of which are window guidance and direct PBC lending (Geiger 2008). Window guidance is known in the market economy as moral suasion. It is a policy of benevolent compulsion to make banks and financial institutions follow the official guideline. And it is currently the most prominent of the quantity-based direct monetary instruments of the PBC (Geiger 2008). It is relatively successful, since in an authoritarian party hierarchy seniority counts and the Governor of the PBC is a higher-ranking official than the leaders of commercial banks. In the last few years window guidance has also increasingly been used to control commercial bank lending to the real-estate sector in order to curb the real-estate bubble in China. Direct PBC lending is used to steer preferential lending to certain areas and industrial sectors, for example as indirect subsidy for rural credit co-operatives with very low lending rates to these institutions. But it can also involve lending to local governments, asset management companies and rural credit co-operatives to help rid them of NPLs (Geiger 2008).

Fiscal policy

In the first 20 years of the Chinese economic reforms fiscal policies played only a limited role as an instrument of macro stabilization. In a market economy macro stabilization is achieved either through automatic stabilization or through discretionary fiscal policy, or a combination of both. China's experimentation with fiscal control can again be divided into two distinct periods. In the first, from 1979 to 1996, it remained inactive due to the fiscal erosion of the government as a result of the decentralization of finance. Budgetary revenues as a share of GDP declined from 33 per cent in 1978 to only 10.3 per cent in 1995 (Naughton 2008; Kuijs and Xu 2008) and the central government's share was reduced to only 3 per cent of GDP (Wong and Bird 2008).

This dwindling of the government's financial resources was due to a combination of the erosion of SOEs' profits, due to greater competition from the NSEs, and the low income elasticity of tax revenue (Blejer et al. 1991). The tax on SOEs' profit had previously been one of the major sources of budget revenue. The low income elasticity of tax revenue was largely the result of the introduction of the contract responsibility system for SOEs, and intergovernmental fiscal relations. The contract responsibility system adopted in SOEs in the mid-1980s was essentially a profit contract system (Chai 1997) where an enterprise guaranteed the state the delivery of a given amount of profit in return for being allowed to retain the excess profit it made. This led to below-quota profits being subject to a flat tax, while above-quota profits were taxed at a lower level or even not at all. Enterprises thus retained an increasing portion of profits as they expanded, resulting in this tax having an income elasticity of less than unity for the enterprise (Blejer et al. 1991).

The contract responsibility system, adopted in the intergovernment fiscal relation in the late 1980s, also changed the revenue-sharing between the different levels of government. Like enterprises, local governments contracted to remit a predetermined amount of revenue to the higher government and were allowed to keep the remaining above-quota revenue. Thus the central government's share in revenue was more or less fixed, whereas that of the local government expanded with increases in output and profits. That is how the decline in revenue of the central government happened.

In sum, during this period the fiscal position of the central government which was responsible for macro stability was declining, and it became so weak that it was incapable of carrying out any discretionary fiscal policy. Worse still, the income inelasticity of the government revenues imparted an automatic destabilizing influence on the fiscal system. Thus in periods of inflation the government's share in tax revenue actually decreased while output and profits increased, fuelling a further increase of aggregate demand and inflation. Conversely, when the economy slowed down the government's share of tax revenue increased perversely and aggravated the decline in aggregate demand. This procyclical pattern of the Chinese fiscal system can be observed in Table 15.6.

The table shows clearly that in the period between 1984 and 88 when the economy was overheated the budget deficit as a share of GDP actually increased from minus 1.6 per cent in 1984 to minus 2.6 per cent in 1988, further fuelling inflationary pressure. Similarly, between 1992 and 1994 as the economy became overheated, and once again after the Southern tour of Deng Xiaoping, the budget deficit measured as share in the GDP did not decline but rose from 1 per cent in 1992 to 1.2 per cent in 1994.

The fiscal position of the Chinese government was much stronger in the second period of reforms from 1997 to 2010 as a result of the tax reform in 1994, which broadened the basis of taxes in that it introduced both direct and indirect taxes into the system. The main taxes introduced were a value-added tax, corporate income tax and an operations tax. At the same time the system of tax collection was improved in that the local government only collected local taxes (Wong and Bird 2008). Taxes are divided into three categories – national, local and joint taxes – which are shared between both levels of government. The reforms significantly improved the income elasticity of tax revenues, and their share in GDP increased from 10.3 per cent in 1995 to 30 per cent in 2010. Consequently, the share of the central government in tax revenues increased.

The greater income elasticity of tax revenues also provided an automatic stabilization mechanism for the Chinese fiscal system. However, the automatic stabilization effect is still relatively small in China. Stabilization in a market economy works mainly through the progressiveness of personal income tax and government expenditure on social welfare. In contrast, China relies mainly on a combination of indirect taxes as well as direct taxes on profits and business activity, which accounted for only 10 per cent of Chinese GDP in 2007, while taxes on personal income generated only 1.3 per cent of GDP (Kuijs and Xu 2008). At the same time the government's expenditures on social welfare

Table 15.6   China's fiscal stance: budget deficits relative to GDP (in %)

	GDP growth deviation from growth trend (percentage point)	Budget deficit as % of GDP
1979	−2.2	−5.2
1980	−2.0	−3.3
1981	−4.6	−1.3
1982	0.1	−1.4
1983	1.3	−1.7
1984	5.4	−1.6
1985	2.4	−0.5
1986	−1.3	−1.9
1987	1.7	−2.0
1988	1.5	−2.6
1989	−5.6	−1.8
1990	−5.6	−0.8
1991	−0.7	−1.1
1992	4.3	−1.0
1993	3.3	−0.8
1994	2.8	−1.2
1995	−0.8	−1.0
1996	0.0	−0.7
1997	−0.5	−0.7
1998	−2.0	−1.1
1999	−2.2	−1.9
2000	−1.4	−2.5
2001	−1.5	−2.3
2002	−0.7	−2.6
2003	0.2	−2.2
2004	0.2	−1.3
2005	0.6	−1.2
2006	1.8	−0.8
2007	3.2	0.7
2008	−0.8	−0.4
2009	−1.5	−3.0

Source: SSB, China Statistical Yearbook (various issues) and OECD (2010).

are still very modest so that the automatic stabilization effect is relatively low. However, the strengthening of its fiscal position now enables the Chinese government to carry out anticyclical discretionary fiscal policies. For example, in the aftermath of the Asian financial crisis in 1997 China adopted an expansionary fiscal policy which substantially increased the government's deficit from 0. 7 per cent of GDP to 2.5 per cent in 2000 (Table 15.6).

As the economy recovered and regained its momentum towards growth from 2001 on, the government withdrew its stimulus and the budget deficit declined steadily from minus 2.3 per cent in 2001 and developed into a surplus of 0.7 per cent in 2007. In 2008, as the GFC threatened to slash China's economic growth significantly the government introduced a 4 trillion RMB stimulus package for 2009 and 2010. At 14 per cent of GDP this dosage is rather large and, as a consequence, the budget deficit in 2009 hit 3 per cent of GDP, the highest in three decades (Yu 2009). The expansionary fiscal policy has been a great success and played a pivotal role in stabilizing and reviving the economy. It also helped China to maintain a healthy growth rate of above 8 per cent in those two difficult years. The risk of a soaring debt crisis similar to that of Greece, Ireland and other European countries is minimal, as China's fiscal position in 2008 was relatively strong with gross government debt amounting to only 21 per cent of GDP (OECD 2010).

Escaping the Reform Trap

The gradual reform strategy that China adopted was meant to minimize disruption to the existing distribution of wealth and power so as to soften opposition to change from vested interest groups and political cadres who had held a monopoly on many privileges and life chances in the old socialist system. The most powerful of these were, of course, the party cadres and bureaucrats who stood to lose power and control when the market started to replace the central planning system (Nee 1989). They were the ones likely to stall any reform in order to protect their own interests and would, if they could, freeze the country permanently in a transition stage. But so far, China has been able to avoid this reform trap for two reasons, one of which is that the government has created an effective incentive mechanism to realign the interests of local cadres with the reform-minded policies of the central government.

To motivate local cadres to pursue reforms and thereby push economic growth, the government started to reward them on the basis of their economic performance in the form of bonus payments and promotion. Though central planning has been abolished in China there is still a quasi development plan at the central level which sets performance targets and directs actions of cadres at the lower levels in the one-year and five-year plans respectively. Local cadres are evaluated at the end of each year on the basis of how they fulfil these targets (Edin 1998).

Edin's study (1998) of the Chinese countryside for the years 1996 to

1998 reveals that the bonuses received by township cadres stood up well in comparison with their salaries. And Wu and Ma (2009) found that the economic performance-based promotion is the key to understanding the nearly double-digit economic growth in the 30 years of reform. However, the empirical evidence for this is still mixed. Chen et al. (2005) find that provincial leaders' chances for promotion were positively related to the relative performance of their predecessors. In contrast, the study by Opper and Brehm (2007) of promotion patterns of China's provincial leadership from 1985 to 2005 shows that network-based promotion played a more important role in China's leadership recruitment than did performance-based promotion.

Another reason why China has been able to escape the reform trap lies in the role change of cadres. Contrary to the expectation that their importance would decline with progressive market reforms, their fortunes actually increased because they were in a position to take advantage of new opportunities opened up by reforms and therefore they were relatively successful in getting ahead (Oi 1986). Empirical evidence suggests that cadres gained through the reform process in two basic ways. First, since the reform movement is still incomplete and government intervention is still pervasive, entrepreneurs need to form at least a loose coalition with cadres in order to reduce transaction costs of doing business. For example, when private property rights are not clearly delineated investors need the cadres' protection against government expropriation. In return, they are often willing to give them a share of the residual income from their enterprises. For example, as mentioned before, in urban areas sitting tenants have *de jure* development rights which allow them to make residual claims over a new development project which replaces the building in which they are tenants. Thus private developers simply give away a portion of shareholding of the property development to local authorities in order to protect themselves from expropriation (Wong and Choy 2010). Similarly, since the state still owns and controls strategic industries and monopolizes the supply and pricing of important production factors, such as bank credit, energy, telecommunication and public utilities, private entrepreneurs need political connections to cadres in order to gain access to these inputs.

Secondly, having formed alliances with entrepreneurs, cadres develop vested interests and directly or indirectly earn high incomes. Often their experience leads them to become entrepreneurs themselves. Burns's (1985–86) study of local cadres in China's countryside shows that during the early phases of the rural reforms former and incumbent cadres made up a disproportionally large segment of the category of new entrepreneurs. The study of a sample of 14440 private entrepreneurs by Choi and Zhou

Table 15.7　China's princelings

Leaders	Relatives engaged in business
I.　2nd generation	
Deng Xiaoping	Relatives, controllers of Poly group
II.　3rd generation	
1. Li Peng	Li Xiaolin (daughter) CEO of China Power International Development
	Li Xiaopeng (son), former head of Huaneng Power, current vice governor of Shanxi province
2. Jiang Zemin	Jian Mianheng (son) former head of Telecommunication Corporation
3. Zhu Rongji	Zhu Yunlai (son) chief executive of China International Capital Corporation
III.　4th generation	
1. Hu Jintao	Hu Haifeng (son) Head of Nuc Tech and Tsinghua Holdings
2. Wen Jiabao	Wen Yunsong (son) executive chairman of Unihub
	Zhang Peili (wife), largest shareholder of Beijing Diamond Jewelry

Sources:　Tai (2010) and Huang (2010).

(2001) in 1993 found that entrepreneurs who had been cadres enjoyed a clear advantage over their non-ex-cadre counterparts. Especially after Deng's famous Southern tour of China in 1992, many cadres became entrepreneurs using their valuable previous government experience as a tool for success.

The most powerful entrepreneurs with a cadre background are the so-called 'princelings', the children of senior cadres. Table 15.7 shows that the offspring of current and former political leaders dominate the boardrooms of many of the nation's biggest firms. According to research by the Chinese Academy of Social Sciences, reported by the *South China Morning Post* (scmp.com, accessed 24 April 2010), 91 per cent of China's richest millionaires, for example those with assets of 100 million RMB or more, fall into this group of princelings.

The greater participation of cadres in business has bred rent-seeking activities and corruption on a fairly massive scale, which is an urgent problem that needs to be addressed and rectified by China's current and future leadership. A study of 120 corruption cases involving higher government and party officials at provincial level and above finds that the number of cases has doubled every five years since 1987 (caijing.com.cn, accessed 10 October 2010). Because of the existence of hidden or 'grey' income associated with corruption and bribery, the real size of the Chinese economy and household income are underestimated to a significant extent by the official data. For instance, in 2008, according to Wang (2010), China's real household income was about 30 per cent higher than the official estimate; and China's real GDP was 10 per cent higher than the official estimate. Since two-thirds of the missing income went to the richest 10 per cent of the population, China's real income inequality is also significantly underestimated by the official data.

CONCLUSION

China's long march to a market economy is not yet complete, though in 2010 after 30 years of reform it had covered about two-thirds of the distance from a centrally planned to a market economy. Its Eastern European counterparts covered this in ten years. However, the gradual strategy adopted by China has paid off since it has been able to avoid the traumatic economic collapse suffered by other transitional economies in the early phase of their reform. It has also been able to remain politically stable in the last 20 years in spite of the Tiananmen Square tragedy in 1989 and recent ethnic unrest in Tibet and Xinjiang. And though the Asian financial crisis in 1997 and the global financial crisis in 2008 hit many countries hard and erased their growth, China has been able to achieve and maintain double-digit growth figures throughout the three decades of reform. Moreover, it has simultaneously kept the rate of inflation at about 3 per cent.

China has achieved the macro stability through a regime combining administrative and indirect monetary and fiscal controls. Most importantly, the reform progressed and deepened without getting bogged down in the reform trap which catches most transitional economies out. This was made possible by motivating the political elite, for example the party cadres and bureaucrats, the pillars of the status quo, to become agents of change. By allowing them to benefit from changes in the opportunity structure and reaping the fruits of reform, they became facilitators of and active participants in the reform process through a changed reward and promotion structure, and eventually often became entrepreneurs themselves.

However, in spite of 30 years of reform China is not home yet. The size of its state sector is still very large, the budget constraints of state enterprises remain weak, and the role of the state sector is still fairly overwhelming. However, most important of all, China's factor markets have yet to be fully developed. The incomplete reforms provide ample opportunities for cadres in rent-seeking. Bribery and corruption among higher government officials has become a serious problem in recent years.

16. Towards a new growth strategy

Much has been written about China's reforms and its open door policy but very little on its new development strategy. Ishikawa (1983) suggests that in the reform period: 'the previous development policy of high growth and high investment is being replaced by a new one which aims at securing a steady increase in personal consumption and in which investment is weighted in favour of light industry and agriculture'. However, this view proved premature, for while the development of heavy industry is no longer emphasized and improvement in consumption is stressed it is not true that the government has abandoned its high growth and investment strategy. Otherwise it would be difficult to explain why the government continues to extol the doubling of China's gross national product (GNP) every ten years as a goal of long-term development (Chai and Roy 2006). Similarly, the allegation that China no longer pursues a high investment policy does not square with the fact that China's fixed investment as a percentage of gross domestic product (GDP) has risen from 23 per cent in 1978 to 40 per cent in 2007 (Brandt and Zhu 2010).

What, then, is China's new development strategy? To begin with, the high-growth goal in order to catch up with developed countries' income per capita has not changed. This is evidenced by the targets set in the 1980–2010 long-term Development Plan which adopted a three-step strategy to achieve the goal, with each first step envisioning to double China's GDP within a decade. This implies an annual growth target rate of 7 per cent per annum. As will be discussed later, these targets have actually been surpassed by the significant margin of 3 per cent, with China posting a 10 per cent growth rate throughout the 30-year reform period.

Secondly, as mentioned, the raising of the consumption standard of China's population has become an important aspect of China's new strategy. For after three decades of emphasizing the development of heavy industry, the rapid growth of consumption – as predicted by the Feldman growth model – had not materialized and Mainland China's standard of living had fallen far behind that of Taiwan, Hong Kong, Singapore, Malaysia and other parts of Southeast Asia. Hence pressure was building for the Chinese government to act in order to bridge this gap urgently or else be faced with the prospect of social unrest and/or political upheaval.

And the Chinese government was well aware that this had led to the downfall of other communist regimes in Eastern Europe.

To achieve the twin objectives of high growth of GDP and consumption, China has changed its growth strategy from extensive to intensive. To accommodate this change, several new policies have been introduced: (1) population control; (2) export orientation; (3) attraction of foreign investment; and (4) promotion of technological progress.

POPULATION CONTROL

China's population policy has evolved through different stages during the post-war years. In the 1950s and 1960s China did not control the growth of its population due to Maoist ideology. According to Mao, the relationship between population growth and per capita income growth is positive, for according to him: 'among all matters in the world, human resources are most precious and as long as we have manpower, any miracle can be achieved' (Mao 1965).

However, Mao's view was criticized by Ma Yinchiu, an economist, as a result of which a vigorous debate ensued in the late 1960s. It ended with a victory of Maoist thought and Ma was severely criticized as a rightist and was fired in 1960 from his job as President of Beijing University. However, the failure of the Great Leap Forward (GLF) and the resultant biggest ever famine in world history confronted Mao with a cruel reality check. As a result a population control policy was formally initiated in the early 1970s. The new measures to reduce the birth and fertility rates included: (1) encouraging couples to marry late, and (2) to defer child bearing to a later age; (3) prolonging the time between births by compulsory implantation of an intra-uterine device (IUD) after the first delivery; and (4) the compulsory sterilization of one partner after the birth of a second child (Bannister 1997).

In Mao's lifetime the birth control policy was never effectively implemented and it was only after his death in 1976 that the government stepped up its efforts to restrict population growth. In 1980 a coercive one-child policy was officially promulgated under which all urban Han Chinese couples were subjugated to the requirement that they have only one child. In contrast, different rules, varying in different locations, applied to Han Chinese in rural areas (Bannister 1997). The population control policy was implemented through administrative coercion backed up by a cadre evaluation system whose sole criterion was the achievement of the regional birth control target. It encouraged officials to compete for lower local birth rates within their jurisdiction and sometimes led to the falsification of birth statistics (Wang and Mason 2008).

Table 16.1   Birth, death, fertility and growth rates of China's population

	1950	1965	1982	1990	2003	Projected 2005	Projected 2025
Crude birth rate per 1000	37.0	37.9	22.3	21.1	12.4	12.0	10.0
Population crude death rate per 1000	18.0	9.5	6.6	6.7	6.4	6.0	9.0
Population total fertility rate	NA	NA	2.9	2.3	NA	1.8	1.6
Average annual population growth	1.9	2.8	1.6	1.4	0.6	0.5	0.0

Sources: Chai and Roy (2006) and US Census Bureau (2010).

Table 16.1 presents the results achieved by the Chinese government in the post-war period with its population control policies. In the first 15 years of the pre-reform period it had failed to arrest the rampant population growth, with the unintended exception of the years of the Great Famine in 1959–61 which resulted from the collapse of the rural economy after the GLF. From 1950 to 1965 the annual growth rate of China's population was in line with other low-income countries and averaged more than 2 per cent. The population growth in China slowed down from 2.8 per cent in 1965 to 1.6 per cent in 1982, which amounts to a reduction of 43 per cent. From then to 2005 it slowed further to a low 0.5 per cent. This success is a remarkable achievement of China's population control policy.

The rate of population growth is measured by the difference between the average birth and death rates of a country. The former is strongly influenced by the fertility rate (average number of children a female bears in her lifetime) and the net reproduction rate (number of girls born per woman). The average death rate, on the other hand, reflects both the standard of a country's health care facilities and their accessibility to the general populace. As evidenced in Table 16.1, one of the distinctive features of the Chinese population was the very high birth rate in the pre-reform period, with 37.9 births per 1000 population in 1965. It is also remarkable that the death rate fell from 18 per 1000 in 1950 to only 9.5, which constitutes a reduction of nearly 50 per cent by 1965. This reflects the great improvements in China's health system with, among others, the introduction of barefoot doctors under Mao. The third important feature is that between

1965 and 1982 China managed to reduce its birth rate by 41 per cent, and cut it by another 46 per cent during the reform period (1982–2005). The policy was so successful that China's fertility rate dropped from 2.9 in 1982 to only 1.8 in 2005, and as of 2010 was below the replacement level of fertility.

The significance of China's population control policies to the world and to the Chinese economy cannot be overemphasized. To begin with, if the growth of the world's most populous country continues to slow, China's population will be overtaken by that of India (Wang and Mason 2008; OECD 2010). Secondly, the population growth control policies contributed significantly to the high rate of economic growth in both the Maoist and the reform periods, taking the form of the first and second 'demographic dividend' (Wang and Mason 2008). Low fertility and rising life expectancy due to the decline in the death rate have altered not only the growth rate but also the age structure of China's population pyramid. To illustrate: in 1980 it was bottom-heavy, typical of a young, growing population, but by 1990 it showed a bulk in the working-age group and a relatively small child population, typical of a more mature population structure. And an increase in the population in the high-productivity age group improves the support ratio, that is, the ratio of the effective number of producers to that of consumers. This leads to an increase per capita income known as the first demographic dividend (Wang and Mason 2008). Given that per capita output is simply a product of support ratio, L/P, and labour productivity, Q/L; and assuming a production function, $Q = F(K, L, t)$ – where Q is output, P is population or consumers, L is labour or producers, K is capital and t technological progress or total factor productivity growth – the rate of growth in per capita output $G(Q/P)$ is equal to the rate of the support ratio (the excess of the rate of growth of labour, $G(L)$, over the rate of growth of the population, $G(P)$), the rate of growth of capital intensity, $G(K/L)$, and output elasticity of capital, (Ek), and the rate of technological progress, t:

$$G(Q/P) = G(L) - G(P) + Ek \, G(K/L) + t \qquad (16.1)$$

The demographic first dividend is measured by the first two right-hand side terms of equation (16.1) which represents the growth in the support ratio.

According to an estimate by Wang and Mason (2008), the support ratio increased in the first reform period from 1982 to 2000 by 28 per cent and accounted for 15 per cent of China's economic growth of 8 per cent in GDP per capita (purchasing power parity adjusted). During the second period between 2000 and 2010 the support ratio continued to climb but at a slower pace, thus its contribution to economic growth declined. It is estimated to reach its peak by 2013 and then turn negative.

The second demographic dividend results from the ageing population, for with a falling fertility rate and rising life expectancy the old-age dependency ratio (the ratio of elderly to those aged 15–64) is expected to increase from its 0.11 level in 2010 to reach 0.24 in 2030 and 0.43 by 2050 (OECD 2010). This means that individuals must accumulate additional wealth or face a significant reduction in their standard of living in their old age. Wealth can be accumulated in different ways, one of which is accumulation of capital. This would lead to capital deepening and an increase of $G\,(K/L)$ in equation (16.1), leading to an increase in per capita output. Another possibility is the accumulation of transfer wealth, or an increase in the obligation of future generations to provide old-age support in the form of either public pension plans or as part of the familial support system. The latter does not create capital, nor does it contribute to intensive growth. Thus, whether China will enjoy a second demographic dividend in the near future depends very much on the kind of pension financing arrangement the country adopts.

Though its birth control has contributed significantly to China's intensive growth, it also has serious social consequences. One of them is rising female infanticide, evident from the rising excess female infant mortality. This jumped from 10 per cent in the late 1970s to the extraordinary level of 60 per cent in 1995 (Wang and Mason 2008). The major reason for it is China's traditional preference for sons (see Chapter 1) which was exacerbated by the one-child policy and economic reforms, especially in rural areas. Since land is periodically contracted to households under the household responsibility system (HRS) on the basis of the number of people in a household, and since daughters still are expected to marry and become members of another family or village, households with daughters stand to lose a portion of their land. In contrast, those with sons can count their potential wives and future children as part of their own lineage and hence improve the households' prospects for land entitlement.

Furthermore, the disbanding of the commune system caused the collapse of the rural welfare system, and while there is a new state-based rural pension system its coverage is inadequate due to the lack of funding at the local government level. Hence, sons are increasingly relied on by their parents to provide for them in their old age. The economic foundation of the traditional bias for sons is still maintained, and since people are only allowed one child they tend to abandon female children, choose sex selective abortion or neglect their daughters. As a result of the higher female infant mortality the sex ratio (of males to females) rose from 1.07 in 1978 to 1.169 in 2000 (Wang and Mason 2008). It has been estimated that at the time of writing in 2010 there were 60 to 100 million women fewer alive than what the natural rate would provide in the absence of gender discrimination at birth. A rising sex ratio implies a shortage of women available for marriage and leads to greater stratification through marriage. The people in rural areas, especially the poor and uneducated, are hardest hit by this shortage. The most recent Census shows that in 2000 only 3.8 per cent of males aged 40 were single but the percentage for the above-mentioned group was 26.5 per cent (Wang and Mason 2008).

EXPORT-ORIENTED STRATEGY

Export-oriented (EO) strategy was adopted to enable China to partici-pate in the international division of labour, leading to intensive growth via an increase in its static and dynamic efficiency. According to Zhao's memoir (2009), this strategy was conceived while he was the party chief of Guangdong province, where he was inspired by the success of neighbour-ing Hong Kong and Taiwan. And while his proposal to adopt the export-oriented strategy to promote China's economic development was backed by Deng Xiaoping and others, some party elders including Yao Yilin, Li Peng and Chen Yun had strong ideological reservations about it. For this reason, but also to smoothe the transition and to minimize any disruption to the existing trade regime, namely the import substitution policies, the EO strategy was implemented only incrementally and carefully.

In the initial stage, special Export Oriented Zones (EOZs) were created and restricted to special areas and enterprises (Naughton 1996), and they were separated from the rest of the country (see Chapter 15). As discussed earlier, in the third phase of the reforms (in 1992) the special EOZs were extended into some of China's interior provinces and, finally, after China's entry into the World Trade Organization (WTO) in 2001, the policy was extended to the whole country.

Reforming the Foreign Trade System

China changed its command trade system to a market-based one in order to stimulate the interest of domestic enterprises in exports. It started with a gradual reduction in the scope and a slow phasing out of the foreign trade planning system. The decentralization of trading rights broke up the foreign trade monopoly of the 12 national foreign trade corporations (FTCs) and opened it up for other enterprises. It succeeded in sharply increasing the number of enterprises with trading rights, from 12 in 1978, to 35000 in 2001 (Branstetter and Lardy 2008). In addition, domestic prices were more and more linked to world market prices through the introduction of the agency system in 1984. Under this the FTCs acted as agents of domestic enterprises with commissions paid on the basis of actual import and export transactions. Without the state absorbing profits and losses from foreign trade, consumers now paid, and domestic producers received, the equivalent amount to the international prices for traded goods. The transition process was, however, very slow and on the eve of the reforms only 20 per cent of all importable and exportable commodities had their domestic prices actually based on world market prices. But their share increased rapidly to between 80 and 90 per cent in the early 1990s (Chai and Roy 2006). The abolition of price controls in China and the entry of the country into the WTO has further pushed the process ahead, so that at the time of writing in 2010 most prices of goods in China are in line with world market prices.

Last but not least, the rigid, centralized foreign exchange control system was loosened with the introduction of a foreign exchange retention system and parallel foreign exchange markets. Under the new system domestic enterprises contributing to foreign exchange earnings were allocated a user quota proportional to their foreign exchange earnings. In order to be able to use this quota enterprises had to use renminbi (RMB) to buy back foreign exchange from the state bank at the official exchange rate. The foreign exchange purchase, subject to the approval of higher authorities, could then be used to import goods or could be sold in exchange for domestic currency at the parallel foreign exchange market. As the parallel market rate was above the official exchange rate, these enterprises were able to receive a certain amount of quota rent (Chai and Sun 1993).

As early as 1985 formal parallel exchange markets or swap centres were introduced at which enterprises could sell the surplus of retained foreign exchange to other enterprises at the market rate. By 1992, more than 100 of these had been established, in all major cities in China, and more than 70 per cent of foreign exchange used by Chinese firms was traded and priced at the market rate (Chai and Sun 1993). With the introduction of the current account convertibility in 1994 swap centres disappeared because the market rate was now identical with the official rate. This constituted the end of foreign exchange control in China's trade transactions.

The Promotion of Export

Under the import substitution (IS) regime exporters have little incentive to export and any export activity faces various acts of discrimination. To begin with, exporters are discriminated against in the use of imported inputs, because high import tariffs push the price of the latter well above world market prices. Hence their goods are not competitive on the international market. Secondly, producers of exportables are also disadvantaged on the output side as the relative price of their output compared with that of importables is lower than its relative world market price because the relative domestic price of importables is kept artificially high by import barriers.[1] Lastly, under the IS regime the official exchange rate tends to be overvalued because it is geared to subsidize the import of capital goods that could not be produced domestically. Again, this discourages exports as the overvalued exchange rate lowers the domestic currency prices of exported goods.

Thus the first step to promote exports had to consist in getting rid of these structural anti-export biases in the system. The policies that China adopted for this purpose were similar to those of the other Asian newly industrialized countries, namely: first, import liberalization; and second, the introduction of compensatory financial and fiscal incentives. A third measure was the devaluation of the exchange rate.

The import liberalization policy was implemented in stages, for initially it applied only to trading activities in the special zones. Firms operating there and specializing in exports were now allowed duty-free imports of raw materials, intermediate products and capital goods as well as the use of tax-free domestic inputs for exports. Later on, when the EO regime was extended to other parts of China, a wholesale import liberalization programme was introduced. This resulted in a steep decline in import tariffs from 56 per cent in 1982 to 43 per cent in 1985. The rate of tariffs was reduced to 15 per cent on the eve of China's entry into the WTO in 2000. In 2007 China's actual tariff rate was 9.4 per cent, which is fairly low compared to other larger emerging economies. For example, India still had an average tariff rate of 13.7 per cent and Russia a rate of 10.7 in 2007 (OECD 2010). In addition, the dispersion of tariff rates over all products was much lower in China than in other emerging markets, indicating that its tariff structure was relatively neutral, and the degree to which tariffs were used to protect particular industries was relatively low (OECD 2010).

Compensatory financial and fiscal incentives were also used in China to promote exports. As mentioned, the country relied heavily on indirect taxes to fund government expenditures. Thus exporters were subject to a relatively heavier indirect tax burden than their counterparts in other countries which rely on direct tax on income. China started to compensate for this disadvantage with rebates on various indirect taxes for exporters. It made intensive use especially of the value-added tax (VAT) tax rebate (Branstetter and Lardy 2008).

The gradual devaluation of the official exchange rate played a major role in China's attempts to promote exports. While in 1981 the official exchange rate was 1.5 RMB to the US dollar, it was down to 8.7 RMB in 1994 when the dual exchange rate was abolished. Between 1995 and 2005 the RMB was effectively pegged to the US dollar at 8.3 to 1 (Branstetter and Lardy 2008). And in 2005 the RMB was revalued by 2.1 per cent against the US dollar, and has since experienced a gradual appreciation. Since August 2008, however, it was again repegged at 6.86 RMB to $1 to counter the negative effects of the global financial crisis (GFC) on Chinese exports. This rate remained unchanged until 2010 when the Chinese government was under mounting pressure from the world community to reduce its huge trade surplus and to allow the RMB to appreciate gradually against the US currency. In 2010, China's currency was estimated to be undervalued by 40 per cent. And this was, of course, one of the major factors behind the increased international competitiveness of Chinese exports to the world market.

Outcome of the Export-oriented Strategy

China has achieved spectacular success with its EO strategy, which saw total exports over the last 30-year period (1979–2008) increase annually by 18.1 per cent (SSB, China Statistical Yearbook 2009). In 2007 China relegated the US to a lower ranking by becoming the world's second-largest exporter, and in 2008 it did the same to Germany. It is now the world's largest exporter, and some people call it the world factory. Exports also account for an increasingly larger share in China's GDP. On the eve of the reform in 1978 exports constituted only 5 per cent of China's GDP (Chai and Roy 2006), while in 2008 they made up around 33 per cent (OECD 2010).

However, the significance of Chinese exports to the world and the Chinese economy should not be overrated, as a large part consists of the export processing trade, which involves processing and assembling imported intermediate products for exports. In 1998, for instance, this kind of trade made up 53 per cent of China's total foreign trade (Chai and Roy 2006). And the importance of this part of China's foreign trade remained unchanged in recent years. This is shown by Naughton (2007) who divides imports into two categories: ordinary imports destined for China's domestic market, and export processing and other imports. He shows that in 1997, the latter made up 73 per cent of Chinese total imports. And while this share has declined somewhat due to a slight increase in ordinary imports as a result of China's entry into the WTO and its subsequent greater import liberalization measures, the imports for export processing and other imports still maintained a staggering 50 per cent share in GDP in 2005.

The relatively huge share of China's export processing trade tempts scholars to overestimate considerably the relevance of China's exports. Increased globalization and the subsequent vertical disintegration of the production chain of multinational corporations (MNCs) breaks production into a series of separate processes and these processes are relocated to different countries according to their comparative advantage. For example, Apple's iPods and iPhones are designed in California; components are sourced from Taiwan and assembled in China. Hence, it becomes increasingly difficult to identify the country of origin of exports. Thus many Chinese exports are actually those of other countries.

To assess the real Chinese content of these exports one needs to estimate the domestic value-added of China's exports. The analysis of Koopman et al. (2008) suggests that the domestic value-added component of high-tech Chinese exports is indeed low, ranging between 4 per cent for computers to 15 per cent for telecommunication equipment. Overall, in 2002, the domestic content of Chinese exports was estimated at 50 per cent only (OECD 2010). The relatively low value-added content of China's exports implies that it is still a long way from beating Germany as the world's number one exporter. It also implies that China's economy is less dependent on exports than it seems. Given that exports of goods in 2008 were equivalent to 33 per cent of GDP in 2008, and that the share of domestic value-added in total export goods was 49 per cent, the share of value-added generated by exports in GDP was only 16 per cent (OECD 2010).

FOREIGN INVESTMENT

Foreign investment in post-1978 China consists essentially of foreign loans and foreign direct investment (FDI) and the former were in the majority up to 1991 (Table 16.2). From 1992 on, FDI became more important.

In 1979 a law was passed allowing joint ventures between Chinese nationals and foreigners and from then on FDI in China underwent three distinct phases. In the first one from 1979 to the mid-1986 FDI was welcome but highly regulated (Chai 1997) with the result that its growth was subdued. The second phase began in 1986 with the introduction of the '22 regulations' which significantly reduced government intervention and offered more incentives to foreign investors. As a result, after the initial slow start, FDI in China started to rise in the second half of the 1980s even though its growth slowed again briefly after the Tiananmen Square incident.

The third phase of growth of FDI in China began after the tour by Deng Xiaoping of the Southern provinces in 1992, with the opening of some of the interior provinces for FDI. This led to its spike after 1992, but its

Table 16.2   Volume and structure of China's realized foreign investment[1]
            (in billion US$)

Year	Volume	Foreign loan	FDI	Other foreign investment[2]
1979–84	181.87	130.41	41.04	10.42
1985	47.60	25.06	19.56	2.98
1986	76.28	50.14	22.44	3.70
1987	84.52	58.05	23.14	3.33
1988	102.26	64.87	31.94	5.45
1989	100.60	62.86	33.92	3.81
1990	102.89	65.34	34.87	2.68
1991	115.54	68.88	43.66	3.00
1992	192.03	79.11	110.08	2.84
1993	389.60	111.89	275.15	2.56
1994	432.13	92.67	337.67	1.79
1995	481.33	103.27	375.21	2.85
1996	548.05	126.69	417.26	4.10
1997	644.08	120.21	452.57	71.30
1998	585.57	110.00	454.63	20.94
1999	526.59	102.12	403.19	21.28
2000	593.56	100.00	407.15	86.41
2001	496.72		468.78	27.94
2002	550.11		527.43	22.68
2003	561.40		535.05	26.35
2004	640.72		606.30	34.42
2005	638.05		603.25	34.80
2006	670.76		630.21	40.55
2007	783.39		747.68	35.72
2008	952.53		923.95	28.58
1979–2008	10498.18	NA	8526.13	500.48

Notes:
1. Realized foreign investments is the total amount of foreign capital actually used. Data on foreign loans are not available after 2000.
2. Other foreign investments include sale of shares, international leasing and compensation trade.

Sources: SSB, China Statistical Yearbook (various issues).

growth was slowed by the Asian financial crisis in 1997. However, with its end FDI soared again and in 2009 China was the second-largest recipient of FDI in the world after the US (UNCTAD 2010).

However, the significance of FDI in China to the world should not be over-rated as China's official FDI statistics contain a significant amount

Table 16.3   China's realized foreign direct investment by type of foreign ownership (%)

Year	Equity JVs	Contract JVs	Co-operative development	WOFEs	Other	Total
1979–81	8.8	47.9	43.2	0.1	0.0	100
1982	8.0	41.3	41.5	9.2	0.0	100
1985	34.9	35.3	29.0	0.8	0.0	100
1988	61.8	24.4	6.6	7.3	0.0	100
1992	55.4	19.1	2.8	22.7	0.0	100
1997	43.1	19.7	0.8	35.8	0.6	100
2001	33.6	13.3	1.1	50.9	1.1	100
2003	28.8	7.3	0.6	62.4	0.9	100
2006	22.8	3.1	0.0	73.4	0.7	100
2008	18.7	2.1	0.0	78.3	0.9	100

Source: SSB, China Statistical Yearbook (various issues).

of the so-called 'round-tripping FDI', which involves the rerouting of China's domestic capital to Hong Kong Chinese enterprises which invest them in Mainland China in order to capture the various fiscal and financial incentives enjoyed by the foreign-invested enterprises (FIEs). The round-tripping FDIs introduce an upward bias in the level of FDI and its growth (Chai and Roy 2006).

The relative importance of various FDIs in China is presented in Table 16.3 which shows that the trend is towards greater foreign ownership and control. In the first phase foreign investors were heavily engaged in a 'lower form' of FDI, such as contractual joint venture (JV) and co-operative development projects, both of which do not involve foreign equity capital. As is evident from Table 16.3, these lower forms of FDI accounted for over 80 per cent of China's actual FDI in the first phase. In the second phase the improved investment environment and changed attitude of China's government towards foreign ownership stimulated an increase in the higher forms of FDI, namely equity JVs and wholly owned foreign enterprises (WOFEs). By the early 1990s they accounted for over 70 per cent of actual FDIs in China. In the third phase WOFEs became increasingly popular among foreign investors and they have become the predominant form at the start of the twenty-first century.

Over the whole period the neighbouring East Asian countries have remained the major source of China's FDI. For example, in 2003 Hong Kong, Macao, Japan, Taiwan and South Korea, together with Singapore and the four core Association of South East Asian Nations (ASEAN) countries, accounted for 63 per cent of China's actual FDI.

Table 16.4   FDI inflow to China by sector (billion US$)

Year	Agri-culture	Manu-facture	Real estate	Finance	Non-real estate	Utilities
1997	1.5680	29.5578	5.169	0	1.6551	2.0719
1998	1.2018	27.6462	6.4101	0	1.6451	3.1028
1999	1.2673	23.5196	5.5883	0	1.5511	3.7027
2000	1.2592	26.7494	4.6575	0.0763	1.0119	2.2421
2001	1.7098	31.7137	5.1366	0.0353	0.9089	2.2728
2002	1.6087	37.5088	5.6628	0.1067	0.9135	1.3751
2003	1.3372	37.5478	5.2356	0.2320	0.8674	1.2954
2004	1.6523	43.7886	5.9502	0.2525	7.6208	1.3653
2005	1.0732	42.9432	5.4181	12.3010	9.1371	1.5335
2006	1.0600	40.7650	8.2295	6.8940	11.1962	1.4766
2007	1.4135	41.2992	17.0890	9.0100	13.3638	1.3454
2008	1.7638	50.9876	18.5900	15.9000	18.4454	2.0363

Source: OECD (2010).

In the first phase FDIs were concentrated in the service sector, especially in real estate, with hotels and other tourism-related projects. But in the second phase, following the Plaza Accord in 1985, foreign investments shifted significantly towards the manufacturing sector due to the growing trend of Asia's newly industrialized countries and Japan to relocate their labour-intensive manufactured exports production bases. With the opening of the service sector to FDI after China's entry into the WTO in the third phase, however, the share in the service sector soared again, especially in real estate and finance, as Table 16.4 shows.

As discussed in Chapter 7, FDI increases a country's rate of growth by increasing employment, capital formation, exports and productivity. But in China the employment contribution of FDI was not significant because of China's huge labour supply. Thus, for instance, in 2005 FIEs employed only 3 per cent of China's urban labour force (Cai et al. 2008). The capital contribution of FDI was more significant and the ratio of FIE invest-ment in total fixed asset investment peaked at 17 per cent in 1994. But it subsequently fell to 10 per cent in 2000, and further to 7 per cent in 2003 (Branstetter and Lardy 2008). The export contribution of FDI to China's economic growth was the most significant element, for in 2008 FIEs accounted for 30 per cent of the output of China's large and medium-sized industrial enterprises and for over 50 per cent of their total exports (SSB, China Statistical Yearbook 2009).

Last but not least, FDI undoubtedly played a critical role in improving Chinese productivity, for after decades of insulation from the world economy its workers and managers benefited immensely from their exposure to foreign technology and management practice, and they were quick to pick up relevant skills. Furthermore, entry of FIEs into the previously insulated domestic market provided a challenge for domestic firms and increased the competitive pressure, as a result of which low-productivity firms were forced to exit and remaining firms had to improve their efficiency to remain competitive.

TECHNOLOGICAL PROGRESS

Ultimately the sustainability of intensive growth in the long run depends on the 'residual' in equation (16.1) or the rate of technological progress. And in the final analysis, this in turn depends on factors such as: (1) the amount of unexploited technology available to a country as a result of the technological gap between it and more advanced countries; and (2) the country's capacity to absorb these technologies. Once the technological gap has disappeared the rate of progress depends on the rate of development of the country's own creative technology.

There is no doubt that China over the 30 years from 1979 to 2009 has been engaged in catching up with the technology of more advanced countries. Since in Mao's era China pursued a policy of self-reliance, the technological gap had actually widened in that period. Thus when in 1979 China embarked on the open door policy and on reform, it had an enormous reservoir of unexploited technology to catch up on by way of imports of foreign technology and absorption of modern technology.

Imports of Technology

Foreign technology can be introduced into an economy in three forms, namely: (1) imports of technology embodied in machinery and equipment; (2) imports of disembodied technology in the form of payment for licences, patents, technological know-how and services provided by foreigners; and (3) FDI. Table 16.5 provides an overview of the development of these modes of technology transfer in China over roughly the last 30 years. In the first ten-year period of reforms, because of China's limited capacity to absorb technology, the main form of transfer was by way of importing machinery and equipment. Thus their net imports to China in 1985–89 were almost quadruple those of the 1980–84 period and accounted for one-third of China's non-housing fixed asset investment. However, international experience shows that this kind of technology

Table 16.5   China's imports of technology, 1980–2008 (billion dollars)

Period	Net imports of machinery and equipment	Payments for imported foreign technology	FDI
1980–84	19.5	7.8	3.1[1]
1985–89	72.2	60.2	12.5
1990–94	71.2	131.4	80.2
1995–99	67.0	4943.1	210.3
2000–2004	−61.5	8196.3	254.6
2005–2008	−557.3	NA	281.3

Note: 1. 1979–84.

Sources: China Statistical Yearbook (various issues), Gao (2003), SSB, *China Statistical Yearbook of Science and Technology* (various issues), Chai and Roy (2006) and OECD (2010).

transfer only makes a limited contribution to domestic learning of foreign technology.

In the early 1990s net imports of machinery and equipment to China stalled, and the trend reversed and turned negative as China's exports of machinery and equipment grew larger than imports, due to the export activity of FIEs. From then on, imports of disembodied technology and FDIs became the dominant form of technology transfer to the country.

Increasing the Domestic Technological Capacity

Imports of foreign technology by themselves are not sufficient to upgrade a country's technological standard, for significant efforts by the importing country are required to optimize the use of imported know-how. During 1979–2009 the Chinese government has stepped up its efforts to help enterprises absorb and assimilate it in two ways: (1) through support from the public sector; and (2) by promoting the domestic generation of technology and its utilization. Government support for technological improvement can be direct or indirect. The most important indirect mechanism is through a very good education system that places emphasis on technical subjects in order to enhance the capacity to absorb new technologies.

As is well known, China has achieved a high level of general education and even prior to the market reforms spent considerable resources on technical education. This emphasis continued through the reforms. Table 16.6 gives an overview of China's efforts and improvements in education since 1952. It shows that China's rate of literacy improved from 20 per

Table 16.6   China's levels of education, 1952, 1980 and 2008

Year	Literacy rate	% enrolled in primary school	% enrolled in secondary school	% enrolled in tertiary education	% of graduates in science and engineering
1952	20	49.2	NA	0.3	40
1980	77[1]	93.9	46.0	2.0	52
2008	93	99.5	86.2	23.3	56[2]

Notes:
1. 1982.
2. 1994.

Sources: Chai and Roy (2006), Hannum et al. (2008) and SSB, China Statistical Yearbook (various issues).

cent in 1952 to 77 per cent at the beginning of the reforms, and reached 93 per cent in 2008. The higher level can also be gathered from the increased enrolment rate in all three levels of China's education system. In 2008 enrolment rates in the primary and secondary levels were in fact approaching those of Japan. Tertiary enrolment saw a huge rise in the reform years, when it jumped from 2 per cent in 1980 to more than 23 per cent in 2008. The greater emphasis on technical education can be seen from the greater share of tertiary graduates in science and engineering, which increased from 40 per cent in 1952 to 56 per cent in 1994. At that level it is even higher than that of the Asian NICs and Japan (Hannum et al. 2008).

Direct action by the government to support technological change included the recent launch of several technology programmes (Hu and Jefferson 2008) of which one group aims at encouraging basic research. This includes the Key Project Program (started in 1982), the 863 Program (started in 1986) and the 973 Program (started in 1997). The last two aim at enhancing China's technological capability in order to catch up with other Organisation for Economic Co-operation and Development (OECD) countries. The second group of programmes is primarily designed to encourage the diffusion of applied technology in industries and rural areas. These include the Spark Program (1986) and the Torch Program (started in 1988). Other government support measures include the micro intervention by the government in the form of grants and subsidies to encourage enterprise spending in research and development (R&D).

The strength of efforts to promote the domestic generation of technology can be gathered from the government's share of spending in R&D and innovation investment. R&D includes actual expenditure on basic,

Table 16.7   Percentage share of R&D and innovation fixed asset investment expenditures in China's GDP, 1980–2008

Year	R&D expenditures	Innovation fixed assets investments
1980	NA	4.1
1985	NA	5.0
1990	0.74	4.5
1995	0.60	5.6
2000	1.00	5.1
2005	1.33	5.8[1]
2008	1.54	NA

Note: 1. 2004.

Sources: SSB, China Statistical Yearbook (various issues) and Hu and Jefferson (2008).

applied and experimental research which aims at developing new products as well as new process technologies. R&D expenditure in latecomer countries tends to focus on incremental changes to borrowed technologies rather than on fundamental innovation. Since the capital-intensive, unmodified modern technology borrowed from more advanced countries is not an optimal solution for latecomers with an abundant labour force, they are prone to modify it to adapt it to their conditions. Two studies of China's R&D show that since the mid-1990s China has mainly been developing in the area of relatively labour-intensive and capital- and energy-saving technologies with the support of R&D (Hu and Jefferson 2008).

Innovation investment is largely geared towards the technical upgrading, transformation and innovation of existing enterprises which are more inclined towards the application of technology. Since the reforms, R&D and innovation investment have experienced rapid increases as shown in Table 16.7, which also shows that R&D intensity in China rose from 0.74 in 1990 to 1.54 per cent in 2008. This is a very high level in view of China's low level of income per capita. Thus China is the only low- and middle-income country in the world whose R&D intensity exceeds 1 per cent (Hu and Jefferson 2008).

Innovation fixed asset investment, which is the renewal of fixed assets and technological innovation of the original facilities by enterprises, has also experienced a rapid rise since the reforms. It accounted consistently for over 5 per cent of China's GDP expenditures and saw a phenomenal annual rate of growth of 16.7 per cent between 1980 and 2004.

Unfortunately, figures beyond 2004 are not available because the State Statistical Bureau (SSB) stopped its publication.

The outcome of China's domestic innovation efforts is impressive and China has in recent years succeeded in launching astronauts into space and in orbiting satellites around the moon. The country now ranks among the top ten countries in R&D expenditures and the number of researchers. According to a report by the information company Thomson Reuters, China in 2009 was ranked second in international scientific publications, up from 17th in 1993 (scmp.com, accessed 11 November 2009).The country's research is concentrated in the physical sciences and technology, especially materials science, chemistry and physics. Similarly, the number of patents granted to Chinese nationals as compared to foreigners has increased by a huge margin: in 2006 this ratio was five to one (SSB, China Statistical Yearbook 2009). Similarly, its high-technology exports as a percentage of total manufactured exports rose from 16.6 to 30.7 per cent in 2006. China's imports of foreign technology and its own innovation efforts contribute significantly to China's total factor productivity. Hu et al's (2005) study of 10 000 industrial large and medium-sized enterprises from 1995 to 2001 shows that R&D complemented borrowed technology and significantly enhanced productivity.

In spite of the impressive results of China's innovative efforts during 1979–2009 the country still has some way to go before it can become a leader in technology. Its R&D intensity still lags behind that of other OECD countries, which spend an average 2.2 per cent of GDP on R&D as compared to China's 1.5 per cent (OECD 2010). And while China has nearly as many scientific publications as the US, their quality still leaves much to be desired: in the rush to publicize, plagiarism is rampant, data are often fabricated or experiments are not properly set up, and so on. Furthermore, in terms of citations, China's ranking is relatively low (Hu and Jefferson 2008). Though China's patent registrations have soared in recent years, most are found to be utility and design patents representing an adaptation of existing technology, and its share in invention patents is limited (OECD 2010). Similarly, while China's high-tech exports have soared in recent years there is still a huge technological gap between it and the advanced OECD countries. This is evidenced from two facts. Firstly, while labour productivity in manufacturing in China has slowly caught up with that of the US, in recent years it was still only 9.6 per cent of the level of US firms (Maddison 2007). Secondly, in technology trade with the world, China's deficits have increased, for example the ratio of the amount paid for technology imports to earnings from technology exports has increased from 6.7 in 1998 to 18.1 in 2008 (SSB, China Statistical Yearbook 2009).

SUMMARY AND CONCLUSION

With the reforms, China shifted from an extensive to an intensive growth strategy in line with the twin objectives of high GDP growth and a rapid increase in the standard of consumption. The government pushed the development by setting the goal of doubling GDP every ten years and catching up as quickly as possible with advanced countries in terms of per capita income. To ensure that most of the extensive growth would be translated into intensive growth – that is, growth of per capita income – the controversial one-child policy was introduced. In addition, the government emphasized the importance of total factor productivity (TFP) as an additional source of growth to the high rate of investment. For this purpose reforms were introduced which got rid of inefficiencies, and an export-oriented strategy was put in place to enable China to participate in the international division of labour and to exploit its comparative advantage. The objective was to increase China's static and dynamic efficiencies in resource allocation and utilization.

In order to accelerate the rate of technological progress China continuously improved its education system to bring it up to world standard. Imports of foreign technology and FDI were encouraged to enhance China's capacity to borrow foreign technology. At the same time, China stepped up its science and technology activities, and the government engaged in direct and indirect investments to induce and promote domestic R&D activity and to enable the country to absorb the transferred technology to its resource endowment.

NOTE

1. Let $P^d x$, $P^d m$, $P^w x$ and $P^w m$ be domestic and world market price of the exportable and importable and r the exchange rate of foreign currency, and t the export tariff, then

$$P^d x / P^d m = P^w x \, r / P^w m \, r \, (1 + t),$$

$$\text{or } P^d x / P^d m = P^w x / P^w m \, (1 + t).$$

$$\text{Hence } P^d x / P^d m < P^w x / P^w m.$$

17. The rise of China

RAPID GROWTH

In its 30 years of reforms and open door strategy from 1979–2009, China achieved and maintained a spectacular real annual growth rate of GDP of nearly 10 per cent according to official statistics. However, official statistics overstate the growth rate because the gross domestic product (GDP) deflator used by China underestimates the actual rate of inflation for the period (Maddison 2007). On the other hand it is possible that the official growth rate is too low because it does not sufficiently take into account the service sector and product quality improvement (Perkins and Rawski 2008). Table 17.1 presents the official growth data and compares them with other estimates. It shows that the official data and estimates are fairly consistent, with the single exception of those by Maddison.

However, with a growth rate between 9 and 10 per cent in the reform period China has achieved double the growth of the period from 1952 to 1978 (Perkins and Rawski 2008). And the comparison with China's East Asian neighbours in their rapid growth periods shows that it outdid them all, as Table 17.2 shows. One of the reasons for this was, of course, China's relative backwardness at the starting point of modern economic growth. The greater this is – measured in terms of GDP per capita as percentage of that of the world's most advanced country, the USA – the faster latecomers can grow because they are able to borrow and adopt advanced technologies. Table 17.3 compares China's per capita income in relative purchasing power with those of its East Asian neighbours, and shows that China was by far the most backward country with only Korea nearly as poorly developed in 1952. Growing from a small base always achieves a good growth rate, but China also enjoyed the greatest advantage in terms of unexploited technology because of its backwardness.

China's fast pace of development coupled with the size of its population make it only a matter of time before China catches up with advanced countries and regains its ranking as the world's biggest economy, which it held at the beginning of the nineteenth century. In fact in the period between 2008 and 2010 China has already overtaken Germany, Japan and the USA in all sorts of fields. China's GDP ranking (measured at conventional exchange

Table 17.1   Comparison of China's official economic growth rate and estimates

	Period	%
China's official growth rate	**1979–2008**	**9.8**
Perkins and Rawski	1978–2005	9.5
Bosworth and Collins	1978–2008	9.3
Brandt and Zhu	1978–2007	9.3
Maddison	1978–2003	7.9

Sources: SSB (annually), Perkins and Rawski (2008), Bosworth and Collins (2008), Brandt and Zhu (2010) and Maddison (2007).

Table 17.2   Comparison of China's and other Asian NICs' growth rates in their period of MEG

	Period	Growth rate (%)
China	1979–2008	9.8
Japan	1952–78	7.9
Taiwan	1960–94	8.5
South Korea	1964–94	8.3
Singapore	1960–94	8.1
Hong Kong	1960–94	7.5

Source: SSB (annually) and Yusuf (2001).

Table 17.3   China's and its Asian neighbours' GDP per capita as % of that of US in 1952 (US = 100)

	GDP per capita
China	5.2
Japan	22.7
Korea	7.3
Singapore	22.1
Hong Kong	23.7
Taiwan	10.3

Source: Maddison (2001).

rate) in 2010 was already higher than that of Japan when it became the world's second-largest economy. And China is set to overtake the USA in 2030. Measured in terms of relative purchasing power China's output is already the second-largest since 2008 and is projected to move to first place in 2015. Moreover, while in recent years the world economy suffered from the global financial crisis (GFC) and the European sovereignty debt crisis, China's rapid economic growth continued thanks to the country's stimulus package, which was the largest in the world. As a result China has now become the engine of world economic growth and its increase in domestic spending in current dollar terms is contributing more to global growth than the US domestic demand. Furthermore, as already mentioned in Chapter 16, in 2008 China replaced Germany as the world's largest exporter. In 2006 it overtook Japan as the country with the largest foreign exchange reserves. In 2010, China and Japan were in joint second place after the US as the world's largest producers of manufactured goods, and China is projected to become the world's leading producer by 2015 or 2017, according to the OECD (2010). Lastly, in 2006 China overtook the US not only as the world's largest car producer, but also as its largest internet user.

In spite of China's growing importance in the world economy, one should not overestimate its geopolitical significance. Even when China becomes the world's largest economy in the next 20 years or so it will still have a long way to go to overtake the world's advanced countries in other areas. I have already discussed the large technological gap between China and the US, and the following discussion shows that China's standard of living in 2030 will still be only less than half that of the USA and about three-quarters of Japan's. To catch up with a higher standard of living China will have to massively increase its productivity, update its technology and undergo further structural changes.

SOURCES OF GROWTH

In simple growth accounting the growth of GDP can be disaggregated into growth resulting from an increase in the amount of capital and labour employed, $G(K)$ and $G(L)$ respectively, and the rate of growth in total factor productivity (TFP) or technical progress expressed as the residual, t. Table 17.4 presents some of the most recent estimates of China's sources of growth for the entire reform period as well for parts of it. The table shows that in the pre-reform period economic growth was factor-intensive, with a low rate of growth for TFP which averaged only 0.5 per cent (Perkins and Rawski 2008) since it mainly relied on greater inputs of labour and capital. In other words, in that period China achieved modern

Table 17.4   Sources of China's economic growth, 1978–2008 (%)

Period	Average annual TFP growth	Growth capital	Contribution labour[1]	TFP
Perkins and Rawski (2008)				
1978–2005	3.8	43.7	16.2	40.1
1978–85	3.2	40.6	26.6	32.8
1985–90	3.1	38.8	21.5	39.7
1990–95	6.7	33.3	9.5	57.3
1995–2000	3.2	52.7	10.5	36.8
2000–2005	3.1	57.1	10.6	32.3
OECD (2010)				
1978–2008	3.8	50.0	10.0	40.0
1988–93	3.6	48.9	7.8	40.0
1993–98	4.0	52.9	4.9	39.2
1998–2003	3.2	54.0	5.8	36.8
2003–2008	4.1	55.6	3.7	38.0

Note: 1. Labour is education enhanced labour in Perkins and Rawski's estimates.

Sources: Perkins and Rawski (2008) and OECD (2010).

economic growth (MEG) at very high cost through the huge sacrifice of leisure on the part of the population and the curtailing of current consumption to a bare minimum. In the reform and open door policy period the factor-intensive growth of China's economy increasingly gave way to growth generated by rising productivity. As shown in Table 17.4 the growth of total factor productivity stayed at around 3.8 per cent a year during 1979–2009, which indicates that 40 per cent of the growth was due to improved TFP. Nevertheless, China's economic growth is still relatively capital-intensive with capital accumulation accounting for 50 per cent of economic growth in this period. And there are indications that it has become more capital-intensive in recent years.

What has caused the accelerated productivity growth of China's economy? As it is both a developing and a transition economy there are two major reasons. As a transition economy China's growth can be attributed to an increase in allocative efficiency, since production factors shift to higher-productivity sectors when barriers to factor mobility are lowered. And as a developing economy productivity can be increased by using previously unexploited (foreign) technology. A study by the OECD (2010) which used a two-sector model for agriculture and non-agriculture estimates that in the period from 1988 to 2008 the relocation of labour away from agriculture to industry and the service sector contributed one-third of China's TFP growth. Two-thirds of TFP growth was accounted for by greater use of advanced technology.

More recently Brandt and Zhu (2010), using a three-sector dynamic model consisting of agriculture, and the state and non-state non-agricultural sectors and applying a counterfactual simulation technique, confirm that the relocation among the three sectors continues to play an important role in China's rapid growth. Thus the relocation efficiency and the rapid growth of TFP in the non-state and non-agricultural sectors were the driving forces of China's rapid economic growth since the start of the reforms.

STRUCTURAL CHANGE

Economic growth requires structural change, which is shaped by two factors in a market economy. One is the change in consumer prefer-ences expressed in the form of different elasticity of demand for different products, and the other is the differential pace of technological advances between the sectors. Since China is still in transition to a market economy its structural change is not only shaped by these market forces but also, to a considerable extent, by government policies. This, plus the fact that China is still a labour-surplus economy, causes its structural change to deviate from the normal pattern of a developing country.

In order to understand the issue we have to look at change in the struc-ture of production. Table 17.5 presents the structure of GDP measured in current prices. It shows that China's economic growth is accompanied by a shift away from agriculture to industry and the service sector, as is

Table 17.5   Distribution of GDP by sectors (in % and current prices)

Year	Agriculture	Industry	Services
1978	28.2	43.9	23.9
1985	28.4	42.9	28.7
1990	27.1	41.3	31.6
1995	19.9	47.2	32.9
2000	15.1	45.9	39.0
2005	12.2	47.7	40.1
2009	10.3	46.3	43.4

Source: SSB (annually).

214An economic history of modern China

Table 17.6   Contribution to GDP growth (%)

Year	Agriculture	Industry	Services
1990	41.7	41.0	17.3
1995	9.1	64.3	26.6
2000	4.4	60.8	34.8
2005	6.1	53.6	40.3
2008	6.5	50.6	42.9

Note: Ratios of the increases in value-added of agriculture, industry and services to GDP in constant prices.

Source: SSB (annually).

normal for a developing economy. In the reform period the percentage share of China's agriculture declined from 28 per cent in 1978 to 10 per cent in 2009. The industrial sector's share dropped initially until 1990 and then picked up again and rose to 46 per cent, whereas services grew significantly from 24 per cent in 1978 to 43 per cent of GDP in 2009. The share of industry is exceptionally high and in 2003 was about 10 per cent above the average 37.3 per cent of other middle-income countries (Heston and Sicular 2008). Whereas China's industry appears to have overdeveloped, its service sector is still underdeveloped.

The average share of the service sector in middle-income countries in 2003 hovered around 54 per cent (Heston and Sinclair 2008), but China's lagged well below that figure with only 43 per cent of GDP. Thus it seems China has not shaken off its legacy of preferential development of industry. While the agricultural sector's relative contribution to GDP growth declined from 41.7 per cent in 1990 to only 6.5 per cent in 2008, that of industry and the services increased accordingly (Table 17.6). The industry's contribution to GDP growth actually increased with the reforms and peaked at 64 per cent in 1995, but declined since then to 50.6 per cent in 2008. The contribution of the service sector grew steadily as well, but remained in second place with 42.9 per cent in 2008. Thus recent growth is mainly industry-led.

In the early phase of the reforms the government's policy to rectify the imbalance in the industrial sector by promoting the development of light industries met with some success, as evidenced from the equal share in GDP of both light and heavy industries in 1990 as Table 17.7 shows. However, since then China's preference for the development of heavy industries re-emerged, and in 2008 the share of heavy industry reached 71 per cent which was even higher than at the beginning of the reforms. Thus there is no doubt that GDP growth since 1990 was heavily industry-led.

Table 17.7   The share of light and heavy industry in China's industrial output (%)

Year	Light industry	Heavy industry
1978	43.1	56.9
1985	47.4	52.6
1990	49.4	50.6
1995	47.3	52.7
2000	39.8	60.2
2005	31.1	68.9
2008	28.9	71.1

Source: SSB (annually).

Table 17.8   Shares and growth contribution of household consumption (C) and government consumption (G), gross capital formation (I) and net exports (X – M) in China's GDP (%)

	1979	1985	1990	1995	2000	2005
1. Share in GDP						
C	49.6	51.1	48.6	45.2	44.8	38.6
G	14.4	14.1	14.1	14.2	15.2	14.2
I	36.4	35.4	37.0	38.8	37.1	41.9
$X - M$	−0.4	−0.6	0.3	1.8	2.9	5.3
2. Growth contribution						
$C + G$	66.1	62.6	54.9	51.6	51.8	40.1
I	36.0	38.8	31.2	41.6	36.2	47.5
$X - M$	−2.1	−3.4	13.9	6.8	11.9	12.4

Note: Figures are based on 7-year moving averages of GDP and annual growth contribution (3-year average for 1979).

Source: SSB (annually).

On the demand side, GDP is made up of personal consumption, C, and government consumption, G, of gross capital formation, I, and net exports $(X - M)$. Their shares in, and relative contributions to, China's GDP are presented in Table 17.8. It shows that on the eve of the reforms in 1979 personal consumption made up nearly 50 per cent of GDP, and its share was larger than that of investment. The contribution of net exports was actually negative at minus 0.4 per cent. The immediate effect of the reform was to increase further the share of personal consumption, and produce a decline in investments. However, in 1990 the trend started to reverse and the share of personal consumption declined and that of investments increased again. In 2005 the latter exceeded the share of personal consumption. Table 17.8 also shows the increasing importance of external demand – that is, of net exports – in the course of the reforms. It grew from a negative value to almost 5 per cent in 2005.

The share of personal consumption in China's GDP in 2005 at 38.6 per cent was relatively low compared to other middle-income countries, where it averaged 58 per cent in 2003 (Heston and Sicular 2008). And conversely the share of investments in China at 41.9 per cent was well above the average 26 per cent in other middle-income countries.

In terms of growth contribution the popular hypothesis that the Chinese economy in recent years was export-led cannot be confirmed. Throughout the reform period the growth in domestic demand (due to consumption and investment) has provided the main impetus for GDP growth. As mentioned, the growth contribution of net exports was negative in the initial years of the reform, but turned positive and grew to 12.4 per cent in 2005. However, it is still relatively modest compared to the growth contribution of domestic demand. And as Table 17.8 shows, the role of consumption in recent years has increasingly been overshadowed by that of investments. Thus China's economic growth is increasingly investment-led.

The persistence of the investment-led growth pattern during the reforms can be attributed to the fact that China during this period was still a labour-surplus economy and, therefore, shares some of Japan's structural features in its high economic growth period (Minami 1994). As in Japan, surplus labour in China causes wage (w) increases to lag behind those of labour productivity (AP) and leads to a decline in labour's share of income ($\pi = w/AP$). This in turn leads to an increase in the rate of savings since the rate of savings from non-wage income is higher than that from wage income. At the same time, as the share of labour (π) falls, the rate of return on capital ($r = (1 - \pi)\ Y/K$) increases and stimulates investment by raising the expected rate of return of capital. Thus a decline in labour's share stimulated both savings and investments and, hence, economic growth.

The declining share of labour in China's GDP is evident from the Organisation for Economic Co-operation and Development (OECD 2010) data which show that the share of compensation of employees in GDP fell from 50 per cent in 1993–97 to only 48 per cent in 2003–07. In the same period the rate of gross domestic saving rose from 37 to 47 per cent and even reached 51 per cent in 2008 (OECD 2010). This is an exceptionally high rate by international standards since the average rate of domestic savings for other middle-income countries stood at only 28 per cent in 2003 (Heston and Sicular 2008).

THE STANDARD OF LIVING

One way of getting an idea of the increased material welfare of a country or its standard of living is by measuring the growth of per capita GDP. In China this averaged 4 per cent in the pre-reform period but more than doubled to 8.6 per cent in the reform period between 1978 and 2008. Thus reforms contributed significantly to the welfare of people in the People's Republic of China (PRC). However, compared with other countries China still has a long way to go before it catches up with the standard of living of advanced countries. In 2005 its per capita GDP, measured at purchasing power parity, was only US$6600 (World Bank, *World Development Report* 2007). This is equivalent to only 15 per cent that of the US, 21 per cent that of Japan and 30 per cent of South Korea's standard of living (Brandt and Rawski 2008).

Following Perkins and Rawski's (2008) relatively optimistic forecast instead of that of Maddison (2007), China's per capita income will reach US$31 123 in 2030 (Table 17.9), but this will still only be less than half of that of the US and about three-quarters of Japan's.

However, GDP is only a rough measure of consumers' welfare since it includes items such as capital formation, taxation, corporate reserves, military expenditure and others which do not constitute per capita income. The private consumption per capita is a much more precise indicator of the standard of living, and according to official statistics this grew at an annual average rate of 7.6 per cent from 1979 to 2009. Thus it increased almost four times faster than it had done in the pre-reform period (1952–75) when it had reached only 2 per cent per annum (Perkins and Rawski

Table 17.9   *Projection of China's growth of per capita income, 2005–30 (US$ at 2005 prices)*

	Per capita GDP, 2005	Projected per capita GDP, 2030	Projected rate of growth, 2005–30 (%)
China	6 600	31 123	6.4
USA	42 038	64 072	1.7
Japan	30 986	42 796	1.3

Note: GDP in relative purchasing power.

Sources: Perkins and Rawski (2008) and Maddison (2007).

*Table 17.10   Coverage of durable consumer goods in China, 1981 and
              2008 (ownership per 100 households)*

	Urban areas 1980–81	2008	Rural areas 1980–81	2008
Air conditioner	0.1 (1985)	100.3	n.a.	9.8
Car	0.3	8.8	n.a.	n.a.
Colour TV	0.6	132.9	0.4	99.2
Washing Machine	6.3	94.7	1.9 (1985)	49.1
Refrigerator	0.2	93.6	0.1 (1985)	30.2
Motorcycle	n.a.	21.4	0.9 (1985)	52.5
Computer	5.9 (1999)	59.3	n.a.	5.4

Source: SSB (annually).

2008). Nevertheless, OECD statistics (2010) show that even in terms of relative purchasing power China's private consumption per capita in 2008 was way behind that of other OECD countries. It amounted to only one-tenth of the average, and between one-fifth and one-quarter that of other low-income countries in the OECD.

However, improvements in the standard of living of China's population show up vividly in the dramatic change of consumption patterns. The proportion of consumption expenditure on foodstuffs is known as the Engel coefficient. According to international norms a country is considered poor when the Engel coefficient is between 50 and 59 per cent, and moderately comfortable when it is between 40 and 50 per cent. China's Engel coefficient for urban households has declined steeply, from 56.7 per cent in 1981 to 37.9 per cent in 2008. However, the decrease was less for rural households where it amounted to 59.7 and 43.7 per cent, respectively (Chai 1992 ; SSB 2010). Thus by international standards China's private consumption level is currently considered as moderately comfortable.

Another significant improvement has been in the area of housing, which in 1978 for urban areas was only 6.7 square metres, and 8.1 for rural areas, measured in terms of gross living space per person. By 2006, these figures had quadrupled and shot up to 27.1 and 30.7 square metres for urban and rural households, respectively.

The consumption of durable consumer goods, such as air conditioners, colour TVs, refrigerators and washing machines, has also risen considerably. Their coverage in 2008 reached almost 100 per cent for urban households (see Table 17.10) and the coverage of computers in cities reached almost 50 per cent. However, car ownership was still limited to

8.8 per cent of urban households. The picture for rural households is not as rosy, for their coverage of durable consumer goods still lagged behind that of their urban counterparts. Thus, while in 2008 all rural households had a colour TV, only half had a washing machine. And consumer goods such as air conditioners, refrigerators and computers were still relatively scarce in China's countryside. Nevertheless, on the whole the higher level of ownership of durable consumer goods indicates a significant reduction of the burden on householders, and potentially increases their leisure time and welfare. It also allows more housewives to join the labour force. While the standard of living of China's rural people still lags behind that of their urban counterparts, their colour TVs provide a considerable source of pleasure for them.

INCOME DISTRIBUTION

A country's economic welfare depends not only on its absolute level of income but also on how the income is distributed, as the same national income distributed more equally means more welfare. The two standard measures of income distribution are absolute and relative inequality. The former measures the rate of poverty defined as the percentage of the population living below the poverty line. And it is in this respect that China's progress is very impressive. According to an estimate by the World Bank using a $1 a day poverty line based on income, the rate of poverty in China declined from 2 per cent in 1981 to 0.3 per cent in 2001 in urban areas. This means that poverty has been practically eradicated in China's cities. However, it remains an issue in rural areas, where the rate was reduced from 79.4 per cent in 1980 to 26.5 per cent in 2001 (Heston and Sicular 2008), indicating that a little more than a quarter of China's rural population is still steeped in absolute poverty. However, if official Chinese figures are to be believed, the rate of rural poverty based on China's official poverty line had declined to only 1.6 per cent in 2007 (SSB 2010).

While the level of absolute poverty has declined over the reform period, relative inequality has increased with development. There are no reliable data for the income distribution for the whole nation since data sets are separated into those for rural and urban households only. However, Chotikapanich et al. (2007) developed a method to transform rural and urban income distribution data into a single continuous national distribution set. Using this, the OECD (2010) estimated the national Gini coefficients for China as shown in Table 17.11.

These estimates show how inequality in China has risen sharply since 1985. From 0.237 in 1985, the national Gini coefficient rose to 0.41 in

Table 17.11   National, rural and urban Gini coefficients, 1985–2007

Year	Rural	Urban	National
1985	0.233494	0.169039	0.237013
1986	0.240261	0.171872	0.250169
1987	0.307624	0.172556	0.297232
1988	0.315373	0.180528	0.300288
1989	0.319982	0.185821	0.311918
1990	0.304181	0.182873	0.300667
1991	0.311831	0.173148	0.310758
1992	0.312055	0.191272	0.319033
1993	0.312384	0.210960	0.332154
1994	0.294804	0.222191	0.328113
1995	0.351344	0.215004	0.345232
1996	0.344369	0.220449	0.336186
1997	0.337395	0.225894	0.327139
1998	0.333541	0.233638	0.328507
1999	0.341841	0.240317	0.340521
2000	0.352345	0.252784	0.354256
2001	0.358282	0.263956	0.365129
2002	0.358612	0.317929	0.390878
2003	0.362299	0.326976	0.401744
2004	0.349260	0.335548	0.404414
2005	0.348705	0.340870	0.410143
2006	0.345396	0.337605	0.409229
2007	0.338519	0.334467	0.407752

Source: OECD (2010).

2005, which reflects a high level of inequality and is similar to that of the US (OECD 2010). The source of the rising inequality was previously identified as the growing rural–urban inequality and regional stratification (World Bank 1997). However, recent studies argue that previously the rural–urban income differences had been overestimated, for two reasons (Sicular et al. 2007; OECD 2010). They have ignored sizeable cost of living differences between urban and rural areas, and also they did not fully capture the number of migrant workers in urban areas. Once these factors are taken into account the importance of spatial inequality and its contribution to overall inequality is reduced. Thus, it is argued, the main cause of inequality lies in the greater intra-rural and intra-urban inequality, which is in turn determined by the difference in factor endowments and their return to rural and urban households.

However, there are indications that inequality in China may have reached its peak and is now in the process of declining, as predicted by the Kuznets inverted u-curve. For example, the Gini coefficient for rural households rose from 0.23 in 1985 to 0.36 in 2003 and then started to decline. It stood at 0.34 in 2007. Similarly, the urban Gini coefficient peaked at 0.34 in 2005, up from the initial 0.17 in 1985, and has started to decrease since then. As a result, the national Gini coefficient also began to stabilize around 2005 and dropped to 0.407 in 2007. However, this optimistic view may not be warranted as it is based on official household income data which, as mentioned in Chapter 15, generally underestimate the degree of income inequality because of the existence of undeclared hidden and 'grey' income which mostly belongs to the upper classes.

Besides the material welfare it is the quality of life which impacts on people's welfare. However, these qualitative aspects can not be directly measured but must be inferred indirectly from indicators such as health, education standard, availability and accessibility of social security, and environmental factors such as population density, pollution and environmental degradation. In the following I will examine just a few of these. The United Nations considers any improvement in people's longevity and knowledge as basic indicators of human development. In respect to these, China's performance in the pre-reform period was most impressive due to Mao's socialist, broad-based development strategy which emphasized the equal availability of health care and education facilities to rural and urban households.

In the reform period the average life expectancy continued to rise from 64 years in 1979 and stood at 73 years in 2007 according to the United Nations Development Programme (UNDP) *Human Development Report* (2009). The same was true for the adult literacy rate, which increased from 66 per cent in 1979 to 93.3 per cent in 2007.

SOCIAL SECURITY

The extent of social security is another important factor in assessing the welfare of a nation. As previously discussed, the system of social security prior to reform was financed by communes in rural areas and by urban enterprises in the cities. This largely protected the population from financial insecurity due to inflation, unemployment, industrial accidents, illness, old age and so on. This system disintegrated with the reforms and leaves social security patchy since a new state-financed social security system is yet to be fully established. Thus the Chinese workers, and peasants especially, are caught in the descending part of the u-curve of the relationship between social security and economic growth, a phenomenon which has also been observed in the development of market economies.

The safety net for the sick faltered during the reforms, and the section of the population hit the hardest was, of course, the people in rural areas. Since the rural safety net relied on the village collective which was financed from farmers' contributions, the amount of money spent on it fell when the income of the collective declined. Thus the rural safety system collapsed, and in the second half of the 1990s half of all village clinics had become private enterprises relying on fees for income (OECD 2010).

In contrast, the system of enterprise-based health care was in the course of the reforms replaced by the basic medical insurance scheme for urban workers (BMIUW) which was financed by contributions from employers and employees. However, its coverage was limited and in 2005 extended to just over 40 per cent of the urban working population. The result was that sick people had to pay a greater share of up to 60 per cent of their medical expenses. The medical insurance situation in China in 2000 was in fact so bad that the World Health Organization (WHO) rated China's health financing system as one of the most inequitable ones in the world, assigning it a rank of 188 out of a total of 191 countries (OECD 2010).

Such a sharp rise in the cost of health services led to misery and considerable decrease in access, with many people not seeking medical treatment when they needed it. In 2007, 38 per cent of the sick were not treated and 70 per cent refused hospitalization despite a referral (Ministry of Health 2009). The government finally rolled out three new medical insurance schemes to rectify the situation. These were the New Rural Cooperative Medical Scheme (NRCMS), the Basic Medical Insurance Scheme for Urban Residents (BMIUR) and the Medical Assistance Program (MA). The NRCMS aimed to provide medical cover for the rural population and BMIUR does the same for the urban population; it covers those that do not benefit from an enterprise scheme. Both are voluntary health insurances financed from contributions by the government and individuals. The MA scheme provides medical benefits for those who receive the minimum living allowance. These schemes together significantly improved and strengthened the safety net and increased the national coverage rate from 20 per cent in 2005 to 80 per cent in 2008. At the same time, the contributions of the sick to their own medical expenses declined from 60 per cent in 2001 to 45 per cent in 2007 (OECD 2010).

While these changes improved the accessibility to health care facilities, the contributions from individuals remain relatively high and China still faces important challenges in this area. The current rate of reimbursement remains relatively small in relation to annual health care expenses for the individual. And the system does not work as well in practice as it is designed to, for patients are paid less than half of the benefits they are entitled to receive, and the proportion of reimbursement declines with the seriousness of an illness (OECD 2010). Thus, those that are worst-off health-wise are also worst off in reimbursements, a factor which markedly increases inequality. In addition, migrant workers living in cities are still not covered by any medical insurance scheme and it is known that many factories employing them do not take particular care to ensure industrial health and safety.

Another part of the population hit hard by structural changes resulting from the reforms were the elderly in rural areas, who had previously been taken care of by the village communes. With their collapse, the elderly could only rely on the traditional system of insurance, namely their family or the land, often with little success. While there was an attempt to organize a rural pension scheme in the form of voluntary saving accounts, the balance of which could be converted into an annuity at age 60, it was not popular and only had a low coverage rate (OECD 2010). In 2009 a new rural pension scheme was rolled out which consists of two parts. One is a flat-rate scheme funded from general taxes which is designed to provide the participant with a pension equivalent to the value of 25 per cent of the average rural per capita household income. The other part is a voluntary contribution scheme which provides 10 per cent of the average rural household income in the area of the participants. This scheme has started to take hold and is expected to progress slowly and to cover all rural households by 2020.

The elderly in urban areas have been more fortunate than their rural counterparts because the urban enterprise-based pension system which paid 80 per cent of the average wage was retained under the reforms. It was only dismantled in the 1990s when state-owned enterprises (SOEs) were forced to downsize and shed surplus workers. And in 1997 the government introduced a new urban employee pension scheme which shifted the responsibility from the retiree's former enterprise to the local government (OECD 2010). This gave rise to thousands of separate pension schemes with different rates of contributions and benefits, by which local governments tried to evade their full responsibility. Nationally the contribution rate averaged only 18.6 per cent in 2003, according to an estimate by the OECD. The coverage rate had been higher, at 48 per cent in 1998. After 2003 it rose again and reached 61 per cent in 2007, but its coverage is still mainly confined to the formal urban sector. The overall rate of coverage of retirement benefits in urban areas is much lower because domestic private enterprises (which would tend to pay less for retirees than state-run enterprises) and migrant workers are largely excluded from these statistics (OECD 2010).

ENVIRONMENTAL PROTECTION

The size of China's population leads to a very high population density with many urban areas comprising 10 million or more people, and a 'town' with 6 million people is considered medium-sized. The high population density has a considerable impact on the quality of life with a minimum of private space and *Lebensraum* at a premium. The high population density together with economic growth based on heavy industry take a high toll on the environment and lead to considerable pollution. China's natural endowments, such as the water level, are highly strained and sinking fast, and environmental degradation is a real threat to the quality of life for China's people as well as for its flora and fauna.

In the pre-reform period the main cause of China's environmental degradation was systemic inefficiency because the planning system lacked any concept of property rights of natural resources, such as clean air, water, forest resources and so on. They were allocated to households as 'free goods' which caused their overuse, depletion and/or deterioration. Enterprises were motivated to fulfil a physical planned output target without due regard to cost and efficiency in the use of resources, let alone environmental deterioration, and they thus used natural resources excessively. This is evident from the high energy and resource intensity of China's GDP which was in general two to three times higher than that of its Asian neighbours. For example, energy consumption per unit of GDP in 1979 in China was 2.7 times higher than that of India (Chai 1990).

The lopsided industrial structure was another important cause of China's environmental problems in the pre-reform era, for the preferential development of heavy industries emphasized the capital- and resource-intensive industries at the expense of light industries and the service sector. Since heavy industries such as iron and steel, metal, chemical and petroleum processing are in general among the most polluting industries, their growth also made China dirtier and more polluted.

While environmental discharge fees were introduced in the late 1970s at the beginning of the reforms, environmental issues did not really catch the attention of the government until the early 1980s. In 1984 China set up its first Environmental Protection Commission at the national level with similar institutions at the local level. It also enacted a large number of laws and regulations dealing with environmental protection, and the environmental discharge fees have gradually been extended and strengthened (Tisdell 1997).

The government's efforts to reduce pollution centred on energy conservation and efficiency. In the period covered by the 11th Five-Year Plan (FYP) (2006–10), energy intensity was to be reduced by 20 per cent, and in 2009 the government announced that it would aim at reducing carbon dioxide (CO_2) emissions per unit of GDP by 2020 by as much as 40 to 45 per cent of the 2005 level (OECD, 2010). In order to achieve this target the government initiated new policies which include measures to close down inefficient and outdated energy-intensive industries, the decentralization of polluting industries away from urban centres, a ban on leaded petrol, stringent new emission requirements for cars, subsidies for energy saving products which flow to consumers, and emission trading, as well as the development of new energies, such as solar, wind, nuclear and hydroelectric power (Roumasset et al. 2008; OECD 2010).

So far China's attempts to control pollution have not met with unqualified success, though some reduction in pollution has been achieved and, for example, the pollution intensities of China's manufacturing industries have been significantly reduced (Chai 2004). Between 1993 and 2009 China's energy intensity per unit of GDP has likewise been significantly reduced, at an average rate of 3.6 per cent per annum, or cut by almost one-half over the whole period. Other studies, such as Roumasset et al. (2008) and Rawski and Sheng (2008), also confirm that air pollution in China's major cities has been significantly reduced in recent years.

On the other hand, China's emission of greenhouse gases (in terms of CO_2) has increased rapidly since the 1980s, in line with the climbing standard of living and increases in the number of households with consumer durables such as refrigerators, air conditioners and cars. In the late 1980s China ranked third in the world in terms of CO_2 emissions, behind the USA and the former Soviet Union (Tisdell 1997). However, with the rapid increase in car ownership, the main emitter of CO_2, estimates indicate that China had already become the largest CO_2 emitter in 2006 (OECD 2010). And these emissions are forecast to increase dramatically in the future when car ownership spreads from urban to rural households.

It also needs to be mentioned that there has been little improvement in water pollution in China and that the government as yet has not addressed this problem systematically. Most of China's coastal waters and many of its major rivers, such as the Yangzi, are heavily polluted. And in general surface water tends to be polluted and even groundwater is contaminated (Economy 2004), due mainly to industrial wastewater, especially in the urban centres. These pollutants include nitrates, sulphates, arsenic and cyanide. Municipal sewerage is the other main contributor to urban water pollution. In rural areas the main source of water pollution results from the use of pesticides and chemicals in agriculture. The heavy use of fertilizers also impacts on water quality by leaching nitrates into groundwater and through run-off into streams. Another major contribution to water pollution comes from China's township- and village-owned enterprises (TVEs) which often are set up along river banks, employ outdated technology, and produce a lot of industrial wastewater which is only inadequately treated before it is flushed into the river system.

Thus the results of China's environmental policies are rather mixed for several reasons, one of which is that it is still a transitional economy where decision-making has been decentralized from the central to regional and local levels but where price signals for decision-making are not yet fully effective, though they are becoming so. On the other hand, property rights in China for most resources are ill-defined, with the consequence that common resources such as air and water have no price or are under-priced. The inadequate regulation of ownership rights coupled with the underpricing of key resources, such as energy, land and other natural resources, encourages their overuse and leads to a lack of maintenance and conservation.

Secondly, due to funding constraints, declining budget revenues and competing demand for scarce capital, the government's budget for environmental protection is rather limited. In the period from 1991 to 2005 it allocated less than 1 per cent of China's GDP for the cleaning-up of the country's polluted environment (Chai and Roy 2006; Perkins and Rawski 2008). In addition, charges and fines imposed on polluters are fairly low and amounted to only a few percentage points of China's annual industrial output. Thus they do not function as a deterrent and made little difference for management decision-making.

Thirdly, since most of the key industrial enterprises are still under government control the government is both the principal polluter and the environmental regulator. Thus it is very difficult for environmental regulators to carry out a review of SOEs or to oppose their practices. For example, the Ministries of Construction, Land and Resources, and Agriculture regularly overrule the decisions of the less powerful State Environmental Protection Agency (SEPA) when projects are in danger of being slowed down due to land use and/or emissions regulations (Roberts 2004).

Fourthly, the greater autonomy of local governments also increases the difficulties SEPA faces in enforcing its regulations. For example, pollution-intensive factories facing stiff new anti-pollution laws in the rich coastal regions often shifted their manufacturing plants to the poor inland regions of China where authorities are more concerned about jobs and tax revenues than the environment (Roberts 2004).

Finally, as mentioned earlier, China's bias towards the preferential development of heavy industries continued through the reforms. Since heavy industries are intensive users of energy and natural resources, this strategy took a heavy toll on China's environment while the cleaner service industries remain relatively underdeveloped.

NATIONAL WELFARE ACCOUNTING

Considering the effects of the standard of living, health, education, income equality, social security and the impact of environment pollution, it is possible to assess how the rapid growth during 1979–2009 has affected the welfare of its people. Net national welfare (NNW) accounting is an attempt to do this quantitatively by taking account of both the beneficial and detrimental aspects of growth. It measures consumption expenditures plus an imputed wage for leisure and the value of services stemming from ownership of consumer durables. From this it subtracts the imputed costs of increased income inequality, social insecurity and environmental pollution.

So far, no estimate of China's NNW is available. But there is no doubt that its per capita level is lower than that of per capita GDP because of the overwhelming detrimental effects of environmental pollution, social insecurity and income inequality. It is, however, unlikely that the growth of NNW per capita lags far behind that of per capita GDP since China has made attempts to rein in the detrimental effects of pollution, and to increase social security and reduce income inequality. Especially in respect to the last two, China has had some success in recent years, so that the growth rate of NNW per capita can be expected to increase and overtake that of per capita GDP. Hence, there is little doubt that the welfare of the Chinese people has improved significantly due to the government's efforts to exploit China's growth potential and to reduce the harm caused by rapid economic growth. This can be illustrated by the partial estimate of China's 'Green GNP' (gross national product) attempted by Roumasset et al. (2008). The partial green net national product (NNP) is estimated from the NNP by adjusting its natural resource depletion (for energy, minerals and forest) from the Net National Product (NNP). However, it does not take pollution into account. The results are shown in Table 17.12 which indicates that in 1975 China's partially adjusted green NNP stood at US$149.4 per capita, which was only 87 per cent of its NNP per capita. It was lower because of the detrimental effect of natural resource deple-tion. In the period from 1975 to 1980 it grew by 3.2 per cent and remained lower than the growth rate of NNP because of the inefficiency in the use of natural resources. However, since 1980 the pattern has reversed with its growth of accelerating 8.8 per cent faster than that of NNP per capita, leading to a narrowing of its difference with NNP. Therefore, if China increases its efforts to rein in the detrimental effects of economic growth, especially of environmental degradation, the welfare of China's people will be improved.

Table 17.12   Partial estimate of China's green net national product per capita (in 2004 US dollars)

Year	NNP per capita	PGNNP per capita
1975	172.2	149.4
1980	216.7	175.3
1985	273.1	231.3
1990	361.1	327.6
1995	589.5	530.0
2000	838.5	810.8

Note: Estimates based on moving 10-year averages with the exception of 2000 which is a 3-year average.

Source: Roumasset et al. (2008).

SUMMARY

China's reforms doubled the previous economic growth rate to almost 10 per cent per annum, topping that of all its East Asian neighbours in their high economic growth period. And while China's growth in the pre-reform period was largely capital-intensive, with capital accumulation accounting for well over half of its growth, the effect of the reforms has been to improve productivity growth significantly. Nevertheless, China's economic development remains relatively capital-intensive with capital accumulation still accounting for nearly 50 per cent of GDP growth. The major driving forces of productivity growth were the exploitation of previously unexploited technology in the non-state sector combined with the open door policy and reforms introduced by the government. A secondary generator of greater productivity growth was the relocation of labour away from the agricultural sector, and within the non-agricultural sector away from the state to the private sector.

The rapid growth enabled China to regain its world number one ranking that it held at the beginning of the nineteenth century because of the size of its population. In 2010 China overtook Japan as the second-largest economy and it is expected to overtake the USA by 2030. Nonetheless, a huge gap in technology and the standard of living will have to be bridged even by then.

The structural changes in China during 1979–2009 reflect its dual characteristics as a transition and labour-surplus economy. Industry, especially the oversized heavy industry, dominated the economic structure on the supply side, whereas the service sector remains relatively undeveloped. On the demand side economic growth continues to be investment-led and the share of wage income and consumption in GDP remains relatively low compared to other countries at a similar stage of development. On the other hand, the share of savings in China's GDP is exceptionally high with the rate of savings tending to exceed that of investments, resulting in the growing current account surplus, which in turn contributes to China's growing trade conflict with the USA.

The rapid economic growth has both detrimental and beneficial effects on the welfare of the Chinese populace. Both the real and per capita income as well as consumption have increased rapidly during 1979–2009 with much higher growth rates than in the past. While the increase in consumption per capita remains lower than the increase in per capita income consumption, patterns have changed, causing a fall in the Engel's coefficient, an increase in housing space per capita and greater coverage of households with consumer durables. The quality of life has also improved with the increase in average life expectancy and the virtual eradication of illiteracy.

However, rapid growth has also produced significant harmful effects for the welfare of the Chinese people, with a greater inequality of income distribution, more social insecurity and massive environmental pollution. Though the government has recognized these problems and has taken measured to address them, some measures have met with less success than others. The safety net for rural and urban residents has been strengthened with provisions for the unemployed, elderly and the sick. Both the income inequality and environmental pollution have been stabilized in recent years and, with some optimism, one can hope that they appear to have reached the turning point of the Kuznets inverted u-curve. Thus 30 years of reform have propelled China into a leading world economy and have significantly improved the people's standard of living, though this remains low in international comparison. Nevertheless, the effects of economic development have significantly improved the welfare of the Chinese populace and outweigh the detrimental effects. Nevertheless the extent of China's pollution and water shortage, if not better controlled, may adversely impact on the health and welfare of its people and limit future economic growth.

18. China's modern economic growth: retrospect and prospect

CHINA'S ECONOMIC GROWTH IN RETROSPECT

China's past can roughly be divided into two major periods. The first, which lasted up to about 1300, had seen growth in both gross domestic product (GDP) and GDP per capita, with the highest growth phase being the Song period (960–1279) when China ranked highest in the world in terms of both criteria. In the second phase, from 1300 onward, China's GDP growth continued and remained the largest in the world in absolute terms, but per capita income stagnated and after roughly 500 years of relative decline it amounted to only half that of Western European countries in the 1820s.

Since the pre-modern economy was dominated by agriculture, the development of China's traditional economy can be analysed in terms of agricultural output growth, which is mainly determined by increase in the yield of land and increase in land availability per capita. Before the 1300s land availability was an important factor because in this period China expanded from the core settlement area in the North China plain to all other areas of the country. Thus the area of land available for cultivation increased considerably over time. However, by far the most important determinant of growth was the rise of China's agricultural productivity, which was much higher than that of Europe at the time. The reason was that China utilized better technologies and had better institutions and government policies.

In the Song period the shift of the population to the South with the addition of land in a warmer climate enabled Chinese farmers to increase the acreage planted with high-yield varieties of crops. It also enabled farmers to introduce from abroad new varieties of seeds with a shorter growth period. This allowed them to use land much more intensively and increased the cropping index. Furthermore, the availability of cheap water transport in the South spurred the development of the market, which facilitated specialization, which in turn contributed to the increase in yield of Song agriculture. Finally, the role of the Song government was important, too. It is credited with being one of the first governments in the world to have recognized the importance of rural development and adopted an integrated approach towards it.

In the second phase of pre-modern growth total output kept increasing but per capita output stagnated. During that time land availability per capita was almost halved since the expansion of the Chinese empire slowed down and the growth in available farmland was only half that of the population growth. Land productivity increased slowly and only at a rate which just offset the declining rate of land availability per capita. Thus per capita output stagnated. The relatively slower increase of land productivity in this period compared to the earlier time was mainly due to the lack of technological change, and most of the yield increase was due to more intensive methods, for example a greater application of labour and capital per unit of land.

Pre-modern economic growth was also accompanied by structural change, although this happened only slowly. Improved farm productivity made for a greater agricultural surplus and supported a greater part of the population in non-agricultural employment. Thus, specialization, urbanization and the development of crafts, especially traditional handicraft industries, and trade were facilitated. And the necessity to exchange between these three parts of the population triggered the development of commercial trade.

However, an agrarian economy has structural limitations which make it difficult to sustain economic growth. Why China failed to industrialize after it hit the brick wall of pre-modern growth has been the subject of much debate. The absence of modern science and technology in traditional China is not a sufficient reason to explain this failure, since China had a lot of scientific discoveries and inventions available which it passed on to the world, such as gunpowder, paper printing, the compass and so on. It can be argued that China did not invent labour-saving machines because it had surplus labour, but that argument is not convincing either. The major stumbling blocks to innovation and economic change in traditional China stemmed from two other reasons, namely from the weak institution of property rights and from a lack of productive entrepreneurs. The latter is due to the biased incentive structure of Chinese traditional society which favoured the allocation of entrepreneurial activities to unproductive pursuits such as rent-seeking instead of innovation.

When the Western countries intruded into China in the mid-nineteenth century, China was jolted out of its traditional economic stagnation for it was forced to open to foreign trade and investments. It carried out a few reforms and tried to catch up with the West, however, modern economic growth (MEG) did not set in until 100 years later, in 1952. The period from the mid-nineteenth to the mid-twentieth centuries is known as the

Period of Great (political) Disturbance, and in it the economy was always in dire straits. China's economy grew slowly and steadily and a little faster than did China's population, allowing for a modest increase in the living standard of the majority of its people.

Economic growth in this period was still in the traditional pattern, fuelled by vigorous growth in agricultural output. This was possible because of a shift in cropping patterns away from grains to higher-yield and higher-value cash crops. The greater commercialization of agriculture was triggered by an improvement in the terms of trade for agricultural products and a greater demand for them. Its main driving force was the growth of the non-agricultural sector and the growing urbanization and industrialization after China's opening to the West. The traditional handicraft industries held their own even with stiffer competition from foreign imports and from the domestic modern manufacturing industries, and even grew due to stronger domestic and foreign demand. Since they were able to absorb a large pool of surplus labour, their wage costs and prices remained relatively low and the traditional crafts remained competitive.

If sources of growth in this period are divided into domestic and foreign ones, the former are actually more important than the latter, for foreign trade grew only slowly, and its contribution to growth was relatively smaller than those of consumption and investment. Its biggest contribution was probably in forcing China's economy to change its structure into the form of catch-up industrialization based on the 'flying geese' pattern. The most important contribution of foreign investment in China's pre-war economy was that it triggered the development of China's modern sector and the country's ensuing industrialization.

The modern industrial sector grew especially rapidly in the period from 1914–18 to 1931–36, due to the First World War which disrupted the supply of foreign imports and increased the competitiveness of China's modern industries against imports due to a currency depreciation and the restoration of China's tariff autonomy. Japanese investments in Manchuria (which Japan had occupied and annexed in 1931) also significantly enhanced the growth of China's modern industry. However, its contribution to China's GDP remained insignificant because of its small size. Since economic growth in this phase largely resulted from the expansion of the traditional sector (agriculture, handicrafts and traditional service industries) it is a debatable point that MEG did not take place in China until the second half of the twentieth century.

Comparing the transition of China's and Japan's economy to MEG, the Japanese experience seems to have been far swifter and smoother. The reason lies in its different capacity to adopt and absorb modern technology – a key determinant for the rate of transition of latecomers to industrialization. It seems that Japan at the eve of its industrialization in the late nineteenth century was more ready for MEG.

Having missed the boat of rapid transition to MEG in the last century, and having re-established itself as the People's Republic of China after the Second World War, China in 1949 did not continue along the capitalist path of MEG but decided to leapfrog and enter directly into the socialist stage of MEG as envisaged by Karl Marx. Under its outspoken leader and chairman of the Chinese Communist Party, Mao Zedong, China pursued for the next three decades the twin objectives of rapid economic growth and socialization. Thus it initially closely followed the development model of the former Soviet Union, which envisaged economic growth by way of a high rate of capital accumulation and gave priority to heavy industries. This went together with a system of state-controlled resource allocation, known as central planning.

However, from the late 1950s on China's development strategy departed significantly from the Soviet model when Mao launched the Great Leap Forward (GLF), which in essence was a radical variant of the Soviet strategy. It aimed at simultaneous economic development and implementing structural change to realize a socialist society, both at maximum speed. To achieve the first Mao mobilized China's abundant resource of surplus labour by forming communes and putting the rural labour force to work on construction and irrigation projects. He also promoted labour-intensive cultivation techniques in agriculture in order to increase its surplus, from which industrialization was to be financed. Small-scale, labour-intensive rural-based industries were promoted in the GLF to boost industrial output.

Mao rejected the Soviet approach of sequential development of socialism, which gave preference to the development of the 'productive forces' in Marxist jargon over that of 'production relations'. He proposed instead the concurrent development of the forces and relations of production because he held – in contrast to orthodox Marxism – that the development of the productive relations would not hamper but facilitate the development of the productive forces. Thus he believed that communism could be realized even in the early stages of MEG.

The GLF did not fulfil Mao's expectations but led instead to the worst famine ever, with a total death toll of between 48 and 76 million people. It sowed the seed for the Great Cultural Revolution during which the country descended into civil war and the People's Liberation Army (PLA) had to be brought in to restore order.

Nevertheless, China under Mao did achieve rapid industrialization and MEG, and quickly caught up with the West in terms of its military (defensive) prowess. And in spite of the ups and downs of the GLF and the Cultural Revolution (CR), it improved its score on the human development index in terms of extending the average life expectancy and raising the rate of adult literacy. But these results, impressive as they were, were achieved at high cost. The standard of living was very low and remained stagnant because MEG was achieved by a massive build-up of capital stock without a corresponding increase in total factor productivity. All in all, the Maoist experiments cost China 30 years in lost opportunities to narrow the gap in the standard of living and technology between China and the West and Japan.

The failure of Mao's experimental strategies produced a backlash against the socialist development model. Thus the second generation of leaders, with Deng Xiaoping and Zhao Ziyang, took the decisive step to change the course of China's economic history and in 1978 started China on the path of capitalist development, following the steps of Japan and other East Asian countries. Their two-pronged strategy undid most of the Maoist legacy and started China on a gradual approach to transition from a planned to a market economy. This occurred relatively smoothly and was successfully implemented, with the single exception of the Tiananmen student protest in 1989 which threatened China's political, social and economic stability.

China's new leaders were no less ambitious than Mao and tried to catch up with the West as fast as possible. In order to make up for the three lost decades under Mao they tried to promulgate intensive economic growth based on growth of per capita income rather than that of GDP. To achieve this objective the controversial population control policy in the form of restricting families to have only one child was introduced. The government also emphasized the importance of increasing total factor productivity as an additional source of growth. In order to boost the latter, an export-oriented strategy was introduced to enable China to participate in the international division of labour and to exploit its comparative advantage, cheap labour. To accelerate the rate of technical progress, imports of foreign technology and foreign direct investment (FDI) were encouraged in the expectation that they would enhance China's capacity to borrow foreign technology. Finally, China stepped up the development of its own science and technology sectors not only for its own sake, but also to enhance the country's ability to absorb and adapt foreign technology. As a result of the implementation of these new strategies China's economic growth skyrocketed compared to what it had been under Mao, and rivalled that of other latecomers like Japan and the East Asian countries in their respective high-growth periods

The high growth during 1979–2009 enabled China to work its way back into the international community and to become a dominant economic, if not as yet political, power. Thus it again has the world's largest population (as at the beginning of the nineteenth century) and has already overtaken Japan as the world's second-largest economy, and is poised to overtake the US soon on that score as well. The fast growth has had benefits and costs for the welfare of China's population. Both real income and personal consumption per capita have increased rapidly. And consumption patterns have changed as well, causing the Engel coefficient to fall, and more housing space per capita and an increase of durable consumer goods for the average household. The quality of life has also improved significantly with people living longer and being more educated. However, income distribution has become more unequal and China's population has experienced a considerable increase in social insecurity, typical for transition economies. China's growing environmental pollution is also a matter of concern. Of late the government has stepped up its efforts to rein in the harmful effects of rapid growth, and has taken measures to strengthen the social security net for the most vulnerable groups, that is, the unemployed, the elderly and the sick. As a result, both income inequality and environment pollution have shown signs of stabilization in recent years. Thus there can be little doubt that during 1979–2009 rapid economic growth has significantly enhanced the living standard and life chances of China's population, and that its beneficial effects far outweigh the detrimental ones.

FUTURE CHALLENGES TO CHINA'S ECONOMIC GROWTH

Climate Change

The industrial revolution fuelled MEG using fossil fuels, the negative side-effects of which become more obvious and serious with development, such as the progressive depletion of resources and the generation and emission of greenhouse gases into the air, which cause global warming. It is only a matter of time until an international energy agreement is put into place which aims at reducing climate change. China, as one of the largest emitters of greenhouse gases, has already pledged to contribute to this global effort by cutting its energy intensity by 20 per cent between 2005 and 2010, and to have reduced greenhouse gas emissions per unit of GDP further in 2020 by 40–45 per cent compared with 2005. It is also set to raise the share of renewable and nuclear energy in total energy supply from 8 per cent in 2008 to 20 per cent in 2020.

But though China has the political will to reduce greenhouse gas emissions it faces an uphill battle to control emissions and achieve the set targets due to its huge population, on the one hand, and its current fairly low level of energy consumption per capita, which is only one-fifth that of the US, on the other hand. With the rising standard of living and the growing expectation of Chinese consumers to catch up with the Western standard of living, the demand for energy has sharply increased as refrigerators, washing machines, air conditioners and cars become available to the population. According to the International Energy Agency's estimate China is already the world's largest consumer of energy, even though Chinese sources, such as the Chinese Energy Authority and the State Statistical Bureau, dispute the figures.

Furthermore, even if China can achieve its planned energy efficiency target, the International Energy Agency predicts that China's emission of greenhouse gases related to energy consumption will by 2020 have grown more than the rest of the world's combined increase (Bradsher 2010). Thus China is likely to face mounting international pressure to reduce its energy consumption targets further. So far, the Chinese government has relied on shutting down outdated and inefficient plants and on administrative restrictions, such as the threat of sacking officials for failing to meet environmental standards. It is likely that in future it will rely more heavily on broad new market-based policy instruments to rein in emissions of greenhouse gases. These include raising the currently relatively low prices of electricity, oil and coal, as well as the introduction of a carbon tax. Thus a rise in production costs and a decline in the rate of economic growth are inevitable.

Completion of Reforms

China's long march towards becoming a market economy is not yet complete. Though it has taken substantial strides in establishing and strengthening product markets, the factor market remains relatively underdeveloped. Similarly, the institution of private property rights and the private sector need further development. The deepening and completion of the reforms will continue to contribute to China's total factor productivity (TFP) growth. However, the possibility of reaping a large allocative and X-efficiency gain through reforms in the future will diminish, as major reforms which yield efficiency gains have already been undertaken.

As mentioned before, China's gradual approach to reforms – in contrast to the approach taken by its East European counterparts – has helped the country to experience a politically, socially and economically relatively stable transition. Economic reforms were introduced early on, while political reforms were delayed. Nevertheless, China will have to face these in the not too distant future, for its authoritarian political system that does not tolerate opposition or guarantee individual rights is incompatible with a market economy. In recent years there has been significant liberalization (Chai and Roy 2006), but the most difficult reform in moving towards a democracy is still waiting to happen. There certainly is pressure on China to become a more democratic state as the country emerges as one of the major economic (and sooner or later political) heavyweights on the international stage. It needs to align itself with the world system and tune in to liberal philosophy because, firstly, a democracy is more helpful to economic development than an authoritarian regime, and so is the better option (UNDP 2002). The reasons are that democratic governance is valuable in its own right, and political freedom and participating in decisions that affect one's life are a fundamental human right and, hence, an integral aspect of human development.

Secondly, democracy increases the efficiency of government and minimizes corruption by officials as they are held accountable to voters. Democracy offers a better way for a peaceful handover of power and of managing conflict, as it provides space for political opposition. Thirdly, democracies are better than authoritarian regimes at avoiding catastrophes and at managing a sudden downturn which could threaten human survival. Sen (1995), for example, provides evidence which proves that India performed better at managing political catastrophes than did China. In the Great Famine of China between 1959 and 1961 casualties reached almost 80 million, but in contrast in post-war India, despite several crop failures, famines have largely been averted as elected politicians responded to famines with public work programmes for the affected people.

However, the transition from an authoritarian to a democratic regime is unlikely to be a peaceful process as it is a tug of war between those in power and those in opposition. Furthermore, even though there is no empirical evidence to support the hypothesis that democracy costs economic growth, there is strong evidence that democracy increases the degree of political instability in the form of protests, demonstrations and riots. Cross-national data as well as China's own experience suggest a negative link between political instability and economic growth (Alesina et al. 1996). Thus the final stages of political reform and the transition to a democratic political system count as another factor that will slow down the rate of economic growth in the future.

Closing the Technological Gap between China and the West

As mentioned, China's rapid economic growth during 1979–2009 has partly been the result of increases in the country's TFP, which was made possible by exploiting foreign technology. However, as China advances further and the technological gap with the developed countries narrows, any technological advance will be more costly as imitation needs to be replaced by innovation. Thus most China experts are forecasting a slowing-down of China's economic growth in the first quarter of the twenty-first century. For example, Maddison (2007) predicts that China's income per capita growth will decrease, from 6.6 per cent per annum over the 25-year period 1978–2003, to 4.5 per cent in the following three decades. And Perkins and Rawski (2008) expect China's GDP growth rate to decline from 9.5 per cent (1978–2005) to 6 per cent in the period from 2016 to 2025.

Population and Labour Supply

Due to its one-child policy, which is unlikely to be abandoned in the near future, the growth of China's population will slow down sharply. But while it will not reach zero it is expected to come close to it by the year 2015 (see Chapter 16, Table 16.1).The growth rate of the population aged 65 and over will, however, increase and the ratio of the elderly to the working-age population (between 15 and 64) is expected to rise from 0.11 to 0.24 by 2030, and to 0.43 by 2050 (OECD 2010). The declining growth rate of the population plus the greater share of the aged will tighten the supply of labour and create labour shortages. This will have the effect of slowing economic growth as wage increases cause the return on capital to decline and investments to fall. The ageing of the population will also slow down the rate of savings due to the savings life cycle. This in turn reduces capital formation. Finally, the ageing population will force the government to spend more on welfare and pensions and, hence, divert resources from growth-promoting activities and reduce economic growth.

Another important factor lies in the disappearance of surplus labour because growth during 1979–2009 has partly been possible because of the migration of surplus rural labour to the cities. Recent labour unrest and demands for higher wages and better working conditions at foreign-invested enterprises, coupled with the fact that the rural real wage rate has grown significantly since 2004, suggest that the previously unlimited supply of labour to the urban sector may have ceased and that China may have already reached the Lewis turning point. The disappearance of surplus labour will negatively affect export growth and the rate of capital formation and, hence, will contribute to a slowing-down of the growth of China's economy.

The International Economic Environment

During 1979–2009 the international environment was extremely favourable to China's economic growth. For example, in the 1980s, when China opened its doors to trade and foreign investments, the Asian newly industrialized countries (NICs) and Japan were in the process of relocating the production base of their labour-intensive industries due to their domestic labour shortage. Another reason was their growing trade conflict with the US and Europe due to their accumulation of foreign exchange reserves as a result of their growing trade surplus with the West. Many moved their factories to China because of its labour surplus. The new FDI brought not only capital but also know-how and export marketing networks, since investors used China as an export platform to send their products to the US and Europe. Later on, factors such as the collapse of communism, the revolution in transport, communication and information technology, the worldwide import liberalization following the Uruguay Round of talks and China's entry into the World Trade Organization (WTO) all helped to integrate China into the international economic network, with specialization in labour-intensive production processes. As a result China overtook both the US and Germany to become the world's largest factory and exporter. In the process it also accumulated the world's largest foreign reserves, ahead of those of Japan.

However, success brings retribution and China currently stands accused of having contributed to the global imbalance of capital. A central feature of this was debt-funded consumption by the US that allowed 5 per cent of the world population to account for 25 per cent of its GDP, 15 per cent of its consumption and 49 per cent of its current account deficit (Das 2009). This consumption was funded by Japan, Germany and especially China. China used its trade surplus to invest heavily in US dollars by purchasing US Treasury bonds and other US security and, hence, helped to finance US trade and budget deficits. It was also Chinese funds which helped to keep the US interest rate low, encouraging higher levels of borrowing which led to the housing and stock market bubbles and contributed to the global financial crisis (GFC) in 2008.

Since China has maintained a fixed exchange rate, its huge current account surplus is a clear symptom of a substantial undervaluation of its currency. And the fact that it accounts for about 39 per cent of the US's total trade gap in 2008–09 (Roach 2010) won the country no friends. It came under increasing pressure from the US, which branded China a 'currency manipulator' and accused it of taking an unfair advantage to increase its exports to the US. And the US Congress expects China to appreciate its currency or else it will impose trade sanctions on China.

It appears that China, in order to avoid a trade conflict does not have any choice but to follow in the footsteps of Japan in the late 1980s, and to appreciate its currency. It will also have to practise self-restraint in terms of the volume of exports to the US, and increase its imports from there. Thus, this factor too will work in the direction of slowing China's economic growth.

Rebalancing China's Growth

Finally, China will have to change its growth strategy, which is also likely to dampen its economic growth rate. In the past Chinese economic growth was quantitative-oriented with a high growth rate set as an absolute priority. However, the launching of the 11th FYP (2006–10) brought a major shift in China's development strategy, for it now aims at qualitative growth by making growth cleaner, less resource-intensive and more sustainable. It also envisages a more people-centred approach with a more equal sharing of the benefits of development (Kuijs and Xu 2008).

As discussed earlier, China's growth in the past was capital- and resource-intensive, investment-led, and gave priority to industry, especially heavy industry. It was sustained by a high rate of savings at the expense of consumption, and neglected the service industries by underpricing key inputs, including capital, energy, natural resources and the environment. This path led to a declining share of wage income and consumption in GDP and an increasing foreign trade surplus which contributed to a serious international trade conflict. The 11th Five-Year Plan (FYP) and the coming 12th FYP (2011–15) are steering a different course to rebalance China's growth pattern. They aim at increasing the role of consumption and of the service industries in economic growth, and making growth less industry-, investment- and export-led. In the coming years the government is expected to introduce a wide range of macroeconomic and structural policies to achieve a rebalancing of the economy and to promote qualitative change. Such a reorientation will have the cost of slowing economic growth – at least in the short run – but it will improve the standard of living and public welfare (Kuijs and Xu 2008).

The change to less capital-intensive growth will allow China to lower savings and to increase consumption. Raising the share of labour income will not only contribute to this, but will also reduce income inequality. And decreasing the resource intensity of China's economy will limit the negative impacts on the environment of China's economic growth.

Finally, the greater role of consumption in economic growth and the lowering of the rate of savings will reduce the pressure for overproduction and the current account surplus and, hence, reduce China's trade conflict with the international community. The shift from quantitative to qualitative growth will slow economic growth but it will also, for the first time, allow a wide section of China's population to enjoy the fruits of economic growth.

Appendix

Table A.1   Chronological chart of Chinese history (with some approximate dates)

Historical period	Approximate dates
1. Shang	1520–1030 BC
2. Zhou	1030–221 BC
a. Western Zhou	1030–771 BC
b. Spring and Autumn	770–476 BC
c. Warring States	475–221 BC
3. Qin	221–207 BC
4. Han	206 BC–220 AD
5. Three Kingdoms	220–280
6. Jin	265–420
7. Northern and Southern Dynasties	420–581
8. Sui	581–618
9. Tang	618–907
10. Five Dynasties	907–960
11. Song	960–1279
12. Yuan	1271–1368
13. Ming	1368–1644
14. Qing	1644–1911
15. Republic	1912–1949
16. People's Republic	1949–

Source: Beijing Foreign Language Institute (1979).

References

Acemoglu, D. and S. Johnson (2005), 'Unbundling Institutions', *Journal of Political Economy*, **113** (5).

Akamatsu, K. (1962), 'A Historical Pattern of Economic Growth', *Developing Economies*, **1**.

Alesina, A., S. Ozler, N. Roubini and P. Swagel (1996), 'Political Instability and Economic Growth', *Journal of Economic Growth*, **1** (2).

Allen, F., J. Qian and M. Qian (2008), 'China's Financial System: Past, Present and Future', in L. Brandt and T.G. Rawski (eds), op. cit.

Allen, R.C. (2004), 'Agriculture during the Industrial Revolution', in R. Flound and P. Johnson (eds), *Cambridge Economic History of Modern Britain*, Vol. 1, Cambridge: Cambridge University Press.

Andors, S. (1977), *China's Industrial Revolution*, New York: Pantheon.

Ash, R. (1976), 'Economic Aspects of Land Reform in Kiangsu', *China Quarterly*, September.

Ash, R. (1993), 'Agricultural Policy under the Impact of Reforms', in Y.Y. Kueh and R.A. Ash (eds), *Economic Trends in Chinese Agriculture*, Oxford: Clarendon Press.

Baker, H.D.R. (1979), *Chinese Family and Kinship*, New York: Columbia University Press.

Balazs, E. (1964), *Chinese Civilization and Bureaucracy*, New Haven, CT: Yale University Press.

Bannister, J. (1997), 'China: Population Dynamics and Economic Implications', Joint Economic Committee, US Congress, *China's Economic Future*, Washington, DC: US Congress.

Barclay, G.W., A.J. Cole, M.A. Stoto and J. Trussel (1976), 'A Reassessment of the Demography of Traditional Rural China', *Population Index*, **42** (4).

Baumol, W.J. (2008), 'Entrepreneurship: Productive, Unproductive and Destructive', in B. Powell (ed.), op. cit.

Becker, J. (1996), *Hungry Ghosts: Mao's Secret Famine 1964–2000*, New York: Free Press.

Beijing Foreign Language Institute (1979), *The Chinese–English Dictionary*, Hong Kong: Commercial Press.

Bernhardt, K. and P.C.C. Huang (1994), *Civil Law in Qing and Republican China*, Stanford, CA: Stanford University Press.

Blejer, M., D. Burton, S. Dunaway and G. Szapary (1991), *China: Economic Reform and Macroeconomic Management*, Washington, DC: IMF.

Bosworth, B. and S.M. Collins (2008), 'Accounting for Growth: Comparing China and India', *Journal of Economic Perspectives*, **22** (1).

Bradsher, K. (2010), 'China's Fears of Warming Effects of Consumer Wants', *New York Times* online, accessed 5 July 2010.

Brandt, L. (1989), *Commercialization and Agricultural Development: Central and Eastern China 1870–1937*, Cambridge: Cambridge University Press.

Brandt, L. (2000), 'Reflection on China's Nineteenth- and Early Twentieth-Century Economy', in F. Wakeman and R.L. Edwards (eds), *Reappraising Republican Economy*, Oxford: Oxford University Press.

Brandt, L., C.T. Hsieh and X.D. Zhu (2008), 'Growth and Structural Transformation in China', in L. Brandt and T.G. Rawski (eds), op. cit.

Brandt, L. and T.G. Rawski (eds) (2008), *China's Great Economic Transformation*, Cambridge: Cambridge University Press.

Brandt, L. and X.D. Zhu (2010), 'Accounting for China's Growth', University of Toronto Department of Economics Working Paper 394.

Branstetter, L. and N.R. Lardy (2008), 'China's Embrace of Globalization', in L. Brandt and T.G. Raswki (eds), op. cit.

Bray, F. (1984), 'Agriculture', in J. Needham (1954–97), *Science and Civilization in China*, Vol. VI, op. cit.

Brockman, R.H. (1980), 'Commercial Contract Law in Late Nineteenth Century Taiwan', in J.A. Cohen, R. Edwards and F.M. Chang Chen (eds), *Essays On China's Legal Tradition*, Princeton, NJ: Princeton University Press.

Buck, J.L. (1937), *Land Utilization in China*, 3 vols, New York: Council on Economic and Cultural Affairs.

Burns, J.P. (1985–86), 'Local Cadre Accomodation to the Responsibility System in Rural China', *Pacific Affairs*, **58** (4).

Cai, F., A. Park and Y.H. Zhao (2008), 'The Chinese Labor Market in the Reform Era', in L. Brandt and T.G. Rawski (eds), op. cit.

Chai, J.C.H. (1990), 'International Impacts of China's Economic Reforms', in D. Cassel (ed.), *Wirtschaftssystem im Umbruch*, Munich: Verlag Vahlen.

Chai, J.C.H. (1992), 'Consumption and Living Standard in China', *China Quarterly*, 131.

Chai, J.C.H. (1997), *China: Transition to a Market Economy*, Oxford: Clarendon Press.

Chai, J.C.H. (2003), 'Privatization in China', in D. Parker and D. Saal (eds), *International Handbook of Privatization*, Cheltenham, UK and Northampton, MA, USA: Edward Elgar.

Chai, J.C.H. (2004), 'Globalization and the Environment: The Chinese Experiment', in C. Tisdell and R.K. Sen (eds), *Economic Globalisation: Social Conflicts, Labor and Environment Issues*, Cheltenham: UK and Northampton, MA, USA: Edward Elgar.

Chai, J.C.H. and K. Roy (2006), *Economic Reform in China and India*, Cheltenham, UK and Northampton, MA, USA: Edward Elgar.

Chai, J.C.H. and H.S. Sun (1993), 'Liberalizing Foreign Trade: Experience of China', University of Queensland Department of Economics Discussion Paper 135.

Chang, C.L. (1955), *The Chinese Gentry*, Seattle: University of Washington Press.

Chang, C.L. (1962), *The Income of the Chinese Gentry*, Seattle: University of Washington Press.

Chang Chen, F.M. and R.H. Myers (1989), 'Coping with Transaction Costs: The Case of Merchant Associations in the Ch'ing Period', in Institute of Economics (ed.), op. cit.

Chang, J. and J. Halliday (2005), *Mao: the Untold Story*, New York: Alfred A. Knopf.

Chao, K. (1981), 'New Data on Land Ownership Patterns in Ming-Ch'ing China – A Research Note', *Journal of Asian Studies*, **40** (4).

Chao, K. (1986), *Man and Land in Chinese History*, Stanford, CA: Stanford University Press.

Chen, F.M. and R.H. Meyers (1989), 'Some Distinctive Features of Commodity Markets in late Imperial China', in Institute of Economics (ed.), op. cit.

Chen, N.R. (1979), 'China's Balance of Payments', in C.M. Hou and T.S. Yu (eds), op. cit.

Chen, N.R. and W. Galenson (eds) (1969), *The Chinese Economy under Communism*, Chicago, IL: Aldine.

Chen, Y. (2009), *Transition and Development in China*, Farnham, UK: Ashgate.

Chen, Y., H. Li and L.A. Zhou (2005), 'Relative Performance Evaluation and the Turnover of Provincial Leaders in China', *Economic Letters*, **88**.

Chen, Z.P. (1995), 'China's Balance of Payments and the Supply of Capital During its Modernization 1896–1936', *Zhongguo Jingji Shih Yangjiu*, **4** (in Chinese).

Cheng, Y.K. (1956), *Foreign Trade and Industrial Development in China*, Seattle, WA: University of Washington Press.

Cheung, S.N.S. (1969), 'Transaction Cost, Risk Aversion and the Choice of Contractual Arrangements', *Journal of Law and Economics*, April.

Chi, Ch'ao Ting (1936), *Key Economic Areas in Chinese History*, London: Allen & Unwin.

Chinn, D.L. (1979), 'Team Cohesion and Collective Labor Supply in Chinese Agriculture', *Journal of Comparative Economics*, **3** (4).

Choi, E.K. and K.X. Zhou (2001), 'Entrepreneurs and Politics in China's Transitional Economy', *The China Review*, **1** (1).

Chotikapanich, D., D.S.P. Rao and K. Tang (2007), 'Estimating Income Inequality in China Using Group Data and the Generalized Beta Distribution', *Review of Income and Wealth*, **53** (1).

Chow, G. (1993), 'Capital Formation and Economic Growth in China', *Quarterly Journal of Economics*, **108** (3).

Clark, D., P. Murrrell and S. Whiting (2008), 'The Role of Law in Chinese Economic Development', in L. Brandt and T.G. Rawski (eds), op cit.

Das, S. (2009), 'Parting the Bamboo Curtain Part 1: The Basis of China's Growth', *Emerging Markets EconoMonitor*, http://www/rgemonitor.com/emergingmarkets-monitor/258053/parting_the_bamboo_curtain, accessed 12 June 2009.

Deng, G. (1999), *Pre-modern Chinese Economy*, London: Routledge.

Dernberger, R.F. (1975), 'The Role of Foreigners in China's Economic Development 1840–1949', in D.H. Perkins (ed.), op. cit.

Djilas, M. (1957), *The New Class*, New York: Praeger.

Donnithorne, A. (1967), *China's Economic System*, New York: Praeger.

Donnithorne, A. (1972), 'China's Cellular Economy: Some Economic Trends since the Cultural Revolution', *China Quarterly*, **52**.

Eastman, L.E. (1988), *Family, Fields and Ancestors*, New York: Oxford University Press.

Eckstein, A. (1966), *Communist China's Economic Growth and Foreign Trade*, New York: McGraw-Hill.

Eckstein, A. (1977), *China's Economic Revolution*, Cambridge: Cambridge University Press.

Eckstein, A., W. Galenson and T.C. Liu (eds) (1968), *Economic Trends in Communist China*, Chicago, IL: Aldine.

Economy, E. (2004), *The River Runs Black*, Ithaca, NY: Cornell University Press.

Edin, M. (1998), 'Why do Chinese Local Cadres Promote Growth?', *Forum for Development Studies*, **1**.

Elvin, M. (1972), 'The High Level Equilibrium Trap: the Causes of the Decline of Invention in the Traditional Chinese Textile Industries', in W.E. Wilmott (ed.), *Economic Organization in Chinese Society*, Stanford, CA: Stanford University Press.

Elvin, M. (1973), *The Pattern of the Chinese Past*, Stanford, CA: Stanford University Press.

Fairbanks, J.K. (1992), *China: A New History*, Cambridge, MA: Harvard University Press.

Fan, X.G. (1987), 'Tariff Reform under Kuomintang's Nanjing Government', in *Jingjishi*, **6** (in Chinese).

Fan Gang (2010), 'Chinese Bubble-wrap', scmp.com, accessed March 2010.

Faure, D. (1984), *The Rural Economy of Pre-liberation China*, Hong Kong: Oxford University Press.

Fei, J.C.H. and T.J. Liu (1979), 'Population Dynamics of Agrarianism in Traditional China', in C.M. Hou and T.S. Yu (eds), op. cit.

Feuerwerker, A. (1958), *China's Early Industrialization*, Cambridge, MA: Harvard University Press.

Feuerwerker, A. (1969), *The Chinese Economy, ca 1870–1911*, Ann Arbor, MI: University of Michigan Press.

Feuerwerker, A. (1976), *State and Society in Eighteenth-Century China: the Ch'ing Empire in its Glory*, Ann Arbor, MI: University of Michigan Press.

Feuerwerker, A. (1977), *Economic Trends in the Republic of China 1912–1949*, Ann Arbour, MI: University of Michigan Press.

Feuerwerker, A. (1984), 'The State and the Economy in Late Imperial China', *Theory and Society*, **13**, 297–326.

Field, R.M. (1996), 'China's Industrial Performance since 1978', in R.F. Ash and Y.Y. Kueh (eds), *The Chinese Economy under Deng Xiaoping*, Oxford: Clarendon Press.

Gao, Z. (2003), 'Technology Transfer in China's Industrial Development', PhD Thesis, Brisbane: School of Economics, University of Queensland.

Geiger, M. (2008), 'Instruments of Monetary Policy in China and their Effectiveness 1994–2006', UNCTAD Discussion Papers No. 187.

Glick, R. and M. Hutchison (2008), 'Navigating the Trilemma: Capital Flows and Monetary Policy in China', Federal Reserve Bank of San Francisco Working Paper 2008-32.

Golas, P.J. (1980), 'Rural China in the Sung', *Journal of Asian Studies*, **39**.

Granato, J., R. Inglehart and D. Leblang (1996), 'The Effect of Cultural Values on Economic Development: Theory, Hypotheses and some Empirical Tests', in M.A. Seligson and T. Passé-Smith (eds), *Development and Underdevelopment*, Boulder, CO: Lynne Rienner.

Gregory, P.R. and R.C. Stuart (1990), *Soviet Economic Structure and Performance*, New York: Harper Collins.

Greif, A. (2001), 'Impersonal Exchange and the Origin of Markets: From the Community Responsibility System to Individual Legal

Responsibility in Pre-Modern Europe', in M. Aoki and Y. Hayami (eds), *Communities and Markets in Economic Development*, Oxford: Oxford University Press, pp. 3–41.

Haggard, S. and Y.S. Huang (2008), 'The Political Economy of Private Sector Development in China', in L. Brandt and T.G. Rawski (eds), op. cit.

Hannum, E., J. Behrman, M. Wang and J.H. Liu (2008), 'Education in the Reform Era', in L. Brandt and T.G. Rawski (eds), op. cit.

Hao, Y.P. (1970), *The Compradore in Nineteenth Century China*, Cambridge, MA: Harvard University Press.

Hao, Y.P. (1986), *The Commercial Revolution in Nineteenth Century China*, Berkeley, CA: University of California Press.

Harding, H. (1987), *China's Second Revolution*, Washington, DC: Brookings Institute.

Hartwell, R.M. (1971), 'Financial Expertise, Examinations and the Formulation of Economic Policy in Northern Sung China', *Journal of Asian Studies*, **30**.

Heston, A. and T. Sicular (2008), 'China and Development Economics', in L. Brandt and T.G. Rawski (eds), op. cit.

Ho, P.T. (1959), *Studies on the Population of China, 1368–1968*, Cambridge, MA: Harvard University Press.

Ho, P.T. (1964), *The Ladder of Success in Imperial China*, Cambridge, MA: Harvard University Press.

Holcombe, R.G. (2008), 'Entrepreneurship and Economic Growth', in B. Powell (ed.), op. cit.

Hollingsworth, T. (1969), *Historical Demography*, Ithaca, NY: Cornell University Press.

Hou, C.M. (1965), *Foreign Investment and Economic Development in China*, Cambridge, MA: Harvard University Press.

Hou C.M. and T.S. Yu (eds) (1979), *Modern Chinese Economic History*, Taipei: Academia Sinica.

Hsiao, L.L. (1974), *China's Foreign Trade Statistics, 1864–1949*, Cambridge, MA: Harvard University Press.

Howe, C. (1971), *Employment and Economic Growth in Urban China 1949–1957*, Cambridge: Cambridge University Press.

Howe, C. (1996), *The Origin of Japanese Trade Supremacy*, Hong Kong: Oxford University Press.

Howe, C. and K.R. Walker (1977), 'The Economist', in D. Wilson (ed.), op. cit.

Howe, C. and K.R. Walker (1989), *The Foundation of the Chinese Planned Economy: A Documentary Survey, 1953–1965*, Basingstoke: Macmillan.

Hu, A.G.Z. and G.H. Jefferson (2008), 'Science and Technology in China', in L. Brandt.and T.G. Rawski (eds), op. cit.

Hu, A.G.Z., G.H. Jefferson and J.C. Qian (2005), 'R&D and Technology Transfer', *Review of Economics and Statistics*, **87** (4).

Huang, C. (2010), 'The Rising Sons', www.scmp.com, accessed 19 April 2010.

Huang, P.C.C. (1985), *The Peasant Economy and Social Change in North China*, Stanford, CA: Stanford University Press.

Huang, P.C.C. (1990), *The Peasant Family and Rural Development in the Yangzi Delta 1350–1988*, Stanford, CA: Stanford University Press.

Huang, P.C.C. (2002), 'Development or Involution in Eighteenth-Century Britain and China?', *Journal of Asian Studies*, **61** (2).

Huang, Y.P. (1992), *Jindai Zhongguo Jingji Bianqian* (Economic Change in Modern China), Shanghai: People's Publishing House.

Institute of Economics (ed.) (1989), *Second Conference on Modern Chinese Economic History*, Taipei: Academia Sinica.

Ishikawa, S. (1972), 'A Note on the Choice of Technology in China', *Journal of Development Studies*, **9** (1).

Ishikawa, S. (1983), 'China's Economic Growth Since 1949', *China Quarterly*, **94**.

Jones, E.L. (1990), 'The Real Question about China: Why was the Song Economic Achievement not Repeated?', *Australian Economic History Review*, **30** (2).

Jones, H.G. (1976), *An Introduction to Modern Theories of Economic Growth*, New York: McGraw-Hill.

Joseph, W.A., C.P. Wong and D. Zweig (eds) (1991), *New Perspectives on the Cultural Revolution*, Cambridge, MA: Harvard University Press.

Kahn, H. (1979), *World Economic Development: 1979 and Beyond*, Indianapolis, IN: Hudson Institute.

Khan, A.R. (1978), 'Taxation, Procurement and Collective Incentives in Chinese Agriculture', *World Development*, **6** (6).

King, F.H.H. (1965), *Money and Monetary Policy in China 1845–1895*, Cambridge, MA: Harvard University Press.

King, F.H.H. (1969), *A Concise Economic History of Modern China*, New York: Praeger.

King, L.P. and I. Szelenyi (2004), *Theories of the New Class*, Minneapolis, MN: University of Minneapolis Press.

Kirzner, I. (1973), *Competition and Entrepreneurship*, Chicago, IL: University of Chicago Press.

Koopman, R., Z. Wang and S.J. Wei (2008), 'How Much of Chinese Exports is Really Made in China?', NBER Working Papers, 14109.

Kraus, R.C. (1981), *Class Conflict in Chinese Socialism*, New York: Columbia University Press.

Krusekopf, C.C. (2002), 'Diversity in Land Tenure Agreements under Household Responsibility System', *China Economic Review*, **13** (2–3).

Kueh, Y.Y. (1995), *Agricultural Instability in China 1931–1991*, Oxford: Clarendon Press.

Kueh, Y.Y. (2008), *China's New Industrialization Strategy*, Cheltenham, UK and Northampton MA, USA: Edward Elgar.

Kuijs, L. and G. Xu (2008), 'China's Fiscal Policy: Moving to Center Stage', paper presented at the Stanford Center for International Development Conference on Social Services, Regulation and Finance, 23–24 October.

Kung, J.K.S. and J.Y.F. Lin (2003), 'The Causes of China's Great leap Forward Famine 1959–1961', *Economic Development and Cultural Change*, **52**.

Kuznets, S. (1971), *Economic Growth of Nations*, Cambridge, MA: Cambridge Belknap Press.

Landes, D.S. (1969), *The Unbound Prometheus; Technological Change and Industrial Development in Western Europe from 1750 to the Present*, Cambridge: Cambridge University Press.

Lardy, N.R. (1984), 'Consumption and Living Standards in China, 1978–83', *China Quarterly*, **100**.

Lardy, N.R. (1998), *China's Unfinished Economic Revolution*, Washington, DC: Brookings Institute.

Lau, L.J., Y.Y. Qian and G. Roland (2001), 'Reform without Losers', *Journal of Political Economy*, **108** (1).

Laurenceson, J. and J.C.H. Chai (2003), *Financial Reform and Economic Development in China*, Cheltenham, UK and Northampton, MA, USA: Edward Elgar.

Lawson, R.A. (2008), 'Economic Freedom and Property Rights: The Institutional Environment of Productive Entrepreneurship', in B. Powell (ed.), *Making Poor Nations Rich*, Stanford, CA: Stanford University Press.

Lee, J. and C. Campbell (1997), *Fate and Fortune in Rural China: Social Organization and Population Behavior in Liaoning 1774–1873*, Cambridge: Cambridge University Press.

Lee, J. and F. Wang (1999), *One Quarter of Humanity: Malthusian Mythology and Chinese Realities, 1700–2000*, Cambridge, MA: Harvard University Press.

Levy, M. (1955), 'Contrasting Factors in the Modernization of China and Japan', in S. Kuznets, W.E. Moore and J.J. Spengler (eds), *Economic Growth in Brazil, India and Japan*, Durham, NC: Duke University Press.

Li, H.L. (2003), 'Economic Reform in the Urban Land System in China', *Journal of Contemporary China*, **12** (34).

Li, Z. (1994), *The Private Life of Chairman Mao*, London: Chatto & Windus.

Lim, L.Y.C. and P.E. Fong (1991), *Foreign Direct Investment and Industrialization in Malaysia, Singapore, Taiwan and Thailand*, Paris: OECD.

Lin, J.Y.F. (1995), 'The Needham Puzzle: Why the Industrial Revolution did not Originate in China', *Economic Development and Cultural Change*, January.

Lin, J.Y.F. and D.T. Yang (2000), 'Food Availability, Entitlements and the Chinese Famine of 1959–61', *Economic Journal*, **110**.

Lippit, V.D. (1978), 'Class Structure and the Development of Underdevelopment in China', *Modern China*, **4** (3).

Liu, G.G. (1984), *Zhongguo Jingji Fazhang Zhanlue Wenti Yanjiu* (Studies of China's Economic Development Strategy), Shanghai: People's Publishing House.

Liu, J.H. and H.X. Wang (2006), 'The Origins of the General Line for the Transition Period and the Acceleration of the Chinese Socialist Transformation in Summer 1955', *China Quarterly*, **187**.

Liu, P.K.C. and K.S. Hwang (1979), 'Population Change and Economic Development in Mainland China since 1400', in C.M. Hou and T.S. Yu (eds), op. cit.

Liu, T.C. and K.C. Yeh (1965), *The Economy of the Chinese Mainland*, Princeton, NJ: Princeton University Press.

Liu, Y.Y. and Q.Q. Fang (1991), *Minquo Shehui Jingji Shi* (Republican Social and Economic History), Beijing: China's Economic Publishing House.

Llewellyn, K. (1931), 'What Price Contract?', *Yale Law Journal*, **40** (5).

Ma, H. and S.Q. Sun (eds) (1987), *Zhongguo Jingjie Jiegou Wenti Yanjiu* (Studies in China's Economic Structural Problems), 2 vols, Beijing: People's Publishing House.

Ma, S.Y. (2010), *Shareholding System Reform in China*, Cheltenham, UK and Northampton, MA, USA: Edward Elgar.

Ma, Z.J. (1987), 'Tariff and Public Finance during the Republican Beijing Government Period', *Jingjishi*, **8** (in Chinese).

Maddison, A. (2001), *The World Economy: A Millennial Perspective*, Paris: OECD.

Maddison, A. (2007), *Chinese Economic Performance in the Long Run, 960–2030AD*, 2nd edn, Paris: OECD.

Mah, F.W. (1979), 'External Influence and Chinese Economic Development', in C.M. Hou and T.S. Yu (eds), op. cit.

Mann, S. (1987), *Local Merchants and Chinese Bureaucracy 1750–1950*, Stanford, CA: Stanford University Press.

Mao, T.T. (1965), *Selected Works*, Beijing: Foreign Language Press.

Mao, T.T. (1977), *A Critique of Soviet Economics*, transl. Moss Roberts, New York: Monthly Review Press.

McClelland, D. (1983), 'The Achievement in Economic Growth', in B.F. Hoselitz and W.E. Moore (eds), *Industrialization and Society*, Paris: UNESCO.

Minami, R. (1994), *The Economic Development of Japan*, 2nd edn, London: Macmillan Press.

Ministry of Health (2009), *The Fourth National Health Service Survey*, Beijing.

Mokyr, J. (1990), *The Lever of Riches*, Oxford: Oxford University Press.

Mosk, C. (2007), *Japanese Economic Development*, London: Routledge.

Myers, R.H. (1970), *The Chinese Peasant Economy: Agricultural Development in Hopei and Shantung 1890–1949*, Cambridge, MA: Harvard University Press.

Naquin, S. and E.S. Rawski (1987), *Chinese Society in the Eighteenth Century*, New Haven, CT: Yale University Press.

Naughton, B. (1995), *Growing out of the Plan: Chinese Economic Reform 1978–1993*, Cambridge: Cambridge University Press.

Naughton, B. (1996), 'China's Emergence and Prospects as a Trading Nation', *Brookings Papers on Economic Activity*, **2**.

Naughton, B. (2007), *The Chinese Economy*, Cambridge, MA: MIT Press.

Naughton, B. (2008), 'A Political Economy of China's Economic Transition', in L. Brandt and T.G. Rawski (eds), op. cit.

Nee, V. (1989), 'A Theory of Market Transition: From Redistributive to Markets in State Socialism', *American Sociological Review*, **54**.

Needham, J. (1954–97), *Science and Civilization in China*, Cambridge: Cambridge University Press.

North, D.C. (1981), *Structure and Change in Economic History*, New York: Norton.

North, D.C. (2003), *Understanding the Process of Economic Change*, Forum Series on the Role of Institutions in Promoting Economic Growth, Forum 7, Arlington, VA: Mercatus Centre at George Mason University.

Ohkawa, K. and M. Shinohara (eds) (1979), *Patterns of Japanese Economic Development*, New Haven, CT: Yale University Press.

OECD (2002), *China in the World Economy*, Paris: OECD.

OECD (2010), *OECD Economic Surveys: China*, Paris: OECD.

Oi, J.C. (1986), 'Commercializing China's Rural Cadres', *Problems of Communism*, **25** (5).

Olson, M. (1982), *The Rise and Decline of Nations*, New Haven, CT: Yale University Press.

Olson, M. (2008), 'Big Bills Left on the Sidewalk: Why Some Nations are Rich and Others are Poor', in B. Powell (ed.), op. cit.

Opper, S. and S. Brehm (2007), 'Networks vs Performance: Political Leadership Promotion in China', unpublished paper.

Palmer, M.J.E. (1987), 'The Surface–Subsoil Form of Divided Ownership in Late Imperial China: Some Examples from the New Territories in Hong Kong', *Modern Asian Studies*, **21**.

Parish, W.L. (1981), 'Egalitarianism in Chinese Society', *Problems of Communism*, Jan–Feb.

Perkins, D.H. (1967), 'Government as an Obstacle to Industrialization: The Case of Nineteenth-Century China', *Journal of Economic History*, **24** (4).

Perkins, D.H. (1969), *Agricultural Development in China, 1368–1968*, Chicago, IL: Aldine.

Perkins, D.H. (ed.) (1975a), *China's Modern Economy in Historical Perspective*, Cambridge, MA: Harvard University Press.

Perkins, D.H. (1975b), 'Growth and Changing Structure of China's Twentieth Century Economy', in D.H. Perkins (ed.), op. cit.

Perkins, D.H. and T.G. Rawski (2008), 'Forecasting China's Economic Growth to 2025', in L. Brandt and T.G. Rawski (eds), op. cit.

Perkins, D.H., S. Radelet, D.R. Snodgrass, M. Gillis and M. Roemer (2001), *Economics of Development*, 5th edn, New York, USA and London, UK: W.W. Norton.

Perkins, D.H. and S. Yusuf (1984), *Rural Development in China*, Baltimore, MD: Johns Hopkins University Press.

Pomeranz, K. (2000), *The Great Divergence*, Princeton, NJ: Princeton University Press.

Powell, B. (ed.) (2008), *Making Poor Nations Rich*, Stanford, CA: Stanford University Press.

Rawski, T.G. (1975a), 'The Growth of Producer Industries 1900–1971', in D. Perkins (ed.), op. cit.

Rawski, T.G. (1975b), 'China's Industrial System', in Joint Economic Committee, US Congress, *China: A Reassessment of the Economy*, Washington, DC: US Government Printing Office.

Rawski, T.G. (1978), 'China's Republican Economy: An Introduction', Discussion Paper No.1, Joint Centre on Modern East Asia, University of Toronto.

Rawski, T.G. (1982), 'The Simple Arithmetic of Chinese Income Distribution', *Keizai Kenkyu*, **31** (1).

Rawski, T.G. (1989), *Economic Growth in Prewar China*, Berkeley, CA: University of California Press.

Rawski, T.G. and Z.X. Sheng (2008), 'Overall Trends in China's Air Quality', unpublished manuscript.

Richardson, P. (1999), *Economic Change in China, ca 1800–1950*, Cambridge: Cambridge University Press.

Riskin, C. (1975), 'Surplus and Stagnation in Modern China', in D.H. Perkins (ed.), *China's Modern Economy in Historical Perspective*, Stanford, CA: Stanford University Press.

Riskin, C. (1987), *China's Political Economy*, New York: Oxford University Press.

Riskin, C. (1998), 'Seven Questions about the Chinese Famine 1959–61', *China Economic Review*, **111** (24).

Roach, S. (2010), 'Passing the Buck', www.scmp.com accessed 14 May 2010.

Roberts, D. (2004), 'The Greening of China', *Business Week*, 27 October.

Roll, C.R. (1980), *The Distribution of Rural Incomes in China*, New York: Garland Publishing.

Roumasset, J., K. Burnett and H. Wang (2008), 'Environmental Resources and Economic Growth', in L. Brandt and T.G. Rawski (eds), op. cit.

Rozman, G. (1973), *Urban Networks in Ch'ing China and Tokugawa Japan*, Princeton, NJ: Princeton University Press.

Schumpeter, J. (1934), *The Theory of Economic Development*, Cambridge, MA: Harvard University Press.

Schurmann, H.F. (1956), 'Traditional Property Concepts in China', *Far Eastern Quarterly*, **15** (4).

Selden, M. (2006), Jack Gray, Mao Zedong and the Political Economy of Chinese Development', *China Quarterly*, **187**.

Sen, A.K. (1977), 'Starvation and Exchange Entitlements: A General Approach and its Application to the Great Bengal Famine', *Cambridge Journal of Economics*, **1**.

Sen, A.K. (1995), 'Economic Development and Social Change: India and China in Comparative Perspective', London School of Economics and Political Sciences Discussion Paper.

Sheridan, J. (1975), *China in Disintegration*, New York: Free Press.

Sicular, T., X. Yue, B. Gustafsson and S. Li (2007), 'The Urban–Rural Income Gap and Inequality in China', *Review of Income and Wealth*, **53** (1).

Skinner, G.W. (1964), 'Marketing and Social Structure in Rural China, Part I', *Journal of Asian Studies*, **24** (1).

Skinner, G.W. (1977), *The City in Late Imperial China*, Stanford, CA: Stanford University Press.

Srinivasan, T.N. (1990), 'External Sector in Development: China and India 1950–1989', *American Economic Review*, **80** (2).

SSB (State Statistical Bureau) (1986), *Zhongguo Nongcun Tongji Daquan* (China Comprehensive Rural Statistics), Beijing: Agricultural Publishing House.

SSB (State Statistical Bureau) (1989), *Zhongguo Gongye Jingji Nianjian* (China Industrial Economic Statistical Yearbook), Beijing: Industry, Transport and Materials Statistics Department.

SSB (State Statistical Bureau) (2010), 'Guanghui De Licheng, Hongwei De Bianzhang' (Serial Report on 60 Years of Economic and Social Development of the New China: Achievements and Retrospect), http://www.stats.gov.cn/tjfx/3tfx/qzxzgc160zn/t20090907_402584869.htm, accessed 17 May 2010.

SSB (State Statistical Bureau) (annually), (*Zhongguo Tongji Nianjian*) (China Statistical Yearbook), Beijing: China Statistical Press.

SSB (State Statistical Bureau) (annually), *China Statistical Yearbook of Science and Technology*, Beijing: China Statistical Press.

Tai, C. (2010), 'The Princelings and China's Corruption Woes', Centre for International Private Enterprise Development Blog, accessed 23 June 2010.

Tang, A.M. (1979), 'China's Agricultural Legacy', *Economic Development and Cultural Change*, October.

Tawney, R.H. (1964), *Land and Labor in China*, New York: Octagon Books.

Telford, T. (1995), 'Fertility and Population Growth in the Lineages of Tongchen County 1520–1661', in S. Harrell (ed.), *Chinese Historical Microdemography*, Berkeley and Los Angeles, CA: University of California Press.

Tisdell, C.A. (1997), 'China's Environmental Problems and its Economic Growth and Transition', in C.A. Tisdell and J.C.H. Chai (eds), *China's Economic Growth and Transition*, Brisbane: University of Queensland.

Tullock, G. (1987), 'Rent-Seeking', *The New Palgrave: A Dictionary of Economics*, London: Macmillan.

UNCTAD (United Nations Conference on Trade and Development) (2010), *World Investment Report*, Geneva: United Nations.

UNDP (United Nations Development Programme) (annually), *Human Development Report*.

US Census Bureau (2010), *International Data Base*, http://www.census.gov/ipc/www/idb/country.php, accessed 6 June 2010.

Van Ness, D. and S. Raicher (1983), 'Dilemmas of Socialist Development: An Analysis of Strategic Lines in China 1949–1981', *Bulletin of Concerned Asian Scholars*, **15** (1).

de Vries, J. (1984), *European Urbanization 1500–1800*, London: Methuen.

Walder, A.G. (1987), 'Wage Reform and the Web of Factory Interest', *China Quarterly*, **23**.

Walder, A.G., B.B. Li and D.J. Treiman (2000), 'Politics and Life Chances in a State Socialist Regime', *American Sociological Review*, **65**.

Wallis, J. and D.C. North (1986), 'Measuring the Transaction Sector in the American Economy 1870–1970', in S.L. Engerman and R. Gallman (eds), *Long-Term Factors in American Economic Growth*, Chicago, IL: Chicago University Press.

Walker, K.R. (1966), 'Collectivization in Retrospect: The Socialist High Tide', *China Quarterly*, **26**.

Walker, K.R. (1984), *Food Grain Procurement and Consumption in China*, New York: Cambridge University Press.

Walker, K.R. (1998), 'Food and Mortality in China during the Great Leap Forward, 1958–61', in R. Ash (ed.), *The Collected Papers of Kenneth R. Walker*, Oxford: Oxford University Press.

Walter, C.E. and F.J.T. Howie (2003), *Privatizing China*, Singapore: Wiley & Sons.

Wang, F. and A. Mason (2008), 'The Demographic Factor in China's Transition', in L. Brandt and T.G. Rawski (eds), op. cit.

Wang, S.L. (2010), 'Grey Income' (in Chinese), http://www.caijing.com.cn, accessed 9 July 2010.

Wang, Y.C. (1973), *Land Taxation in Imperial China, 1750–1911*, Cambridge, MA: Harvard University Press.

Wang, Y.C. (1979), 'Evolution of the Chinese Monetary System 1644–1850', in C.M. Hou and T.S. Yu (eds), op. cit.

Watson, J.L. (1977), 'Hereditary Tenancy and Corporate Landlordism in Traditional China: A Case Study', *Modern Asian Studies*, **2** (2).

Will, P.E. and R.B. Wong (1991), *Nourish the People: the State Civilian Granary System in China 1650–1850*, Ann Arbor, MI: Michigan University Press.

Wilson, D. (ed.) (1977), *Mao Tse-Tung in the Scale of History*, Cambridge: Cambridge University Press.

Wong, C. and R.M. Bird (2008), 'China's Fiscal System', in L. Brandt and T.G. Rawski (eds), op. cit.

Wong, M.C.W. and L.H.T. Choy (2010), 'The Role of Chinese Enterprises in the Economic Transformation of China through Foreign Direct Investment', in N. Wang (ed.), *China's Economic Transformation*, Hong Kong: University of Hong Kong Press.

World Bank (1983), *China: Socialist Economic Development*, Washington, DC: World Bank.

World Bank (1985), *China: Long-term Development Issues and Options*, Baltimore, MD: Johns Hopkins University Press.

World Bank (1988), *External Trade and Capital*, Washington, DC: World Bank.

World Bank (1997), *China 2020*, Washington, DC: World Bank.

World Bank (annually), *World Development Report*, Washington, DC: World Bank.

Wrigley, E.A. (1988), *Community, Chance and Change: The Character of the Industrial Revolution in England*, Cambridge: Cambridge University Press.

Wrigley, E.A. (2002), 'Country and Town: The Primary, Secondary and Tertiary Peopling of England in the Early Modern Period', in P. Slack and R. Ward (eds), *The Peopling of Britain*, Oxford: Oxford University Press.

Wrigley, E.A., R.S. Davies, J. Oeppen and R.S. Schofield (1997), *English Population History from Family Reconstitution, 1580–1837*, Cambridge: Cambridge University Press.

Wu, C.M. (1994), 'Domestic Market and the Movement to Imitate the West', *Jingjishi*, **2** (in Chinese).

Wu, J.N. and L. Ma (2009), 'Does Government Performance Really Matter', paper presented at the 10th Public Management Research Association Conference, J. Glenn School of Public Afffairs, Ohio State University, 1–3 October.

Xing, F. (2000), 'The Retarded Development of Capitalism', in D. Xu and C.M. Wu (eds), op. cit.

Xu, D.X. and C.M. Wu (2000), *Chinese Capitalism, 1522–1840*, London: Macmillan.

Yamazawa, I., A. Hirata and K. Yokota (1991), 'Evolving Patterns of Comparative Advantage in the Pacific Economies', in M. Ariff (ed.), *The Pacific Economy*, Sydney: Allen & Unwin.

Yang, J.S. (2009), *Mubei* (Tombstone), Hong Kong: Cosmos Books.

Yeh, K.C. (1968), 'Capital Formation', in A. Eckstein, W. Galenson and T.C. Liu (eds), op. cit.

Yeh, K.C. (1979), 'China's National Income', in C.M. Hou and T.S. Yu (eds), op. cit.

Yu, Y.D. (2009), *China's Policy Responses to the Global Financial Crisis*, Melbourne: Australian Productivity Commission.

Yuan, X. (1996), 'Modern China's Foreign Trade and Import Substitution Industrialization', *Jingjishi*, **3** (in Chinese).

Yusuf, S. (2001), 'The East Asian Miracle at the Millennium', in J.E. Stiglitz and S. Yusuf (eds), *Rethinking the East Asian Miracle*, Washington, DC: World Bank.

Zhang, Y.F. (1992), *History of Industrial Development in Modern China* (in Chinese), Taipei: Guiguan Book Company.

Zhao, Z.Y. (2009), *The Secret Journal of Zhao Ziyang* (in Chinese), Hong Kong: Century Press.

Zhu, J.M. (2004), 'From Land Use Right to Land Development Right: Institutional Change in China's Urban Development', *Urban Studies*, **41** (7).

Zweig, D. (1991), 'Agrarian Radicalism as a Rural Development Strategy 1968–1978', in W.A. Joseph, C.P.W. Wong and D. Zweig (eds), op. cit.

Index

Note: subheadings of historical periods are listed chronologically.

Acemoglu, D. 54
active planning concept 125–6
advanced agricultural co-operatives
    (AACs) 112–13
agrarian economies 50, 231
agriculture
    overview 230–31
    traditional economy
        institution compared with
            Europe
        free peasantry 18
        land transaction 18–19
        landlord–tenant relationship
            16–17
        property rights 15–16
    technology compared with
        Europe
        cash crops 86, 232
        cotton and Champa rice
            introduced 21
        fallow land 13–14
        fertilizer and irrigation 14–15
        high-level equilibrium trap
            theory 51–3
        seeds 15
        sowing methods 14
        tools 14, 15
    territorial expansion 7–8
Song period
    government assistance and policy
        19–20, 21–3
    per capita agricultural output
        growth 20–21, 23
    Wang An Shi reform 19
Ming–Qing period
    cottage industry 28
    grain output performance 23
    land–man ratio 23–4, 36–7
    limit to specialization 36

new crops and multiple cropping
    24
stagnation 24
late Qing/Republican period
    GDP share compared with Japan
        94
    land cultivation rights 84
    land ownership 85–6
    output growth estimates 35–6, 83–5
    source of growth 85
Socialist period
    '3–3' system of land use 135–6
    agricultural tax 114–15
    changed cultivation techniques
        135
        lack of autonomy 158
    collectivization and land reform
        111–13
        labour diversion 134–5
        people's commune system
            122–4, 136–7
        private plots 124, 142, 143
    Learn from Dazhai Campaign 146
    liberalization policies following
        Great Famine 142–4
        responsible farm system 142,
            143, 146
        'three freedoms one guarantee'
            142–3 146
        'three guarantees one reward'
            142
    surplus as fuel for industrialization
        113–15
Reform period
    abolition of agricultural tax 177
    contribution to GDP growth
        213–14
    household responsibility system
        (HRS) 164, 168, 169, 176

transfer of land rights 168,
176–7
Asian countries 152–3, 155, 201, 210,
239

banking system, *see* financial system;
money
Baumol, W.J. 58–9
Becker, J. 131
bonds and securities 175–6
international 239
Boxer Rebellion 72
Brandt, L. 83–5, 86–7, 213
Brockman, R.H. 42
Burns, J.P. 186

cadres 156–7, 185–8
capital market 175–6
central banking 102, 175
central planning
active planning 125–6
allocation of labour and capital
116–17
foreign trade corporations (FTCs)
118–19
incentives to enterprises and workers
116
resource allocation 115–16
Chang, C.L. 45, 49, 55–6
Chao, K. 26–7
Chen Yun 143, 163–4
Cheng He, Admiral 35
Chotikapanich, D. 219
Chow, G. 152
Civil War 86
closed economies 109–10
co-operatives 112, 123
Coase theorem 99–100
collectivization 111–13
and decollectivization 168
people's communes 122–4, 136–7
communications 82–3
communism 120, 165
compradores 79, 80–81
Confucianism 51, 58, 98, 103
consumption
consumer goods 109–10
environmental issues and 225
material welfare measurement 152,
221

private consumption per capita
217–19
price index (1979–2009) 109–10
raising standard 190–91
rates 152–3, 190–91
shares and growth contribution
215–16
Western 239
contract law 42
contracting institution 54–5
contracting-out system 38
copper, export and coinage 40
cottage industry 28–32
output and labour supply 29–30
handicraft workshops and 31–2,
87–8
cotton industry 21, 68–9
hand loom production 87–8
credit institutions, traditional period 41
Cultural Revolution 115, 116, 121,
144–8

death rates, *see* population
debt ratio, late Qing/Republican period
73–4
democracy 237
demographic changes, *see* population
Deng Xiaoping 143, 146, 163, 165
Development Plan (1980–2010) 190

economic growth
Song and traditional economy
period 230–31
Socialist period
estimates of growth rate 151–2
heavy industry prioritized 110–11
manufacturing growth and 149–50
outcome of policies 149–60
self-reliance principle 123, 147–8
Reform period
allocative efficiency as source of
growth 211–13
demographic dividends 193–4
development strategy 190–91
foreign trade reforms 195–6,
198–9
growth rate 209–10
township- and village-owned
enterprises 169, 225–6
Feldman model 109–10

see also GDP figures; modern
  economic growth (MEG)
Edin, M. 185–6
Elvin, M. 31, 52–3
environmental issues
  climate change 235–6
  energy intensity per unit of GDP
    224, 225
  government policy 226
  greenhouse gas emissions 225
  water pollution 225
  welfare of the population and 227–8
Environmental Protection Agency 224
examination system 48–9, 81, 103
Export Oriented Zones (EOZs) 195
export-oriented strategy 195–9
  foreign trade system reforms 195–6
  liberalization and incentives 196–8
  outcome of 198–9

factor allocation 116–17
Feldman model of industrialization
  109–10, 126
female infanticide 10–11, 194–5
fertility rates, *see* population
Feuerwerker, A. 47
financial system
  traditional economy
    credit institutions 41
    native banks 41
    pawn shops 38, 41
    self-help mutual financial
      associations 41
  late-Qing/early Republican period
    modern banking 81, 88, 96, 102–4
  Reform period
    bank reforms 175–6
    financial market
      bonds 175–6, 239
      private enterprise access 164,
        169, 171
      shares 166, 170, 175–6
      Shenzhen Stock Exchange 176
    loans 175, 178–80
    marketization and 175–6
    transitional regulations 178–80
    non-bank financial institutions
      175
    non-performing loans 175
    policy loans 175

People's Bank of China 179–80,
    181–2
  see also fiscal policies; money
First World War 81, 232
fiscal policies
  traditional economy 36–8
    land tax 56
    sales tax 37, 38
  late Qing/Republican period
    domestic custom tax 37
    taxes 36–7, 102
    transit tax 104
  Socialist period
    agricultural/land tax 114–15
    government revenues 117
    state-owned enterprise profits 115
    turn-over tax and government
      bonds 117
  Reform period 162–3
    automatic stabilization 182, 183–4
    contract responsibility system 182
    discretionary fiscal policy 182–3,
      184–5
    dual pricing system 164, 166,
      171–2
    import tariffs/indirect export tax
      197
    inflation control 178, 180
    outward direct investment (ODI)
      181
    R&D expenditure 205–6
    reopening of financial market
      175–6
    state-owned enterprises 166, 169,
      170–71, 175, 182
    tax reform 183
    window guidance 181–2
  see also financial system
Five-Year Plan 110, 240
floods 11
'flying geese pattern' of economic
    development 67–9
foreign direct investment (FDI)
  late Qing/Republican period
    benefits of 76–7
    treaty ports 75–6
  Socialist period 119
  Reform period 180
    growth of 199–201
    inflow by sector 202

'round-tripping' 201
trend to foreign ownership 201
foreign invasions 100–101
foreign investment 199–203
  foreign investment enterprises (FIEs)
    166–7, 169, 201
  volume and structure (1979–2008)
    200
foreign loans
  late Qing/Republican period 71–4
    debt ratio 73–4
    indemnity payments 71–3
    net resource transfer 74
  Reform period, volume and
    structure of 200
  Socialist period, Soviet contribution
    119
foreign trade 63–78
  export-oriented strategy 195–9
    foreign trade system reforms
      195–6
    liberalization and incentives
      196–8
    outcome of 198–9
  late Qing/Republican period 73–4
    agricultural 87
    effect on industrialization 67–9
    growth contribution 65–7
      share in GDP 66
    import structure 70, 76
    import substitution 68–9
    trade share 64–5
    trade structure changes 69–71
  Socialist period
    exports during Great Famine
      134
    import substitution 195, 196–7
    Preisausgleich 119
    separation of domestic from
      foreign prices 118
  Reform period 166
    agency system 196
    current account surplus 229
    decentralizing of trading rights
      195
    domestic value-added of exports
      199
    export processing trade 198
    export promotion 196–8
    import liberalization 197

special export-oriented zones 195
strategy results 198–9
see also trade
foreign trade corporations (FTCs)
  118–19, 195–6
'Four Clean-up Campaign' 145

Gang of Four 163
Gao, Z. 131–4
GDP figures
  late Qing/Republican period 13
    economic structure, percentage
      shares 95
    growth contribution percentages
      66, 81
    per capita GDP 90, 93–4
    sectoral shares 29, 88, 89
      comparisons 35
      growth rates (1914–18 and
        1931–36) 90
    share of government revenues
      104–5
  Socialist period
    growth rates per capita 152–3
    manufacturing share, comparisons
      149–50
    sources of growth 154
  Reform period
    Green GNP 227
    deflator underestimates 209
    distribution by sectors 213–14
    projected decline 238
    rate of growth, and consumer
      price index 179
    share of consumption 215–16
    share of labour 216–17
  see also economic growth
Gerschenkron model 100
Gini coefficients
  China's urban households (1981)
    154–6
  national, rural and urban coefficients
    (1985–2007) 219–20
governments
  authoritarianism to democracy 237
  traditional society, minor officialdom
    45, 47
  Song period, assistance to
    agriculture 19–20, 21–3
  Qing/Republican

foreign borrowing 71
land law proposal 85
non-intervention and taxes
    36–7
performance compared with
    Japan 100–105
regulation of business 37
Nanjing, loans 72
Socialist
    building of socialism 120–28
    egalitarianism 154, 168
    Lushan Conference (1959) 141
    revenues 117
    see also state-owned enterprises
        (SOEs)
Reform
    bank control 175
    environmental budget 226
    investment policy 190
    welfare schemes 222–3
Granato, J. 58
Great Drought (1877–78) 11
Great Famine 129–41
    death toll 127–8, 137–8
    decline in food availability as cause
        129–30
    causes of decline 130–37
    urban and rural comparisons 138,
        139
    entitlement failure 137–9
    causes of rural entitlement failure
        139–41
    Sen's hypothesis 129
    weather patterns data 131–4
    see also Great Leap Forward (GLF)
Great Flood (1933–35) 11
Great Leap Forward (GLF)
    aim of 121–2, 233
    diversion of labour 134–5
    rates of investment under 126–7
    targets and outcome 110, 116,
        127–8, 233
    see also Great Famine
Great Leap Outward 163
Greif, A. 43
growth strategy
    Maoist strategy 110–11, 122
    agricultural output 85–6
    'walking on two legs' 124–5
    new growth strategy 190–91

rebalancing growth 240–41
Soviet growth model 120–25, 233
see also modern economic growth
    (MEG)
guilds 43

handicraft workshops 31–2, 87–8
Ho, P.T. 7, 45
household registration system 173
household responsibility system (HRS)
    164, 168, 169, 176
Hu Yaoband 165
Hua Guofeng 163
Huang, P.C.C. 86
hyperinflation 104

import substitution (IS) regime 69,
    196–7
imports and exports, *see* foreign trade
incentive system 116, 136
income distribution
    absolute and relative inequality
        219–21
    traditional economy, gentry's share
        86
    late Qing/Republican period 86
    Socialist period
        during collectivization 112–13
        equality gains 154–6
        incentives 116, 136, 144
        per capita 152
        stratification and benefits 157–8
        work point system 136–7, 142,
            147
    Reform period
        continuous national distribution
            data 219–21
        Kuznets inverted u-curve 221
        local cadres' bonuses 185–6
        national Gini coefficients 154–6,
            219–20
        per capita projections 217
        rate of poverty 219
        subsidies 174
        three-step strategy 190
        see also labour markets
indemnity payments 71–3, 101
industrialization
    traditional period, causes of failure
        of

entrepreneurial performance 57–9
  Baumol's allocation theory 58–9
  n-achievement 58
  high-level equilibrium trap 51–3
  institutional failure: property
    rights
    and contracting institution 54–5
    local government rent-seeking
      55–7, 59
  overview of 231
  technological constraints 50–51
late Qing/Republican period
  early development and
    entrepreneurs 79–81
  'flying geese pattern' 67–9
  ownership structure 80
Socialist period
  backyard iron and steel furnaces
    135
  effect on rural population 138–9,
    155
  effect on the environment 224
  Great Leap Forward 121, 122
  rate of growth 149–50
  third front construction 148
  'three red flags' strategy 122
  'walking on two legs' 124–5
Reform period
  export-oriented strategy 195–9
  foreign investment 199–203
  industry-led growth 213–15
    heavy industry 214–15
  technological catch-up, *see*
    technology
  township- and village-owned
    enterprises 169, 225–6
see also modern industry
inflation 104, 117–18, 164–5, 178, 180
infrastructure industries 77, 82–3, 134
international economic environment
  239–40
investment policy, Reform period 190
Ishikawa, S. 190

Japan 66–71, 75–8, 93–106, 150, 216,
  232–3, 239
  investments 81
  social and industrial development
    96–7, 98–9
Jiang Jishi, General 101

Jiang Qing (Madam Mao) 146, 163
Jiang Zemin 165
Jinshi 47
Johnson, S. 54
judicial system 42, 48, 55
Juren 47

Kirzner, I. 57–8
Koopman, R. 199
Kuznets, S. 65, 94, 221

labour markets
  centralization and 116–17
  rural free markets 142
  Reform period
    decline in surplus 238
    effect of foreign investment 202
    labour income share in GDP
      216–17, 238
    worker mobility 173–4
  see also income distribution
land cultivation rights 84, 176–7
land ownership 85–6
land tax 36, 56, 104
Learn from Dazhai Campaign 146
Lin 'Tiger' 146
Lin Piao 143, 145, 146
Lin, J.Y.F. 51
Liu Shaoqi 143, 144–5, 146
Liu, G.G. 83, 84, 85
Llewellyn, K 43
Lushan Conference (1959) 143

Ma Yinchiu 191
Ma, L. 186
Maddison, A. 88, 90, 149, 152, 238
major macro-regions 8
Manchuria 81
Mao Zedong 86
  death 163
  'Four Clean-up Campaign' 145
  policies 110–13, 233–4
  purges of liberals 143, 145–6
  strategy of socialist development
    121–8, 156–9
Mao, Madam 146, 163
market area, traditional period 31
market brokers 38
Marxist theory 85–6, 120–21, 233
Mason, A. 193–4

May Seventh Cadre Schools 145–6
McClelland, D. 58
medical insurance 222–3
modern economic growth (MEG)
    achievement of 150–52
        effect upon society 212–13
    agricultural output 83
    future challenges to 235–41
        and strategic rebalancing 240–41
        international environment 139–40
    government role 99–105
        and policies, post-Mao 234–5
    growth rate estimates 151, 238
    social effects upon 98–9
        changing population and labour
            supply 238
    time scale 88–91, 231–2, 233–4
    trade structure compared with Japan
        70–71, 93–6
    see also economic growth; growth
        strategy
modern industry
    Gerschenkron model 100
    growth rate 81, 232
    impact on economic growth 88–91
        sectoral shares of GDP 88–91,
            215
    infrastructure industries 77, 82–3,
        134
    investment and outputs retraction
        144
    see also industrialization
money
    traditional economy 39–41
        bimetallic types and supply 39–40
        paper currency 40–41
    Qing/Republican banking reform
        103–4
    hyperinflation 104
    Socialist period, inflation control
        117–18
    Reform period 178–82
        adjustment to market rate 166
        credit quota 180
        fixed rate exchange 239–40
        'impossible trinity' 180
        interest rate policy 179–80
        open market operation 175,
            180–81
        reserve requirements 178–9

sterilization 181
stop-and-go growth 178, 180
see also fiscal system
Mongol invasion 11
Mutual Aid Teams (MATs) 112
Myers, R.H. 86

Nanjing government 72–1, 76
national welfare accounting 227–8
Needham, J. 50–51
non-state enterprises (NSEs) 164, 168,
    169, 175–6
North, D.C. 54, 96–7
Northern Expedition 12, 101

outward direct investment (ODI) 181

Peng Dehuai, Marshall 143
pension scheme 223
people's communes (PCs) 122–4, 136–7
    during Cultural Revolution 147
    structure modification 142
People's Liberation Army (PLA) 146
Perkins, D.H. 23–4, 27, 35–6, 83, 84,
    85, 90, 151, 217, 238
politics, *see* government
population
    overview
        compared with Japan 94
        estimates, traditional and modern
            8–9
        rates (1950–2025) 192
    traditional economy
        death rates 11
        early expansion and migration
            patterns 7–8
        female infanticide 10–11
        fertility rate 9–10
        growth rate 12
        late Song to early Ming period 53
        lineage system 10, 18, 98–9
        war and natural disasters 11–12
    Socialist period
        control policy 191–2
        death tolls 127–8, 137–8
        female infanticide 194
        industrial workforce increases
            135
    Reform period
        controls 192–4

gender discrimination at birth
194–5
growth rate and ratios 238
see also society
poverty rates 219
pricing system 164, 166, 171–2, 178–80
privatization 166, 168–71
agriculture, household responsibility
system (HRS) 164, 168, 169,
176
foreign investment enterprises (FIEs)
166–7, 169, 201
non-wholly state funded shareholding firms 169
non-state enterprises (NSEs) 164,
168, 175–6
management contract system
182
private enterprises 164, 169, 171
of state-owned enterprises (SOEs)
166, 169
township- and village-owned
enterprises 169, 225–6
see also reform policies
property rights 156, 166, 171
agriculture and land 15–16
land cultivation rights 84, 176–7
industrialization and 54–7
environmental issues 226
urban areas 177–8, 186

Rawski, T.G. 66, 88–9, 151, 155, 217,
238
Red Guard and Rebel Groups 145–6
reform policies
economic importance of 236–7
evolution of strategies 163–4
marketization 171–3
opening to the West 165–7
Qing period reforms 103
setback triggered by student unrest
164–5
see also privatization
responsible farm system 142, 143, 146
rice crops 21
Riskin, C. 53
Roll, C.R. 112
Roumasset, J. 227
Russia, *see* Union of Socialist Soviet
Republics (USSR)

'Save China Movement' 103
Schumpeter, J. 57
Science and Civilization in China
(1945–97) 50–51
sciences 51
self-reliance principle 123, 147–8
Sen, A.K. 129
service sector 214
Shengyuan 46–7
Shimonoseki, Treaty of 63
silk industry 70, 88
silver coinage 40
silver standard 104
Sino-Japanese War 71
Skinner, G.W. 31
socialism, *see* growth strategies
society
traditional
commoners 47–8
formation and economic
development 98–9
gentry
degree holders 45–7
examination system 48–9,
81
income 49, 56
privileges 48
rent-seeking 55–7
imperial nobility 45, 46, 55
lineage system 10, 18, 89–9
social mobility 48
warlordism 101–2
Socialist period
cadres 156–7
categories of workers 157
egalitarianism 124
establishment of people's
communes 122–4
human development
153–4
social mobility 159
standard of living 152–3
stratification 156–9
traditional period 45–9
Reform period
cadres 185–8
princelings 187
social security 221–3
standard of living 217–19
housing 218

Tiananmen Square
demonstrations 164–5
see also population
Southern Tour 165
Soviet Union, *see* Union of Socialist
Soviet Republics (USSR)
standard of living 152–3, 217–19
national welfare accounting 227–8
see also welfare system
state-owned enterprises (SOEs) 115,
144, 147, 164
contract responsibility system 182
labour mobility and 174
privatization 166, 169–71
profitability deterioration 175, 182
regulation, international comparison
172–3
state-owned shares in listed
companies 170
stratification of society 156–9, 220
structural change 213–17
traditional economy 231
*Structure and Change in Economic
History* 54
swap markets 196

Taiping Rebellion (1850–64) 11, 71,
100
Taiwan, contract enforcement 42
tea 70
technological transfer 67, 203–4
technology 50–51
traditional economy 13–15, 50–51,
86, 231
high-level equilibrium trap theory
51–3
late Qing/Republican period 102–3
Socialist co-operatives and 112
Reform period
achievements 207
economic importance of 237–8
embodied and disembodied
imports 203
growth of domestic capacity
204–7
introduction of foreign
technologies 203–4
R&D and innovation expenditures
205–7
technology programmes 205–6

Ten-Year Plan 163
third front construction 148
'three big differences' 124, 147–8, 155–6
'three freedoms and one guarantee'
142–3, 146
'three guarantees and one reward'
system 142
Tiananmen Square 164–5
total factor productivity (TFP) 153
township- and village-owned
enterprises (TVEs) 169, 225–6
trade
in traditional economy
brokerage system 38
infrastructure for trade
contracting institution 54–5
informal settlement and guilds
42–4
monetary system 39–41
weights and measures 38–9
local market 34
long distance, volume and
commodities 34–5
marketed agricultural output 35–6
restricted limits of 44
taxes and regulation 37–8
Yahang and *Hangtous* 38
late Qing/Republican period 87
infrastructure industries
supporting 77, 82–3, 134
Reform period
capital market 175–6
factor market development 173–4,
189
land market 176–8
marketization 171–3
liberalization of prices 164–5
dual-track system 172
see also foreign trade
transaction sector 96–7
transport 27, 82
Treaty Ports 75–6, 79–81
Tullock, G. 57
'two participations, one reform and
triple combination' policy 147

UN Development Programme 153–4
Union of Socialist Soviet Republics
(USSR) 109–11
central planning 115–16

Index

Great Famine and 134
industrial strategy 123, 124–5
socialist strategy 120–21, 233
United States of America 239–40
urbanization, rate of 26–33
  cottage industry and 28–32
  Ming–Qing period 27–8
  Tang–Ming period 26–7
  two stages compared with Europe
    28

Wang, F. 193–4
warlordism 101–2
wars and uprisings 11–12, 100–101
wealth accumulation 194
weights and measures, Qing period
  38–9
welfare system 174–5, 194–5

medical insurance and pension
  scheme 222–3
social security 221–3
see also standard of living
Wen Jiabao 187
Westernization movements 103–4, 165–6
Working Conference, Central Party
  Committee (1962) 144–5
World Trade Organization (WTO)
  165–6, 196
Wu, J.N. 186

Yang, J.S. 129, 131, 137
Yeh, K.C. 83, 84, 85, 90

Zhao Ziyang 163–5, 195
Zhu Rongji 165, 187
Zhu, X.D. 213